DRINKING

Anthropological Approaches

....

Edited by
Igor and Valerie de Garine

Berghahn Books
New York • Oxford

First published in 2001 by Berghahn Books

www.berghahnbooks.com

© 2001 Igor and Valerie de Garine

Library of Congress Cataloging-in-Publication Data

Garine, I. de.
Drinking : anthropological approaches / Igor and Valerie de Garine.
    p. cm. -- (The anthropology of food and nutrition ; v. 4)
Includes bibliographical references and index.
ISBN 1-57181-809-X (alk. paper) -- ISBN 1-57181-315-2 (pbk. : alk. paper)
1. Drinking behaviour. I. Garine, Valerie de. II. Title. III. Series.

GT2880.G34 2001
394.1'3--dc21   200035608

British Library Cataloguing in Publication Data
A catalogue record for this book is available from the British Library.

Printed in the United States on acid-free paper

ISBN 1-57181-809-X (hardback)
1-57181-315-2 (paperback)

CONTENTS

ILLUSTRATIONS

FIGURES AND MAP

TABLES

PREFACE

The International Commission on the Anthropology of Food (I.C.A.F.) is a commission launched in 1978 under the auspices of the International Union of Anthropological and Ethnological Sciences (I.U.A.E.S.). In the framework of the 14th international congress of the IUAES held in Williamsburg, Virginia, USA (26 July – 1 August 1998), ICAF organised a symposium on 'Drinking: An Anthropological Approach'. The meeting was pluridisciplinary and accepted papers from both the biological and social sciences. It dealt with all categories of beverages: water, milk, natural juices, infusions, fermented and distilled drinks of all kinds …. Topics included the biological consequences of liquid intake, drinking patterns relating to various types of drinks in different cultures among a variety of biological and social groups, and the socio-economic and cultural aspects of drinking dealing with material as well as symbolic and psychopathological dimensions.

Over the last two decades many anthropological books have been devoted to drinking. They are mostly concerned with alcohol and reflect the views of social anthropologists. This volume, which arises from the papers presented at the symposium, tries to avoid moralistic afterthoughts but presents pluridisciplinary aspects of the ingestion of liquids at large. It covers a fair range of societies from rural and urban environments, involving Europe, Africa, Latin America, Malaysia and the Pacific.

Many of the overt and covert meanings of drinking are addressed: from satisfying biological needs to communicating with humans and the hereafter, attempting to reach a differential emotional state or seeking good health and longevity through the ingestion of appropriate beverages. This book attempts to broaden the common knowledge about drinking and show the complexity of the factors concerned.

ICAF is grateful to Berghahn Books for their encouragement and for creating this series devoted to The Anthropology of Food and Nutrition. We would also like to thank all the contributors and participants in the Williamsburg symposium. We hope they remember the practical work we had to do on beverages as fondly as we do.

Igor and Valerie de Garine
December 1999

1. FOR A PLURIDISCIPLINARY APPROACH TO DRINKING

Igor de Garine

Introduction

Drinking is a primary human need. However, whereas many studies have been carried out on food intake, few are available on drinking (Claudian 1970). Although the human being can subsist much longer without food than without water, quantitative data on liquid intake is seldom sought when food consumption studies are carried out.

Drinking has a biological function which goes beyond nutrition and is related to adapting to environmental conditions and energy expenditure. Each culture has its own particular drinking behaviour (Vargas, this volume), and access to drinking water may even be a stressful matter (Pollock, this volume). It is probable that degrees of thirst and the accepted stage of urgency in quenching it may not be the same in every society. For instance, in Mauritania, the camelback traveller will be welcomed with a large calabash of water mixed with whey, to which a handful of straw stems has been added in order to prevent him from swallowing the vessel's contents in one gulp. Travellers in the desert begin their journey before sunrise and refrain from drinking as long as possible, which is not in accordance with scientific recommendations about hydration.

Looking at the question of ingestion of liquids challenges the optimistic views of the human ecologists of the 1960s in relation to the adaptability and fitness of hunter- gatherers (Sahlins 1974). Considerable water loss caused by the blazing sun results in low working capacity, which should not be mistaken for leading a leisurely life (Ulijaszek, this volume). A tall and lean figure, which is valued in our civilisation, is the result of low energy intake; it leads also, among East African pastoralists, to reduced lean mass and muscles, and to the inability to work for lengthy periods (Little, this volume). Taking into account not only solid foods but also liquids sheds a new light on nutritional adaptation and biological fitness.

When drinking is considered, the focus is mostly on alcoholic beverages, with a moralistic, welfare concern going back to the nineteenth century and reflecting certain Northern European puritanical views still active today in the economically and culturally dominant powers of the West. A large amount of data has been published on alcoholic drinking, intoxication and its various causes and consequences, with special reference to culturally and psychologically vulnerable groups such as ethnic, tribal and socio-economic minorities.

... drinking arki brings pleasure ... (Muzey, N. Cameroon).

Since the 1970s, a number of anthropologists have considered the topic in a less negative way, for instance, Everett, Waddel and Heath (1976), Marshall (1979), and Heath (1995). Significantly, Mary Douglas entitled the book she edited in 1987 'Constructive drinking: Perspectives on drink from anthropology'. Drinking brings pleasure and acts as a social lubricant in many gatherings.

However, drinking is not necessarily a positive activity. This negative aspect has been widely publicised (see the publications of the Rutgers Center of Alcohol Studies, for instance, Wolcott 1974; Sadoun et al. 1965). Drinking to the point of intoxication has become a notable element in contemporary societies, probably related to the worldwide process of socio-economic and cultural change, and to its psychological consequences in an aggressive world of unequal opportunities (Hubert, this volume).

One might wonder if the temptation to escape the harsh realities of life by using both the energising and soothing properties of alcohol could be considered a feature of many human beings, allowing them to reach a psychological stage in which inhibitions diminish in an amiable and understanding in-group. This might be interpreted as a consequence of the self-consciousness of the human being and his craving to escape it. Loosening his self-control through a feeling of repletion (enjoying digestive euphoria together), intoxication and drugs may help to alleviate the daily grind.

Rather than focusing on the dramatic consequences of a worldwide increase in alcoholic drinking behaviour, it might be fruitful to envisage drinking from both the biological and the social science perspectives, and in the general framework of ingestion, liquid intake and nutrition. Drinking fulfils a biological need, i.e., quenching thirst, primarily with water. It may also have a ludic aspect (Millan, this volume). Drinks are part of the diet; they answer biological needs as well as hedonic organoleptic expectations, and reflect many specific cultural wants.

Through their physical characteristics, drinks provide fluid substances. One may refer here to the moisturising properties of liquid sauces which enable bulky food to be swallowed easily. Drink is food which does not need to be chewed. What are the differences between a light porridge and a thick drink? Are soups drinks or food? To which category belongs the fresh cattle blood consumed by a number of East African pastoral tribes such as the Turkana? (Little et al. 1988: 297). It is not easy to draw a line, and each culture has its own outlook.

In each human group all ingested liquids should be taken into account according to various viewpoints.

Physical and Biochemical Aspects

- Physical stage at which drinks are considered acceptable: thickness, ability to provide satiation, temperature adequacy, ability to quench thirst, or to cool down or warm up the body.
- Nutritional value of the various biochemical components should be examined, mentioning also those which are enhanced or destroyed by the technological process involved, such as fermentation, brewing or boiling.
- According to the technology involved, drinks can be divided into beverages which need:

  1. No technological intervention: natural drinks such as water, milk, blood.
  2. Traditional household technology: local beers, wine, alcohol, kava, fruit juices, paps, fermented gruels, hydromel. It should be mentioned that in traditional societies, which have loose seasonal and daily evaluations of the time dimension, brewing and fermenting introduce the notion of a more precise computation of time.

... and to seal a marriage ... among the Yasa and Mvae of Southern Cameroon.

3. Modern manufacturing: carbonated water, soft drinks and fruit juices, industrial beers, wines, spirits.
4. Special mention should be made of the medicinal and pharmacological uses of drinks.

Macerations, infusions and decoctions using various plants are drunk to cure ailments. Medicinal drinks not only take care of the body, they are also reputed to have a psychoactive aspect. Stimulants, sedatives, and hypnotics can be drunk and may lead to various kinds of disorders. The medical use of alcohol is a very rich and complex field and its image is positive in many cultures.

Time and Place

A parallel can be drawn between eating and drinking behaviour. They do not necessarily entail the same ingestion episode. In many cases alcoholic drinking does not occur during meals. In most traditional contexts, there are few drinking bouts during meals since satiation is the aim. For instance, among the Masa, Muzey, Tupuri and other populations we have studied in Cameroon, water is drunk before and after the meal. Accompanying foods with drinks, and carefully matching wines to dishes, are features of the Southern European cultures of the wine belt, especially French, Italian and Spanish, rather than a general trend.

These aspects should be investigated: drinking during meals, drinking between meals, drinking when socialising and while consuming ordinary fare such as snacks, or at teatime, cocktails or brandy time; the 'apéritif' and 'digestif' of the French should be included here as well as the 'quick one for the road' gulped down by some British men before returning home after a day's work. The systematic, lonely drinking of some alcoholics should probably also be mentioned.

Drinking also occurs on irregular occasions such as attending markets, fairs and other crowd gatherings. The nature of the drink varies. Tea and soft drinks are likely to be used during religious meetings, charity sales, and during garden parties. In Europe, alcohol – chiefly beer – accompanies soccer matches and is part of hooliganism.

Drinking, and especially alcoholic drinking, has become a worldwide marker of festive occasions: social events at the individual level (inviting a colleague for drinks), at the family level (birthdays, weddings etc.), or within the neighbourhood, community or any other social grouping.

It is difficult to trace the borderline between ritual and profane occasions, which are both religious and social and correspond to each culture's own calendar.

Differences may also be perceived according to the location where drinking occurs: at home, outside the home in specific places such as bars, cafés and brasseries or street stands.

In relation to social organisation, one should mention the nature of the participants and the size of the group involved in drinking: individuals, family, peers, colleagues, neighbours and special drinking partners. Any type of grouping may be encountered here.

In short: a pluridisciplinary holistic approach to drinking in any culture and social group should answer the following questions: Who drinks? Which drink? In what quantity? With what physiological and psychological results? How? Where? When? Why (for which overt and covert purpose, biological, hedonic, cultural, psychological)? All etic and emic aspects should be taken into account. It may be possible to distinguish between:

1. Drinking to quench thirst, to satisfy biological needs.
2. Drinking to enjoy subtle organoleptic qualities.
3. Drinking to facilitate social and religious relationships.
4. Drinking to obtain psychoactive effects ranging from the various stages of intoxication to loss of consciousness.

Drink, even more than food, is a socialising agent and has various culturally appraised consequences (Chatwin, this volume).

From the economic aspect, drinks, and especially alcohol, are important commodities. Their production generates high income and profit. This prospect is taken advantage of at both governmental and individual level, as is their commercialisation and diffusion. Owning a teashop, a pub, a *cantina*, a café or a bar is a profitable venture anywhere in the world. In rural African societies, such as those of Northern Cameroon, beer brewing and distillation of sorghum grain are the best ways of obtaining cash in the bush. For an inside view from Kenya, see Subbo (this volume).

Drinks can be exchanged for work. In most cultures they are a compulsory ingredient for working parties and important assets to achieving economic and social status (E. Garine, this volume).

They may be part of the bridewealth and used to seal a marriage. This is, for instance, the case with palm wine, red wine and whisky among the Yasa and Mvae of Southern Cameroon.

Drinking, even more than eating, has a status-conferring and status-displaying function in which prohibitions and preferences operate. It is a socio-economic and cultural marker (Smith, this volume). This aspect is well substantiated. In most societies, the rich and the elite may consume sophisticated expensive drinks (often alcohol), the poor drink crude ones (including methylated spirits) and long to imitate the upper strata's behaviour. It is a conspicuous consumption activity: offering drinks, serving chosen wines or spirits during a reception, or paying for rounds for fellow drinkers enhances prestige and is sometimes a means of wooing clientèle.

Drinks can also be status markers in terms of age and gender (Cantarero, Ibrahim, this volume). It is commonplace that women and children have a more limited access to alcohol in traditional societies, and that the increasing consumption of alcoholic drinks among women appears to be a universal trend in the contemporary use of liquids.

What one drinks can also reflect moral creeds and religious affiliations. Wilson (this volume) mentions innocent alcoholic ingestion in a Muslim society. The cultural ethos plays a major role in the dynamics of drinking. Today, the adhesion by some to temperance-style groups in the Western world is a way of trying to counteract a general tendency towards permissiveness where alcohol is concerned.

Drinks are a means of establishing and maintaining contact with human and also supernatural powers, whether they be ancestors or Lord Jesus Christ, whose blood is symbolised by wine in the Holy Communion. In many religious and magical rituals, liquid offerings are made to the supernatural powers (I. de Garine, this volume). They consist of natural drinks – water, milk, blood (the drink of many supernatural powers in Africa), beer and wine – and more recently spirits. Among drinks, water is a magico-religious ingredient. As Leslie White wrote some years ago (White 1959: 1) : 'Man is the only animal able to distinguish between drinking water and Holy water'. It can be ingested to cool off the bad influences which are often considered hot, or the pollution resulting from contact with the evil, or, as among the Muzey of Cameroon, the impurity resulting from contiguity with the holy world at the end of important rituals. It has also the property of cleansing malevolent thoughts or spells.

Water is used to refresh the body in the case of a fever. It is also used to cure symbolically 'hot' episodes in human life, such as pregnancy or the post-partum period for women, or anger, violence and even the consequences of witchcraft among men (for instance, among the Masa and Muzey).

Eating and drinking together reinforce a sense of communion between individuals. Among humans, drinking, especially the consumption of alcoholic beverages, defines social relations. It is a feature of festive gatherings whether they be sacred or profane, ritual or informal.

The stimulant properties of alcohol are taken advantage of to induce mirth, release inhibitions and to allow social barriers and formal attitudes to be loosened in a joyful ambience. Being tipsy is in many cultures considered a positive state. As we mentioned, alcoholic drinking is determined by time and location. It is a time slot and a locus in which attitudes and behaviours which challenge the ordinary, formal rules of social life, and even the political order, are tolerated. Pubs, taverns and cafés have often played a role in social upheavals, riots, strikes and revolutions.

The sedative, hypnotic attributions of alcohol are not the only ones to be sought. In the Pacific, in Vanuatu (ex New Hebrides), the analgesic and tranquillising properties of *Piper methysticum,* from which kava is made, are used in the same way to create a privileged moment at sunset in a secluded place – the men's enclosure *(nakamal)* – allowing for quiet chatting, evocation of family memories, and contacts with the hereafter, without the distractions of women, children, pigs and the turmoils of daily life. It is being promoted in the Pacific region to fight stress and alcoholism (Lebot and Levesque 1997).

At the next stage, the emotional aspect of interpersonal intercourse rises, permissive attitudes in relation to the social order and sex begin to appear, behaviour which is an outlet to frustration; joking and conflict display may help in catalysing violence. These aspects can be ritualised. Among the Koma of Northern Cameroon, this is a time when traditional joking relationships between groups and individuals come alive. During the tipsy and slightly high time of millet threshing, initiation partners are expected to joke so crudely and loudly about each other that they would appear to the outsider to be clashing violently. This sequence is followed by a time for erotic singing between men and women which may result, as the night deepens, quite often in sexual intercourse. No fighting takes place, but total inebriation can result in accidental deaths in this mountainous and perilous environment.

In many societies, loud singing, shouting and fighting do take place. This is a time for aggressive behaviour (Avila, this volume). Increasing the fighting spirit of soldiers through the distribution of alcohol was practised in the First World War as well as in the Napoleonic armies. According to Falewicz (1978), the expression 'drunk as a Pole' is a compliment referring to the military efficiency of the Polish cavalry while intoxicated as compared to the French.

This questioning of the social order may, in general terms, be an outlet to escape the constraints of social rules, social shame and, as mentioned above, to break away from the harsh realities of the daily grind. In this respect, a number of societies resolutely seek drunkenness, a revigorating state in which they 'feel like a lion', as the Masa say.

Attitudes towards intoxication and offensive behaviour resulting in violence also vary widely according to different cultures, as well as in relation to social status, gender, time etc. These aspects have been widely studied. It is obvious that the importance of this stage is related to the general tone of social life, its aggressivity and degree of repression. In constraining religious and moral systems, such as those operating in the West, some people feel the need for an outlet. In these countries, where Protestant cultures (which favour self-control and responsibility) dominate and advocate liberation from the beastly impulses of humans, weekly binge drinking, aimed at reaching inebriation, has become a cultural feature. Nowadays this aspect characterises the world pattern spread by the trendsetting, economically overwhelming cultures of the West. The consumption of alcohol plays a strong cathartic role in modern urban life and is repressed. This is less the case in many traditional societies and among the generally more lenient Catholic cultures of Southern Europe. Here extraversion is favoured, drinking and constant mild alcoholisation, mostly through the consumption of wine (Gonzalez Turmo, this volume), are considered a normal aspect of daily life, in which no feeling of guilt is involved.

In relation to alcoholic drinking in the present day, four general styles appear:

1. Seeking mild inebriation simply for the pleasure of being with friends and other participating individuals during many kinds of social gatherings, either at home or in the jovial atmosphere of pubs, tapas bars and similar places. After all, Dionysus was a joyful deity.
2. Permanent, everyday alcoholisation, characterised by little inebriation and a subtle hedonistic perception of drinks. This is considered as a sign of 'distinction' (in Bourdieu's sense, (Bourdieu 1979)) and commonly accompanies food consumption. Tipsiness is accepted, intoxication frowned upon. The general attitude towards drinking which is frequent, but moderate, is lenient. The main drink concerned here is wine, considered as part of the diet.

3. Binge drinking, often of the lost-weekend type, among Anglo-Saxon and Scandinavian societies, in a highly competitive culture where temperance and the restraint of beastly pulsions in the human being are enforced. This pattern mainly involves drinking beer and spirits. The intoxicating effect of alcohol and its psychoactive properties are clearly sought.
4. Seeking intoxication – what I would call 'despair drinking', deliberately reaching drunkenness to escape the unbearable hardships of life, in which alcohol is used in a similar way to drugs. This is the case in many underprivileged minorities throughout the world and among individual social cases (see, for instance, Waddel and Everett 1980).

It should be remembered that there are no clearcut limits between these four aspects of alcohol consumption.

Beer drinking is spreading throughout the world and wine expertise is permeating northern cultures. Pathological drinking occurs everywhere in reaction to the stresses of modern life, especially in groups where social change is occurring with little hope of socio-economic success. All these types of drinking have medical and socially negative consequences on which there is no need to elaborate. The frequent and regular drinking considered as normal behaviour in southern culture is not unrelated to high levels of liver cirrhosis. However, what is called the 'French paradox' (Troncoso et al., this volume) is not solely linked to the antioxidant properties of wine but to a general permissive and hedonistic attitude towards eating and drinking, perceived as having a much broader function than satisfying primary nutritional needs.

Alcoholisation is a worldwide trend and the Christian religions which encourage temperance are helpless in combatting the general tendency, whereas Islam and the style of life it imposes upon its followers, on the grounds of religious and moral beliefs, appears as a barrier against alcohol consumption, considered 'despicable'. In Western industrial societies, far from being spurned, its consumption seems to be perceived as a pleasant, stress-relieving activity linked to socio-economic success and modernity, as well being a profitable entreprise. Alongside Islam, the rising concern in seeking positive biological consequences from eating and drinking according to contemporary scientific findings (den Hartog, Macbeth, this volume) is a new widespread contribution to what Mary Douglas (1987) has termed 'constructive drinking'. The future will show if it is able to counteract the effect of increasing alcohol consumption linked, among other things, to the emotional insecurity of modern life, a problem to which anthropologists should not remain indifferent.

References

Bourdieu, P. (1979) *La distinction – Critique Sociale du Jugement.* Paris, Editions de Minuit.

Claudian, J. (1970) Comportement de l'Homme Vis-à-Vis du Liquide. *Cahiers de Nutrition et de Diététique* V, 2: 25–40.

Douglas, M. (1987) *Constructive Drinking: Perspectives on Drink from Anthropology.* Cambridge University Press, Cambridge.

Everett, M.W., Waddel, J.O. and Heath, D.B. (Eds) (1976) *Cross Cultural Approaches to the Study of Alcohol: An Interdisciplinary Perspective.* Mouton, The Hague.

Falewicz, J.K. (1978) Rzecz o pijanstwie. *Kultura i spoleczenstwo* 3: 307–22, quoted by Moskalewicz, J. and Zielinski, A. (1995: 224) in Heath 1995.

Heath, D.B. (1995) *International Handbook on Alcohol and Culture.* Greenwood Press, Westport, U.S.A.

Lebot, V. and Levesque, J. (1997) Le Kava, un remède contre le stress? *La Recherche,* 295, Feb. 1997: 84–88.

Little, M.M., Galvin, K. and Leslie, P.W. (1988) Health and energy requirements of nomadic Turkana pastoralists. In, I. de Garine and G.A. Harrison, (Eds.) *Coping with Uncertainty in Food Supply.* Clarendon Press, Oxford: 210–60.

Marshall, M. (1979) (Ed.) *Beliefs, Behaviors and Alcoholic Beverages: A Cross-Cultural Survey.* The University of Michigan Press, Ann Arbor.

Sadoun, R., Lolli, G. and Silverman, M., (1965) *Drinking in French Culture.* Monograph of the Rutgers Center of Alcohol Studies, n° 5, New Brunswick, New Jersey. Distributed by College and University Press, New Haven, Conn.

Sahlins, M.D. (1972) *Stone Age Economics.* Tavistock, London.

Waddel, J.O. and Everett, M.W. (1980) *Drinking Behavior among Southwestern Indians. An Anthropological Perspective.* The University of Arizona Press, Tucson.

White, L.A. (1959) *The Evolution of Culture: The Development of Civilization to the Fall of Rome.* McGraw-Hill, New York.

Wolcott, H.F. (1974) *The African Beer Gardens of Bulawayo. Integrated Drinking in a Segregated Society.* Monograph of the Rutgers Center of Alcohol Studies, n° 10, New Brunswick, New Jersey. Distributed by College and University Press, New Haven, Conn.

2. THIRST AND DRINKING AS A BIO-CULTURAL PROCESS

Luis Alberto Vargas

Introduction

The human body has a series of functions that arise from its biological nature, most of them are interpreted, have special significance, and are carried out in particular ways which are clearly influenced by culture. These are known as biocultural processes. Thirst and drinking are part of our animal physiology, but their fulfillment is attained by a learned social process, and modified by our individual experiences and emotions.

Our need for water is only second to our need for air. We can only live for minutes without air, days without water and weeks without food. Some anecdotal information can be found in Harris (1989). Water is the main constituent of our body and plays a host of roles, in addition to being the main solvent and means of transportation of the elements that are essential to our life.

This paper deals with thirst, drinking and beverages, and our first task is to define them. Thirst is the sensation of craving for water, felt in the mouth and pharynx, that occurs when the osmolarity (ratio of water to solute) in our body rises by about one or two percent. Drinking is simply taking a liquid into the mouth and swallowing it. Beverages are liquids that are drunk; they may be hot or cold and usually consist of something other than plain water. With these very simple definitions we can start analysing the interaction between our biological nature and culture with regard to these three items.

Water Balance in the Human Body

Losing and regaining water is a constant function throughout human life. On average, an adult loses 1.5 litres of water daily as urine; 50 millilitres (ml) forming part of faeces, and 800 ml through skin and respiratory evaporation. Normally we recuperate daily from these losses by drinking about 1.3 litres, eating food with a content of about 800 ml of water, and by oxidation of the hydrogen in our food, also known as metabolic water, which accounts for about 250 ml. This delicate equilibrium can be lost through several mechanisms (see, for instance, chapter 5 of Passmore and Robson 1971). A person may be unable to find water or to drink it, for instance if in a desert, unconscious, having a disease that interferes with swallowing, or if voluntarily avoiding drinking, as in some religious celebrations. There may be excessive losses through diarrhea, vomiting, sweating, fever due to illness, or simply high environmental temperatures. This is the case in infectious diseases or when people are trapped in a very hot place. It is less common to lose water excessively through the respiratory system in places which are very high above sea level, due to the low oxygen levels in the atmosphere and the cooler temperatures. Finally, there can be extraordinary production of urine, as in some kidney diseases, Addisson's disease, or among people taking abnormal amounts of diuretic drugs.

The human body has different ways of reacting to water loss. Since this is a continuous process, thirst is the sensation that we feel whenever we have lost up to about two litres of fluids. This threshold varies from person to person, depending on previous experience, personal expectations and a host of other physiological and psychological factors. Losses of up to four litres of water produce distress, and death occurs with deficits near eight litres (Frisancho 1981), or 15–25 percent of body weight. When environmental temperatures are mild, a person can withstand about four to six days without drinking. During the 1985 earthquake in Mexico City, newborn babies were found reasonably healthy, despite having been buried alive for a week, and thus without food or drink. Of course, when environmental temperatures are higher, dehydration occurs faster since sweating can produce losses of up to twelve litres daily, or four litres per hour – but only for periods of around three to four hours. When water is being lost, thirst will normally force the process to stop. It is also interesting to remember that the consumption of liquids in humans is normally higher during daytime than at night.

Thirst

Thirst is a complex function, and is not only a craving to drink in response to the rising osmolarity in our body (Fitzsimons 1991). At the same time the body starts an antidiuretic function, which restrains urine production and thus the loss of water. Vasopressin and other substances are also released and enable the kidneys to receive enough blood, conserve electrolytes or minerals, and thus stabilise the immediate environment of the cells that constitute the body. Cell dehydration stimulates pressure receptors in the basal forebrain and the renin-angiotensin renal system, and contributes to the appearance of the sensation of thirst. At the same time, adjustments are made to blood pressure. Mineralocorticoids are also secreted and affect our craving for sodium. During pregnancy and lactation, hormones such as estrogens, ACTH (adrenocorticotrophic hormone), cortisol, corticosterone, prolactin, oxytocin and relaxin also affect the craving for water and sodium.

Experimentally it has been demonstrated that thirst can be modified either by drinking water or changing the ratio between body water and its solutes. Of course, the most available and common way to do so is by drinking.

There is also a second type of thirst that can appear under artificial conditions, allowing a person to sweat profusely and providing enough water, but free of sodium. During the first stages of this experiment, water was lost, in order to maintain a normal osmolarity, but as more sodium was lost, the excretion of water changed (McCance 1936). The body maintained its extracellular volume, or the amount of fluids outside of the cells, at the expense of the falling sodium concentration and osmolarity. The subjects experienced a special kind of thirst that could not be quenched with water, but only with hypertonic solutions of salt. This type of thirst may appear in cases of acute hemorrhage, due to the concomitant loss of salts in the blood. In ordinary conditions, when water is freely available, people tend to drink larger amounts than those they have lost. This ensures an adequate production of urine and the elimination of waste products.

Coping with Loss of Water or Maintaining the Homeostasis of Body Fluids

With the exception of the threshold of thirst, what we have presented above are the physiological responses of the human body, which are similar for the whole of humanity, in all times and spaces. However, the means through which we maintain the homeostasis of body fluids combine both physiological and cultural or behavioural responses.

The amounts of water and salt that come into our body are controlled by the physiology of thirst and sodium appetite. Our first response is to drink a liquid. At the same time, our body may start a series of actions. Among them are water-saving devices such as closing the skin blood vessels, in order to restrict the loss of water and solutes from this surface. The kidneys start concentrating urine, that is to say, eliminating an equivalent amount of salts diluted in less water. Nitrogen wastes may be eliminated as highly soluble urea or less soluble uric acid. The osmolarity of the fluids surrounding the body cells is enhanced by increasing the concentration of free aminoacids. If liquids are not drunk and the imbalance gets worse, the body will try to maintain the plasma volume, and reduce the evaporative loss of water by reducing the metabolic rate. Body temperature may be lowered, reducing the amount of water lost due to respiration, through the countercurrent heat exchange in the nasal passages (Frisancho 1981). Finally, if dehydration persists, the person may become unconscious and die.

It must be taken into account that in children, and in small people and fat people there is a lower surface-to-volume ratio, and they need proportionally more water to maintain constant body heat. In addition to these purely physiological mechanisms, each person responds to water loss by behaving in certain ways. The most evident one is looking for something to drink. The body also adapts in the long term by allowing its temperature to rise during the day, and dissipating heat at night by conduction and radiation, thus losing less water.

Humans also tend to look for shade or cooler environments, where they will reduce sweating and the loss of water through the respiratory process. The body may also be insulated by clothing, reducing heat gain by radiation and conduction from the sun and surroundings.

There are also some ways to cope with loss of liquids, which can be labelled as biocultural since they are regulated by culture, although adopted by specific persons. For instance, some human groups practise voluntary dehydration under intense sweating, drinking less than that which they lose, at an amount equivalent to about 2–4 percent of their body weight (Engell and Hirsch 1991). This has no relation to the temperature, composition or taste of the liquids to which they have access, but the remainder of the needed water is taken during meals. We have little idea of the effect of this practice on the body, but it is not believed to be harmful.

Some people who live in hot climates also tend to time their drinking to certain episodes of their daily life, despite the fact that they feel thirsty and have access to beverages. For instance, drinking may be restricted to pauses during work or to mealtimes. Normally they do not interrupt an activity to drink.

Others regulate the velocity of drinking, in order not to gulp down large amounts of liquid in a short time. This has been observed in nomadic groups upon arrival at a source of water. They may throw water on their faces and swallow the small quantity that falls into their mouths, or cup their hands to hold water, but do not make use of available vessels with larger capacity. In still other cases, herbs are put in large quantities in their water receptacles to make drinking difficult on purpose. This may be done to prevent the rapid dilation of the stomach with a mixture of air and water.

Some cultures differ in their choice of the temperature of drinks, according to the conditions of the environment. For instance, people in the United States of America prefer iced drinks to combat heat, and hot drinks such as coffee, tea or infusions when it is cold. In the Near East, however, hot tea, sometimes with large amounts of sugar, is preferred when the temperature is high. Looking for iced drinks to quench thirst is far from being universal, but North Americans have developed its availability through ice-dispensing machines or as ice cubes sold in plastic bags almost everywhere. In other regions of the world ice is not available with the same ease, and this has to do not only with their level of industrialisation, but with cultural preferences. In Mexico, three categories are established for drinks: *frío* (cold), *caliente* (hot) or *al tiempo* (at environmental temperature). In this country it is a common belief that ice is very harmful if you have a cold.

The very nature of drinks is another matter of choice. In many places plain water is preferred but in others, due to easy access to manufactured beverages, some may prefer a soft drink such as Coca-Cola, Pepsi-Cola, so-called mineral water, or the new thirst quenchers which contain small amounts of minerals which are supposed to be more physiological. The choice of what to drink in specific circumstances is in need of more research.

Human behaviour as a response to thirst is very complex, due to the great number of conditions in which it occurs, but it is even more interesting to find that people drink in situations that have little to do with thirst.

Beverages to Quench Thirst and Other Human Needs

Water has been a constant for the evolution of life on earth, and the natural beverage for humans. We perceive it as the most neutral substance: without taste, odour or colour, but not all the water found on our planet is fit to drink. For example, sea water is too salty, some may be muddy, dirty, and nowadays more and more of it is polluted. Finding potable water has been a common task for humans all through their history. Fortunately, nature offered water in abundance to our ancestors, but with the increase in the number of humans it has become a scarce resource. Mexico City, at 2,200 metres above sea level and with about eighteen million inhabitants, provides a perfect example of the huge public works that have had to be installed to make water available for people in our times.

One of the limitations of our body is its incapacity for storing water. If we are preparing for a long trip, and suppose that we will feel thirsty and it will be difficult to obtain water, it is useless to drink large amounts beforehand. Our system will eliminate the excess liquid very fast. Thus one of humankind's greatest discoveries has been to find ways to carry water, starting probably with empty gourds or containers made from leather, and continuing through a long process using ceramics, glass, metals, and plastics.

Humans have also been finding ways to change the characteristics of water, and create beverages. They have become a stimulating way to consume water, and at the same time, fulfill psychological and sociocultural needs. Nature also offers ready-to-drink beverages such as milk, fruit juices or *aguamiel*, the sap of the maguey plant *(Agave atrovirens Kawr)* (Ruvalcaba Mercado 1983) and others. At the same time, there are many natural resources that can be added to cold or boiling water to change its taste, such as honey, flowers, or herbs. Sugared liquids left alone for some time tend to ferment spontaneously and produce alcoholic beverages, which with time turn into vinegar. Later in human history, of course, distillation was discovered and more potent alcoholic beverages began to be produced. People highly appreciate their beverages, and have developed a sensibility for their odour, texture, temperature and colour. In Western culture, this can be perceived by studying the subtle descriptions of wines, in which every aspect is analysed with all of the senses, even up to the point of having professional tasters, whose subjective opinions can have important consequences, such as the inclusion of a certain wine on the list of a restaurant or fixing its commercial price! This is not an exceptional case since we also have professional tasters of tea, coffee or even the Mexican beverage, *pulque*, for which every barrel's price was fixed by a taster as it entered the train station to be distributed in several large cities (Guerrero 1980).

Most cultures have a basic food, which becomes the axis of their cuisine. In many cases this is either a grain or a root, such as wheat, maize, rice, potatoes, or yams. This food may also be the source of beverages, a product of a sustained relationship between humans and the plant. This is the case in Mexico, where corn provides beverages made from its tassels, stalk, and of course, the grain. An infusion of corn tassels is used as a medicinal beverage, and the sweet juice from the stalk can be drunk directly or used to prepare alcoholic beverages. The grain can be ground after being soaked in a hot solution of water and lime and the product is known as *masa*. A small ball of this dough can be diluted in water or milk and become *atole*, or can be left to ferment to make *atole agrio*, or *pozol* (Ulloa 1987). Mexicans also discovered centuries ago that they could toast maize, grind it and, by adding other products, prepare a fine powder, known as *pinole*, which also may be diluted in water, as we do with today's 'instant drinks'. Corn can also be fermented, of course, producing Mexican *tesgüino*, or some of the beers found in other parts of the world.

These Mexican beverages can be used as an example of the many contexts of drinking. For instance, *atole* is a food-drink, it is not only a source of water, but also of energy and nutrients, it is used as a weaning food, but also as a beverage to be consumed early in the morning or late at night. *Pozol* has the advantage that it can be carried as a ball of dough, wrapped in leaves, and prepared away from home as a beverage, just by diluting it in water. This makes it ideal for peasants who work in the fields and eat and refresh themselves with a single product. *Atole agrio*, after undergoing fermentation, has the advantage not only of having a different taste, but of being enriched in its protein content by nitrogen fixation from the air used for the growth and reproduction of the same micro-organisms responsible for its fermentation. Atole began as a domestic drink, but with the growth of cities it has reappeared in the hands of street-food vendors, as a convenient item for an early morning breakfast before arriving at school or work. Its taste can be enhanced by adding cinnamon or many varieties of fruits. In contrast, tesgüino, being mildly alcoholic, is a religious and ceremonial drink among the Tarahumara Indians, in the state of Chihuahua, Mexico.

Mexican time is tuned to the beverages that accompany certain activities. For instance, warm milk with coffee is a popular breakfast drink; coffee usually ends the midday meal; soft drinks or *refrescos* are preferred as a snack; hot chocolate is mandatory for the First Communion feast; *ponche* (water boiled with fruits, cinnamon and other spices, to which alcoholic beverages may be added) is to be drunk during the festivities preceding Christmas; and coffee with a shot of rum or brandy is common during wakes for the dead in rural homes. Tequila is the drink for a man who has just been jilted, and champagne, or *sidra* (a fermented apple drink), is used to celebrate happy moments. Beer is most usual to relieve thirst in hot climates, and in Mexico it must be served very cold, to the point that a round of six to ten very small bottles *(ampolletas)* may be offered on ice, to ensure that they do not get warm while being drunk.

Some beverages, such as Mexican pulque (the fermented sap of *Agave atrovirens*) and tequila, have been the centre of whole ways of life in the regions in which they are produced (Guerrero 1980), much in the way that wine has for the Old World. For instance, pulque is produced in specially built haciendas, that have spaces to store and ferment the raw sap or *aguamiel*. This requires experts who know each phase of its collection, fermentation and transportation process. *Pulque* is drunk in special bars known as *pulquerías*, that have very particular, and mostly ironic, names, in addition to a decoration that is not found elsewhere. There are even games which are not played outside the *pulquería*. *Pulque* requires special vessels, some of which, with a conical shape, were used in ancient Mesoamerica. The modern ones are made of glass and have particular forms and shapes, and some of their names are *cacarizas, tornillos, catrinas* or *chivos*. Again, these glasses are not used for any other beverage.

In contrast, tequila is drunk in a small cylindrical glass known as *caballito*. Some of these glasses were originally used to hold candles in churches and had the face of Christ engraved on the bottom. Hence, if you gulped down your tequila all at once, it was common to say *'hasta verte Jesús mio'* ('til I see you, Jesus my Lord'), since you did not finish drinking until the face appeared. Traditionally tequila is not drunk on its own, but with a pinch of salt and lemon juice. Salt is put on the base of the thumb which is brought close to the mouth and tapped in order to allow it to drop directly into the mouth. After swallowing tequila you may drink a shot of *sangrita*, another beverage made with lemon and tomato juice, and spiced with hot peppers.

Sometimes the container of the beverage adds to the taste. This is the case of *café de olla*, a boiled coffee, spiced with cinnamon, and served in *jarros* or earthenware vessels that give a special flavour. In other cases, such as wine, glass is sought so as not to add any taste.

As seen in these examples, beverages may require special circumstances to be consumed. This concerns the place, the people around you, the food that goes with the drinks, the vessel that holds what is to be drunk, and sometimes even the music that goes with it. Some drinks are ceremonial, others are used as medicine, and yet others are simply sought to quench thirst and refresh a hot or tired body.

As we can see from the above examples, drinking can be a complex biocultural process, of immense variability among humans.

Tasks for the Future

This paper's only purpose has been to present the complexity of drinking among humans. As anthropologists we find that this is an issue that needs more research, due to its great potential. We will give some examples:

1. All over the world there are a variety of native beverages, which are safe and adequate for human consumption. For instance, in places

where there is poor hygiene, fermented drinks made from milk or fruits have the advantage of inhibiting the growth of most micro-organisms that cause disease. Thus they may represent an advantage over polluted water, and they are already part of some cultures and well accepted (Ulloa 1987). More needs to be known about their potential as an alternative to more expensive products such as bottled water or manufactured soft drinks.

2. Many cultures have developed beverages for weaning children (see, for example, Jelliffe 1968, 1974). Some of them work very well and are easily available and culturally acceptable. This is the case with different types of atoles in Mexico (see the variety of atoles in Echeverria and Arroyo 1982). They are made not only of maize, but also of rice, oats, etc. We need to explore their properties and limitations, in contrast to other products that are being introduced on a commercial basis. For instance, some Mexican mothers wean with Coca-Cola, which clearly does not have the nutritional qualities of atoles.

3. We have already given the Mexican example of *pozol* as a native instant drink with good nutritional qualities. The same can be said for *tascalate*, a powder made with the fine flour of maize, cocoa, and *achiote (Bixa orellana)*. Diluted in water it becomes deep red and a very tasty and nutritious drink. These native instant-beverages have great potential not only as food-beverages, but to start local industries and thus contribute to the welfare of those who produce them.

4. Studies of fermented beverages show their potential in inhibiting the growth of pathogens. It seems that the germ producing cholera cannot grow in fermented drinks such as yoghurt (Steinkraus 1983; McGee 1984). More research is needed about their use in epidemics or to prevent water-borne diseases.

5. Since beverages and their vessels go together, some insight has been gained on their possible interaction. For example, it has been shown that ceramics that are glazed with lead products in low temperature kilns release this poisonous metal when in contact with acidic drinks, such as fruit juices or the vinegar in salads. This is quite toxic, and campaigns (e.g., in Mexico through the newspapers) are being run all over the world to encourage the use of other products in glazing, and to use higher oven temperatures (Schnaas 1998).

6. There are some studies concerning the physiology of dehydration after very stressful situations such as extreme heat or intense work (Greenleaf 1991). Anthropologists have observed different types of practices, but we still have insufficient knowledge of the most adequate composition, the temperature, the timing, and the rate of ingestion of beverages. Industry has produced 'thirst quenchers' with water and minerals and commercialised them for people who practise sports. Most of their users forget that the minerals contained in these

beverages can also be obtained with food. More physiological studies are needed in this domain.

7. Little has been done in analysing the effects of the role of industrialised societies in substituting native beverages with mild alcoholic content for beers, rums, brandies and others. A good example is found in Mexico, where *pulque*, a beverage with centuries of tradition, is nearly being eliminated by other, easily available drinks of higher alcoholic content. The social context of drinking alcohol has not been taken into account and this has favoured excessive consumption. Our modern worries on the negative effects of alcoholisation among many human groups imply that we have to investigate further the whole context of this issue.

8. In contrast, much is being done in analysing the medicinal properties of some beverages such as infusions. The results show clearly the benefits that some of them offer. For instance, studies carried out in Mexico show that guava leaves *(Psidium guajava)* have the same antidiarrheal properties as commercial mixtures of pectin and kaolin (see, for example, Lozoya 1998). On the other hand, several medicinal infusions have been found to be toxic in high dosages, or can have serious health consequences when another species is used instead of the medicinal one, due to their morphological similarity.

9. Anthropologists have yet to make a deeper analysis of what makes some beverages acceptable and others to be rejected. This has been largely the domain of marketing experts, but there are more profound motivations than those of interest to industry. Foods and beverages are one of the main influences on health, and finding ways to better the diet of those who need it should be considered a priority.

10. It is also worthwhile studying the artifacts of culture that surround beverages and drinking. With modernisation, most of these objects are being lost, but they are part of our heritage as humans. For instance, *mancerinas* were used in Latin America and Spain to drink chocolate. They are cups embedded in a dish, in such a way that the cup can be picked up easily, while the dish holds pastries or other sweets. It is said that they were designed during the government in New Spain (1664–73) for the father of Viceroy Mancera, whose hands shook involuntarily and who was afraid of spilling his chocolate (Diccionario Porrúa de historia, biografica y geografía de México 1971). These objects are found in museums, but are not in use any more; they are witnesses to a certain moment in Mexican history.

11. Another area that has been understudied is the beverage-food complex. *Tapas* in Spain, and *botanas* in Mexico are examples of foods made to be consumed with beverages, alcoholic or otherwise. In many instances these foods play a significant role in the diet and are a source of culinary innovation and the introduction of new foods.

12. Still more research is needed on the role of beverages and drinking as enhancers of social relationships. Coffee shops, pubs, *cantinas*, bars, *pulquerías* and others are places created by most societies in which one can drink in a social environment. As we have stated above, these sites have their own material culture and social rules that sometimes favour, and in other instances control, the excessive consumption of alcohol. More needs to be known about them in a world where the pathological consumption of alcohol, linked to loneliness and desperation, is becoming more common.

13. The world of native beverages is starting to be analysed in depth. We are finding more and more information on ways to prepare them, and on their nutritional, medicinal, and social properties. Some of them seem to have qualities that would permit their wider diffusion. One of the tasks for anthropologists is to continue their research along these lines. ●

14. As a last example of the many avenues for investigations on beverages, it is interesting to consider them as a sort of marker for history. For example, a fermented drink from the palm tree called *tuba* is found in Mexico and the Philippines. We have scanty information on its place of origin, but finding its production on the Pacific coast of Mexico is a living relic of the past contacts of both regions during the times when ships covered the route from the Philippines to Mexico, bringing people, goods and ideas that crossed the country, before leaving from Veracruz to Spanish ports. Centuries of this trade have left their influence in both countries, and this beverage is one of them.

Conclusion

Clearly drinking has a physiological basis, but it is modified by each individual's personality and culture. Being such a common act, it has been largely overlooked by anthropologists and social scientists, except when it has to do with some of the major problems of humanity, such as excessive alcohol consumption, or the attempted substitution of human lactation for industrialised formulas with modified cow's milk.

We know quite a lot about the physiological mechanisms that control water equilibrium and thirst in the human body, less about the consequences of different ways of drinking, and little concerning the material and social context of it. Clearly there is a need for much ethnographical work all over the world, in order to gain insight into its variability. At the same time, more research has to be conducted on the contents and properties of beverages.

It is interesting to note that, despite the interest that food has aroused in the scientific field and its overflow into the media, beverages have been of lesser concern. We hope that the studies presented in this book begin a new stage in this field.

References

Diccionario Porrúa de historia, biografía y geografía de México (1971). Editorial Porrúa, México D.F., 2 vols.

Echeverría, M. E., Arroyo, L.E. (1982) *Recetario mexicano del maíz*. Museo de Culturas Populares, S.E.P., México D.F: 195–203.

Engell, D. and E. Hirsch (1991) Environmental and sensory modulation of fluid intake in humans. In, D.J. Ramsay and D.Booth, *Thirst: physiological and psychological aspects*. Springer Verlag, London: 382–90.

Fitzsimons, J.T. (1991) Evolution of physiological and behavioural mechanisms in vertebrate body fluid homeostasis. In, D.J. Ramsay and D. Booth, *Thirst: physiological and psychological aspects*. Springer Verlag, London: 3–22.

Frisancho, A. Roberto (1981) *Human adaptation. A functional interpretation*. The University of Michigan Press, Ann Arbor: 11–23.

Greenleaf, J.E. (1991) The consequences of exercise on thirst and fluid intake. In, D.J. Ramsay and D. Booth, *Thirst: physiological and psychological aspects*. Springer Verlag, London: 412–21.

Guerrero Guerrero, Raúl (1980) *El pulque, religión, cultura, folklore*. Instituto Nacional de Antropología e Historia, Mexico D.F.

Harris, Marvin (1989) *Nuestra especie*. Alianza Editorial, El libro de bolsillo, Madrid, España: 144–9. The original title of this book in English is *Our kind*.

Jelliffe, D.B. (1968) *La evaluación del estado nutricional de la comunidad*. Geneva, World Health Organisation, Monograph 53.

Jelliffe, D. B. (1974) *Nutrición infantil en países en desarrollo*. Editorial Limusa, México, Both books are originally in English and have been translated into several languages.

Lozoya, Xavier (1998) *La herbolaria en México*. Consejo Nacional para la Cultura y las Artes, Colección Tercer Milenio, México D.F.

McGee, Harold (1984) *On food and cooking. The science and lore of the kitchen*. Collier Books, Macmillan Publishing Company, New York: 31–6.

McCance, R.A. (1936) Experimental sodium chloride deficiency in man. *Proc. Roy. Soc. Lond. B.* 119: 245–68.

Passmore, R. and J.S. Robson: A. (1971) *Companion to medical studies, volume 1, Anatomy, biochemistry, physiology and related subjects*. Blackwell Scientific Publications, Oxford.

Ruvalcaba Mercado, Jesús (1983) *El maguey manso. Historia y presente de Epazoyucan, Hidalgo, Texcoco*. Universidad Autónoma, Chapingo.

Schnaas, Maria de Lourdes (1998) Plomo y nutricion. *Cuadernos de Nutricion*, 21, 1: 9–12.

Steinkraus, R.H. (1983) *Handbook of indigenous fermented foods*. Microbiological Series 9, Marcel Dekker, New York.

Ulloa, M., Herrera, T. and Lappe, P. (1987) *Fermentaciones tradicionales indígenas de México*. Instituto Nacional Indigenista, México D.F.

3. WATER AND DRINKING IN AN ECOLOGICAL CONTEXT AMONG AUSTRALIAN ABORIGINAL PEOPLE PRACTISING TRADITIONAL SUBSISTENCE METHODS

Stanley J. Ulijaszek

Introduction

The physiological mechanisms controlling thirst are well-known (Rolls and Rolls 1982), and include response to water loss as sweat and urine (Belding 1972), resulting in more concentrated cellular and extracellular fluid. Such water loss is a consequence of the maintenance of a constant internal thermal and biochemical environment (Robertshaw 1985), and is a physiological given. While heat can be transferred between body and environment by way of conduction, convection, radiation, and evaporation (Mount 1979), in hot external environments, evaporative heat loss is the most efficient means of dissipating metabolically generated heat (Frisancho 1993). For example, the proportion of total heat loss by way of evaporation in a sample of adult males at a temperature of 25° celsius is about 23 percent, while at a temperature of 35° celsius, it is 90 percent (Folk 1974). It has been proposed that the evolution of sweating came with increased body size, in association with increased exposure of early endotherms, to periods of solar radiation as their ecological success took their range beyond the forest boundaries of their early habitats (Robertshaw 1985). The loss of body hair across human evolution was associated with the spread of eccrine glands, which facilitated the even spread of sweat across the body to ensure efficient evaporative heat loss (Robertshaw 1985). In warm environments, naked animals have the lowest metabolic and water requirements for optimal thermoregulation (McArthur and Clark 1987); accepting an 'out of Africa' explanation for the origins of humanity (Tobias 1994), a lack of body hair in the hot environmental conditions extant during human evolution may have conferred some selective advantage.

While drinking has clear social aims and consequences, the physiological aspects of water requirements cannot be neglected, especially in environments that may be water-limited for some parts of the year. Since human beings are largely unable to store water (Rolls and Rolls 1982), thirst rapidly follows water depletion, usually initiating behaviours that lead to replenishment of water balance. Water loss of up to 4 percent of body weight can be sustained without loss of physiological function (Mount 1979; Frisancho 1993). Signs of thirst are strong when as little as 2 percent of body weight has been lost, but these do not become worse as dehydration proceeds. After 4 percent water loss, the mouth becomes very dry, and at 8 percent loss, the tongue becomes swollen and speech is difficult (Mount 1979). A water deficit of 20 percent (range 15–25 percent) of body weight will result in death (Adolph 1947). There is little tendency for the sweat rate to be reduced during dehydration (Mount 1979). Although evaporative water losses are very effective in maintaining the body within the thermoneutral range for optimal physiological function in hot environments, there are ecological situations where water availability and drinking to aid the replenishment of water balance cannot be assumed. This is particularly the case among populations that experience heat stress in environments where water availability is marginal; this includes pastoralists in arid and semi-arid regions of the world, as well as hunter-gatherer groups practising traditional subsistence.

While sweating is an extremely efficient means of heat loss, it is possible that under some ecological conditions it may not be possible to stay adequately hydrated for proper physiological function, including adequate work output. Thus, while individuals may be able to work for prolonged periods at low environmental temperatures, the water loss needed to dissipate the metabolic heat generated by work at high environmental temperatures may be in excess of immediate water availability, and may in this way limit the extent of work possible. This may be one way in which human groups are limited in their subsistence scheduling and time-space use by water availability. In this article, the interrelationships between water needs and time scheduling for work are examined for hunter-gatherer populations living in marginal environments which potentially carry both a high heat stress threat, and a high water intake requirement to cope with that threat. Specifically, water requirements and heat stress among Aboriginal people in Central, Northern, and North-Western Australia are considered. The choice of area lies in the detailed ethnographic observations of time-space use among populations traditionally living there, and the availability of detailed data on the thermal environment of this region. The approach taken is one of ecological modelling, using a computer programme developed by the United States Army for the prediction of heat stress and water loss among its personnel (Pandolf et al. 1986). By predicting water losses of Australian Aboriginal people carrying out traditional subsistence practices, the possibility that the short working day of Arnhem Land adults reported by McCarthy and McArthur (1960) might reflect ecologically limited work scheduling by way of high water loss, is examined. If this is the case, then the notion that the short working day is a marker of the leisured society characteristic of hunter-gatherer groups (Sahlins 1972) is challenged.

Time Scheduling and Water Needs

Among traditional societies, work is the physical exertion that has as its aim the generation of subsistence. A common view of traditional Australian Aboriginal subsistence is that it involves less work than in the industrialised West. In this view, leisure is abundant, and there is a greater amount of daytime sleep per capita than among other types of society (Sahlins 1972).

Table 3.1 shows the daily variation in the number of hours spent in work among adult males and females in Arnhem Land (McCarthy and McArthur 1960) at the end of the dry season. Mean values for the two groups range between 3.7 and 5.1 hours per day respectively, with women working slightly longer per day than men. While it has been assumed that Australian Aboriginal people traditionally underused their objective economic possibilities (Sahlins 1972), the eventuality that the subsistence quest might be limited by water availability to support sweat loss has not been considered. Physiological studies of water-loss among Aboriginal peoples are limited to classical studies of sweat rates in response to heat stress by Wyndham et al. (1964), who showed that the sweat rate of Aboriginal people (237ml/m2/hr) was significantly less than that produced by Europeans (384 ml/m2/hr). Although Sahlins did not consider the possibility, the notion that work may be limited by heat stress is plausible given the extent and timing of daytime sleep among the Arnhem Land Fish Creek group (McCarthy and McArthur 1960) used to support his

Table 3.1 Hours spent per day in food-getting activities, among two groups of Australian Aboriginal People in Arnhem Land (from McCarthy and McArthur 1960)

| Day | Fish Creek | | Hemple Bay | |
	male	female	male	female
1	5.3	7.1	6.7	5.0
2	6.5	3.0	2.0	3.3
3	0	0	5.0	1.6
4	3.4	7.0	5.2	5.3
5	6.7	6.7	6.8	5.8
6	5.9	0.8	3.5	7.2
7	4.5	4.5	6.7	7.8
8	0.3	0.2		
9	4.8	6.0		
10	4.8	4.4		
11	3.0	0		
12	3.6	6.5		
13	2.5	7.4		
14	0.3	1.7		
Mean	3.7	4.0	4.7	5.1
CV	59%	70%	34%	39%

own argument. For six of the fourteen days of the study of McCarthy and McArthur, most males and females slept during the afternoon, a time when environmental temperatures are highest and potential heat stress the greatest. Studies of relationships between work output, work scheduling, and water-loss in response to heat stress are absent from the literature, and the present analysis attempts to redress this shortcoming. It is possible to model the influence of work and heat load on the degree of water loss, using the United States Army Heat Stress Model, developed by the United States Army Research Institute of Environmental Medicine (Pandolf et al. 1986). In the present analysis, this model is used to predict the extent to which subsistence activity and scheduling of Australian Aboriginal people may have been limited by the water requirements needed to carry out subsistence tasks in the hot environments of Central, Northern and North-Western Australia.

The Modelling of Water Loss

Models are simplifications of reality, but have proved useful in the study of complex subsistence work and output relationships (Ulijaszek 1995). Most models use optimisation procedures, in some sort of cost-benefit analysis. Such procedures have been used in the study of hunter-gatherer societies, following the postulates of synthetic evolutionary theory (Pianka 1988; Smith 1983). While this is not possible in the present analysis, it can be argued that optimisation of work time scheduling to minimise water loss might have adaptive significance. Many foraging strategy models are based on geometric representations of the relationships of foragers to resources, with solutions found by graphs or by differential calculus (Cody 1974). Once the currency is chosen, an appropriate cost-benefit function must be adopted, and the function solved for an optimum. It is usually assumed that fitness varies directly with the rate of net energy capture which can be achieved while foraging (Pyke et al. 1977). Although a number of factors can intervene to influence this relationship (Schoener 1971), in general it holds true. The present case considers the minimisation of water loss as the key variable, although it is acknowledged that other variables could be chosen as alternatives.

Of the various components of human energy expenditure, the largest among most populations living traditional lifestyles is that of workload and physical activity (Ulijaszek 1996). Importantly, for populations living in hot environments, physical work output is accompanied by the need to dissipate heat. Under conditions of excessive external temperature, the most effective way of losing heat is by way of evaporation from the skin (Robertshaw 1985). Subsistence productivity can be affected by seasonality of climate, and in most communities where climatic seasonality might affect human biology in some stressful way, strategies are employed to reduce its impact. Such strategies may be complex and graded, and involve social and cultural factors and patterns of behaviour which change according to level of stress. With respect to heat stress, patterns of subsistence may alter during times of the year when the combined effects of heat and humidity may preclude extensive work periods, or intensive workloads. Among Australian Aboriginal populations, varying the work schedule could be an effective way of coping with seasonality in heat stress.

The experience of heat stress may also vary with different environments and ecological settings. Most studies of traditional subsistence among Australian Aboriginal groups have been carried out in North and North-Western Australia (e.g., McCarthy and McArthur 1960; Hart and Pilling 1960; Peterson 1973; Sackett 1979; Meehan 1982; Walsh 1990; Tonkinson 1991), where climate and ecology vary enormously: from humid rainforest, to open forest and woodland and low woodland, to arid shrubland, grassland and desert where humidity is the lowest and solar radiation the greatest among these areas (Leeper 1970; Calaby 1980). The first stage of the modelling procedure was therefore to identify climatic regions, using data available from the Australian Bureau of Meteorology (Commonwealth of Australia 1998; website: http://www.bom.gov.au/climate). Sites of meteorological collection for four different ecological zones in the North of Western Australia and in the Northern Territory were identified, and these are given in Table 3.2. The classification into the four zones was carried out by the author on the basis of clear geographical and climatic differences between them. Daily maximum and minimum temperatures were averaged for the four zones, as was relative humidity. Data from the month of January was chosen as being representative of one of the hottest times of the year, when heat-stress limited work scheduling was most likely to occur. Climatic characteristics of the four zones are given in Table 3.3. The greatest variation across these zones is with respect to relative humidity, which ranges between 28 and 74 percent, and rainfall, which varies between 37 and 350mm. The tropical coastal ecological zone shows the least diurnal variation in temperature, while arid inland and central zones show the most. The arid inland zone has the highest maximum and minimum temperatures, exceeding those of the arid central region by 3° celsius.

A number of mathematical models of human thermoregulation have been developed (Woodcock et al. 1958; Wyndham and Atkins 1960; Wissier 1961; Hardy et al. 1971). The software employed in the present analysis was the United States Army Heat Strain Model. Unlike earlier models, this is the first

Table 3.2 Sites of collection of meteorological data, by ecological zone

Ecological zone	Sites
Tropical coastal	Darwin, Gove, Mitchell Plateau
Arid coastal	Broome, Port Hediand, Learmonth, Carnarvon
Arid inland	Tennant Creek, Halls Creek, Rabbit Flat, Balgo Hills, Marde Bar, Wittenoom, Paraburdoo
Arid central	Giles, Alice Springs

Table 3.3 Average climatic characteristics of the four ecological zones
chosen for heat stress and water loss analysis, during the month of January

Ecological zone	Temperature Max (C)	Min (C)	Relative Humidity (%)	Monthly Rainfall (mm)
Tropical coastal	32	25	74	350
Arid coastal	35	24	55	66
Arid inland	40	25	34	88
Arid central	37	22	28	37

comprehensive model which incorporates the theoretical physics of heat transfer, the biophysics of clothing, the physiology of metabolic heat production,
distribution and elimination, and related meteorological factors including relative humidity, wind speed and environmental temperature (Pandolf et al.
1986). The mathematical basis of the model is the integration of three sets of
equations:

1. The three component equation of Givoni and Goldman (1972) for the
   prediction of rectal temperature.
2. The general equation of Shapiro et al. (1982) for the prediction of
   sweat loss response as a function of exercise, environmental and clothing interactions.
3. The general formulae of Givoni and Goldman (1973) for the prediction of final equilibrium heart rate.

The superiority of this model relative to others is its ability to predict physiological responses and human physical performance in the heat, under a greater
variety of conditions than any other model. Access to the modelling procedure
was made to the author by William Matthews, of the United States Army
Research Institute of Environmental Medicine, Natick, Massachusetts.

Assumptions made with respect to workload and time scheduling were
inevitably simplifications of reality, and were as follows. The model Aboriginal man was acclimatised to the heat, wore minimal clothing, and worked constantly at a moderate rate of 440 watts. In the first cycle of the modelling
procedure, he worked for a four-hour period, and took rest for the remaining
eight hours of the hypothetical twelve-hour day. In the second cycle of the procedure, he worked for five hours and rested for seven. Wind speed was
assumed to be low, at 1.5m/sec. Water loss through sweating was predicted for
the model man for the twelve-hour day in the four ecological zones, under two
sets of conditions: firstly on an overcast day in which there was no radiant heat
load; and secondly on a sunny day, in which radiant heat load was incorporated within the model. The model man was then assumed to start at different

Figure 3.1   Modelling sweat loss in Australian hunter-gatherers. The 12-hour water loss at work load of 440 watts, and a four-hour work period, according to the time of start of the working day. Overcast day.

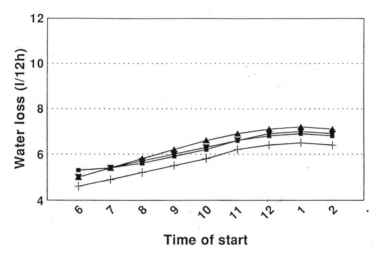

Figure 3.2   Modelling sweat loss in Australian hunter-gatherers. The 12-hour water loss at work load of 440 watts, and a four-hour work period, according to the time of start of the working day. Sunny day (high solar radiation).

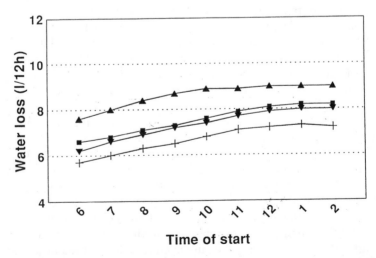

times of the day, such that work initiated later in the day might carry higher water loss, as the environmental temperatures were higher. The time of year chosen was January, when heat stress was highest. Thus, even if water loss was deemed excessive in a particular ecological zone by this model, this would not imply that the populations traditionally living there would have been water-limited all year round. Body weight was set at 59 kg, a weight commensurate with average stature of 172 cm (Brown and Townsend 1982) and a body mass index of 20, typical of adult Australian Aboriginal people (Norgan 1993). Results of this procedure for the four-hour working day are given in Figures 3.1 and 3.2.

On an overcast day (Figure 3.1), twelve-hour water loss is lower in the arid central zone than in the other three zones, regardless of the time of day when work is started. If work is started by 7.00 am, then twelve-hour water loss does not exceed the baseline value of 5.4 litres/twelve-hours calculated on the basis of known sweat rate and surface area (Macpherson 1966) of adult Australian Aboriginal males. For the arid central zone, twelve-hour sweat loss stays below this value if work is started at any time before 9.00 am. If work starts at, or after midday, twelve-hour water loss exceeds seven litres for all zones apart from the arid central zone. Human beings can suffer dehydration to the extent of 4 percent of body weight in the course of a day's work, without impairment of physiological function (Mount 1979; Frisancho 1993). This represents about three litres in the case of the 59 kg model Aboriginal man. Acknowledging that water consumption in the course of the working day is minimal among

Figure 3.3   Modelling sweat loss in Australian hunter-gatherers. The 12-hour water loss at work load of 440 watts, and a five-hour work period, according to the time of start of the working day. Overcast day.

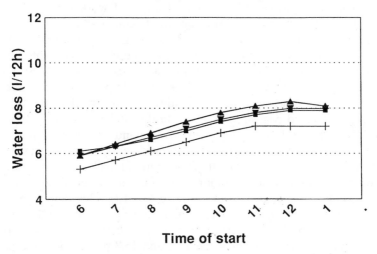

Time of start

-**Arid coastal**   -**Arid inland**   +**Arid central**   -**Tropical coastal**

Figure 3.4 Modelling sweat loss in Australian hunter-gatherers. The 12-hour water loss at work load of 440 watts, and a five-hour work period, according to the time of start of the working day. Sunny day.

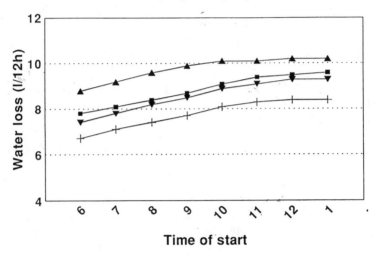

Time of start

-▼- **Arid coastal**   -▲- **Arid inland**   + **Arid central**   -■- **Tropical coastal**

Aboriginal people practising traditional subsistence (Macpherson 1966), the extent of dehydration that these levels of water loss represent for the four ecological zones are: between 7.6 and 12.4 percent if work is started at 6.00 am, between 9.5 and 10.3 percent if it is started at 9.00 am, and between 10.7 and 12.0 percent, if work is started at midday. Thus on cloudy days, adult Aboriginal males are likely to become dehydrated to the point of impaired physiological function regardless of the time of day that work is started, but are unlikely to be stressed by water shortage in the course of a day's subsistence, to the limit of survival, or 20 percent of body weight (Adolph 1947).

On a sunny day with high radiant heat load, there is considerable spread in the twelve-hour sweat rate across ecological zones (Figure 3.2). In the arid inland zone, the twelve-hour sweat rate is about 25 percent greater than that in the arid central zone, regardless of the time at which work starts. Values for the tropical and arid coastal regions are fairly similar, and are intermediate between the two extreme values for arid inland and arid central zones. Although the low water loss value for the arid central zone appears surprisingly low, it is easily explained by the low minimum daily temperatures of this area, which are the lowest of all four zones. For all four ecological zones, the twelve-hour sweat rate exceeds the 5.4 litre sweat-rate baseline regardless of the time of day at which work starts. The extent of dehydration lies between 8.1 and 13.0 percent if work starts at 6.00 am, between 10.8 and 14.7 percent if work starts at 9.00 am, and between 11.2 and 15.3 percent if work starts at noon. The level of dehydration stress is considerably higher if there is a high radiant heat load from direct sunlight, than if there is not. However, in neither case is water loss so high that death by dehydration is threatened.

Results of the modelling procedure for the five-hour working day are given in Figures 3.3 and 3.4. The trends in twelve-hour water loss are similar to those for the four-hour working day model, although the extent of water loss is greater. On an overcast day (Figure 3.3) twelve-hour water loss exceeds the 5.4 litres baseline value regardless of the time of day that work is started, with the exception of the arid central ecological zone. In this zone, twelve-hour water loss is below 5.4 litres only if the five-hour work period starts at 6.00 am. The extent of dehydration that the twelve-hour water losses represent for the four ecological zones are: between 8.8 and 10.3 percent if work is started at 6.00 am, between 10.8 and 12.5 percent if it is started at 9.00 am, and between 12.1 and 14.2 percent if work begins at midday. Thus, a five-hour work period marginally increases the extent of impairment of physiological function due to dehydration, but not to the extent that it becomes life-threatening. On a sunny day, the twelve-hour water loss for the five-hour work period (Figure 3.4) exceeds the 5.4 litre baseline value for all four ecological zones regardless of the time of day that work starts. The extent of dehydration that the twelve-hour water losses represent are between 11.5 and 14.9 percent if work is started at 6.00 am, between 13.1 and 16.8 percent if work starts at 9.00 am, and between 14.1 and 17.1 percent if work starts at noon. Thus, the degree of dehydration is physiologically significant, if not life-threatening, across all four ecological zones.

Water Requirements and Work Scheduling: Reconciling the Model with Knowledge of Australian Aboriginal Subsistence Scheduling

The water loss model presented in this article is consistent with observations of Aboriginal subsistence practices in the arid inland regions of Australia. The Mardu of the Western Desert live by means of a highly mobile adaptation that allows them to exploit scattered food and water resources at different times (Tonkinson 1991). In January, not only is it hot, but water sources are intermittent and ephemeral, and foraging is largely limited to areas surrounding the drying waterholes, which are to all intents and purposes clay-pans. Group size is small, the larger population having dispersed in response to the severity of the environment (Walsh 1990). In summer, people hunt and gather food very early in the day, before it becomes too hot, while in winter they wait until the sun is well up before leaving the warmth of their fires (Tonkinson 1991). The results of the predictive modelling (Figures 3.1–3.4) suggest that a later start would carry considerable physiological costs in this arid inland zone, especially on days with limited or no cloud cover.

In tropical coastal areas of Australia, the average length of time spent working was traditionally four or five hours per day respectively (McCarthy and McArthur 1960). This data, and that of Lee (1968) for subsistence time spent by the !Kung, were used by Sahlins (1972) in developing his 'original affluence' argument. This has been criticised by Altman (1984) who suggested that Sahlins grossly overestimated the amount of leisure time available to Aboriginal people, and that in Arnhem Land affluence is more likely to be a modern phenomenon than one found in more traditional times. Working among a band of coastal Gunwinggu in Arnhem Land in 1979–80, Altman found that men spent an average of 2.9 hours in the subsistence quest. However, the Gunwinggu were by this time dependent upon this market economy for a substantial portion of their subsistence. Indeed, 54 percent of their dietary energy intake came from market sources. In calculating the extra work needed to meet the shortfall in dietary energy availability in the absence of the market economy, Altman (1984) showed that under traditional conditions, time spent in the subsistence quest would have exceeded the values observed during his field study. Furthermore, he showed that at most times of year the time spent in the subsistence quest would have had to be greater than the daily time available for work, in order to attain adequate dietary energy intakes. This suggests that nutritional availability was likely to have been severely constrained in the past in this population. In the present analysis, the results of the predictive modelling of water loss in the tropical coastal zone suggest that the work scheduling and time spent at work by Arnhem Landers would have been limited by water availability at the peak of summer. A four-hour work period on an overcast day would not have resulted in any significant dehydration. However, excessive evaporative water loss to maintain thermoneutrality due to a longer work period, a start after 6.00 am, or working on a sunny day, would have compromised optimal physiological work performance. Thus, while extended work times may have been needed to acquire adequate food under traditional conditions, work output may have been limited by dehydration under most conditions likely to prevail. Notably, the short working day of Arnhem Landers observed by McCarthy and McArthur (1960) may be less a marker of a leisured society (Sahlins 1972) than of a heat-stressed one.

References

Adolph, A.F. (1947) *Physiology of Man in the Desert.* Interscience Publishers, New York.

Altman, J.C. (1984) Hunter-gatherer subsistence production in Arnhem Land: the original affluence hypothesis re-examined. *Mankind* 14: 179–90.

Belding, H.S. (1972) Biophysical principles of acclimatization to heat. In, M.K. Yousef, S.M. Horvath and R.W. Builard (Eds.) *Physiological Adaptations.* Academic Press, New York: 9–21.

Brown, T. and Townsend, G.C. (1982) Adolescent growth in height of Australian Aboriginals analysed by the Preece-Baines function: a longitudinal study, 1961–71.
Annals of Human Biology 9: 495–506.

Calaby, J. (1980) Ecology and human use of the Australian savanna environment. In, D.R. Hards (Ed.) *Human Ecology in Savanna Environments.* Academic Press, London: 321–37.

Cody, M.L. (1974) Optimisation in ecology. *Science* 183: 1156–64.

Commonwealth of Australia (1998) *Monthly Climatic Statistics for Australia.* Bureau of Meteorology, Canberra.

Folk, G.E. (1974) *Textbook of Environmental Physiology.* Lea and Febiger, Philadelphia.

Frisancho, A.R. (1993) *Human Adaptation and Accommodation.* University of Michigan Press, Ann Arbor.

Givoni, B. and Goldman, R.F. (1972) Predicting rectal temperature response to work, environment and clothing. *Journal of Applied Physiology* 32: 812–22.

Givoni, B. and Goldman R.F. (1973) Predicting heart rate response to work, environment, and clothing. *Journal of Applied Physiology* 34: 201–4.

Hardy, J.D., Stolwijk, J.A.J. and Gagge, A.P. (1971) Man. In, D.C. Whittow (Ed.) *Comparative Physiology of Thermoregulation.* Volume III, Academic Press, New York: 327–8.

Hart, C.W.M. and Pilling, A.R. (1960) *The Tiwi of North Australia.* Holt, Rinehart and Winston, New York.

Jones, R. (1980) Hunters in the Australian coastal savanna. In, D.R. Harrs (Ed.) *Human Ecology in Savanna Environments.* Academic Press, London: 107–46.

Lee, R.B. (1968) What hunters do for a living. In, R. Lee and I. Devore (Eds.) *Man the Hunter.* Aidine de Gruyter, Chicago: 30–48.

Leeper, G.W. (Ed.) (1970) *The Australian Environment.* Melbourne CSIRO and Melbourne University Press, Melbourne.

Macpherson, R.K. (1966) Physiological adaptation, fitness, and nutrition in the peoples of the Australian and New Guinea regions. In, P.T. Baker and J.S. Weiner (Eds) *The Biology of Human Adaptability.* Oxford University Press, Oxford: 431–68.

McArthur, A.J. and Clark, J.A. (1987) Body temperature and heat and water balance. *Nature* 326: 647–8.

McCarthy, F.D. and McArthur, M. (1960) The food quest and time factor in Aboriginal economic life. In, C.P. Mountford (Ed.) *Records of the American-Australian Scientific Expedition to Arnhem Land.* Volume 2, Anthropology and Nutrition, Melbourne University Press, Melbourne.

Meehan, B. (1982) *Shell Bed to Shell Midden.* Australian Institute of Aboriginal Studies, Canberra.

Mount, L.E. (1979) *Adaptation to Thermal Environment.* Edward Arnold, London.

Norgan, N.G. (1993) Relative sitting height and the interpretation of the body mass index. *Annals of Human Biology* 21: 79–82.

Pandolf, K.B., Stroschein, L.A., Drolet, L.L., Gonzalez, R.R., and Sawka, M.N. (1986) Prediction modeling of physiological responses and human performance in the heat. *Computers in Biology and Medicine* 16: 319–29.

Peterson, N. (1973) Camp site location among Australian hunter-gatherers: archaeological and ethnographic evidence for a key determinant. *Archaeology and Physical Anthropology in Oceania* 8: 173–93.

Pianka, E.R. (1988) *Evolutionary Ecology.* Fourth Edition. Harper & Row, Publishers, New York.

Pyke, G.H., Pulliam, H.R. and Charnov, E.L. (1977) Optimal foraging: A selective review of theory and tests. *Quarterly Rev. Biology* 52: 137–54.

Robertshaw, D. (1985). Sweat and heat exchange in man and other mammals. *Journal of Human Evolution* 14: 63–73.

Rolls, B.J. and Rolls, E.T. (1982) *Thirst.* Cambridge University Press, New York.

Sackett, L. (1979) The pursuit of prominence: hunting in an Australian Aboriginal community. *Anthropologica* 21: 223–46.

Sahlins, M. (1972) *Stone Age Economics.* Aldine/Atherton, Chicago.

Schoener, T.W. (1971) Theory of feeding strategies. *Annu. Rev. Ecol. Systematics* 2: 369–404.

Shapiro, Y., Pandolf, K.B. and Goldman, R.F. (1982) Predicting sweat loss response to exercise, environment and clothing. *European Journal of Applied Physiology* 48: 83–96.

Smith, E.A. (1983) Optimal foraging theory and hunter-gatherer societies. *Current Anthropology* 24: 625–51.

Tobias, P.V. (1994) The evolution of early hominids. In, T. Ingold (Ed.) *Companion Encyclopedia of Anthropology.* Routledge, London: 33–78.

Tonkinson, R. (1991) *The Mardu Aborigines. Living the Dream in Australia's Desert.* Holt, Rinehart and Winston, Inc., Fort Worth.

Ulijaszek, S.J. (1995) *Human Energetics in Biological Anthropology.* Cambridge University Press, Cambridge.

Ulijaszek, S.J. (1996) Energetics, adaptation, and adaptability. *Am. J. Hum. Biol.* 8: 169–82.

Walsh, F.J. (1990) An ecological study of traditional Aboriginal use of 'country': Martu in the Great and Little Sandy Deserts, Western Australia. *Proceedings of the Ecological Society of Australia* 16: 23–37.

Wissier, E.H. (1961) *An analysis of factors affecting temperature levels in the nude human. Mathematical Studies in Thermal Physiology.* Report Number 4, University of Texas Austin, Texas.

Woodcock, A., Thwaites, H. and Breckenridge, J. (1958) *An electrical analogue for the studying of heat transfer in dynamic situations.* Report Number TR-EP-86, Headquarters of the Quartermaster Research and Engineering Command, Natick, Massachusetts.

Wyndham, C. and Atkins, A. (1960) An approach to the solution of human biothermal problems with the aid of an analog computer. Paper Number 27, *Third International Conference on Medical Electronics.*

Wyndham, C.H., Macpherson, R.K. and Munro, A. (1964) Reactions to heat of Aborigines and Caucasians. *Journal of Applied Physiology* 19: 1055–8.

4. NOR ANY DROP TO DRINK
EVERYDAY DRINKING HABITS IN PACIFIC AND NEW ZEALAND SOCIETIES

Nancy J. Pollock

Water, water everywhere
and all the boards did shrink
Water, water everywhere
Nor any drop to drink

Coleridge
Rime of the Ancyent Marinere

There is a lot of water in the Pacific Ocean, but Pacific island spaces provide very little potable water. Fresh water is a scarce resource and it is not surprising that access is carefully controlled by cultural means.

The social and cultural context in which various beverages are drunk has not yet been closely examined, even though every anthropologist must have notes regarding potable and non-potable substances and be aware of the cultural rules governing drinking, even if only for personal comfort. As the concept of 'drink' has become associated in the literature almost solely with alcoholic substances (see Douglas 1987; Heath and Cooper 1981; and Marshall 1979), we have a large hole in our understanding of the cultural settings in which non-alcoholic beverages are consumed. Among the few works that focus on non-alcoholic beverages there are even fewer from an anthropological perspective. Wilson's (1993) edited volume entitled 'Liquid Nourishment' is a compilation of papers on both non-alcoholic (including yoghurt) and alcoholic beverages in Britain and Europe in historical terms. Thornton (1987: 105) clearly distinguishes two categories of alcoholic consumption from that of non-alcoholic beverages. Miller's (1997) Ethnography of Capitalism includes discussion of the 'sweet drink' industry in Trinidad that affords us a view of that industry as it links producer and consumer (Chap.4: 104). Sweet drinks are 'a core necessity' for Trinidadians within their wider field of beverages that includes milk drinks, fruit drinks and home made juice and sweet drinks. Miller traces the links between several sweet drink producer companies and the state, foreign suppliers and the retail trade, and thus consumers. His concern is to demonstrate how trends in the sweet drink beverage industry are driven by contradictions in consumer culture that 'uses goods to objectify its discourses' (Miller

1997: 151). The central issue he confronts is whether consumption is best viewed as a derivative merely of business or more generally of capitalism (ibid: 311). This focus on the consumer aspects of capitalism is very useful for a wide range of societies, especially where beverages are mainly purchased rather than locally available.

However, much of the other literature omits reference to what people drink even to quench thirst. Bindon's (1981) list of various beverages among his record of total consumption by his Samoan informants, and Rosemary Firth's early work (1930s) on Malay household consumption patterns referring to Kelantan village people drinking juice and water, and the existence of coffee houses (1963), are exceptions whereas Lee's detailed account (1979: 485) of !Kung consumption patterns passes over the beverage question, other than to draw attention to the !Xwa, which he glosses as water root, that serves double duty as a food, and 'more important, as a source of water'. These ethnographic accounts give us tantalising glimpses of a significant area of study but we are not told the basis on which these substances are chosen, nor their appropriateness to various cultural settings, their place within local cultural discourse. Many ethnographers who discuss foods omit references to the social context of beverages in daily lives.

We will use the term beverages here to distinguish the non-alcoholic substances discussed in this paper from 'drinks' as the term that is widely used in the literature to refer to alcoholic substances. In a generic sense in many English-speaking cultures drink is very closely linked cognitively with food. Food and drink are accepted together as vital means of satisfying basic biological needs, appetite and thirst (Malinowski 1923). But whereas we are accumulating a wide range of analyses of food consumption, there is an impoverished record of drink consumption, which may accompany that of food consumption. The focus on alcoholic drinks as a sub-set of generalised drinking behaviour, whether normative or deviant, has thus covered up the lack of data on the consumption of other liquid substances.

In this paper we will focus on spatial associations of these non-alcoholic beverages in order to show how each setting, whether outer Pacific island or urban, or metropolitan New Zealand, has its own limitations that are culturally prescribed. Cultural rules prescribe who may drink together, as well as the places where drinks are obtained, the containers which are used for drinking, and the circumstances in which certain drinks are appropriate. Not only is place particularly important for Pacific island people, but the location of the resource (coconut tree, well or store) is also marked for the consumer by ownership or control. In Pacific societies the range of beverage choices increases from outer islands to urban settings, but other factors such as shortage of money may limit accessibility. Store displays and advertising of key brands may also influence choice of beverage, subtly and not readily expressed.

From this brief ethnographic description of local as distinct from commercial drinks available in the Pacific Islands, as compared with New Zealand, we can consider in more detail the contexts in which those beverages are consumed, and factors affecting selection. Three key concepts will be used in analysis: *accessibility* including factors affecting entitlement (Sen 1981) is the key concern here. Rights to wells, streams, coconut trees and thirst quenching plants are culturally prescribed. *Portability* is a linked phenomenon that draws on the relationship between the drinker and the culturally prescribed tools of access to beverages. Utensils for carrying the liquid, selected culturally, form part of the spatial setting of drinking, as any drinking substance has to be carried from well, or other source, thereby linking the drinker to the source of the beverage. The taste of the beverage is an important variable, allowing for alternative sources to meet taste requirements, and including safety and its appropriateness, particularly for children; hence *potability* is our third concern.

Two key generalisations must be carried forward in the analysis of consumption of beverages (in their broadest sense) and consumption of food. Firstly the cultural context in which both food and drink are consumed is an integral part of social organisation. Food in the Pacific and Southeast Asia symbolises many key values in those societies, such as generosity and communal responsibilities, so that the contexts in which food and drink are consumed, and the appropriate social spaces, have to be understood within the larger worldview. 'Real' food in Fiji refers specifically to taro, and in Malaysia and other parts of Southeast Asia to rice. Other substances are consumed, but they do not have the same satisfaction value as 'real' food (Pollock 1992). The place of beverages in this worldview needs clarifying. Secondly, the entitlement, or rights, to obtain 'drinkables' is also culturally specific. Sen (1981) has proposed the term entitlements to include the ability to command and obtain food (and I assume includes drink) which is so often lacking and thus a basis of famine. Thirst, or lack of potable water, is part of the same concern. Access to basic drinkables such as water, a coconut, or a bottle of soft drink, is culturally controlled, hence the emphasis on spatiality that runs through this paper.

Beverages – Local

In the Pacific potable water on atolls, particularly, is a scarce resource. Coconuts, wells and catchments provide the 'sweet water' that is considered potable, but all of these sources are subject to variations in rainfall and cyclone damage. Pollution by rats and children also occurs so the coconut is the safest drinking source.

'The beverage required by man was supplied by the coconut' (Buck 1938:139). Carefully packaged by nature, its fresh, cool, refreshing, pure liquid becomes 'ready to drink' with the deft swish of a machete. The immature nut is produced by each palm roughly once every thirty days; ripe nuts absorb most of the liquid. The green nuts must be cut down with a machete, usually the task of young boys, so a family household needs a goodly array of trees to meet the needs of its fifteen or twenty members. The trees and the nuts they produce are thus valued property.

A coconut palm also yields a second form of beverage, known as toddy. When the spathe of the inflorescence is cut, sap drips slowly into a container, attached by a young boy who has climbed the tree the evening before. Toddy is a special morning beverage. If left for twenty-four hours or longer, the substance, which contains yeasts, will ferment and yield an intoxicating beverage. In the Marshall Islands it is illegal to make toddy. Its introduction to Nauru from Kiribati is said to have led to lethal fights between factions, further fuelled by gin which the traders introduced. The syrup may also be boiled to yield a form of molasses (see Intoh 1991 for greater detail).

But cutting toddy reduces the yield of nuts a tree produces, so toddy represents an alternative to nuts. Control of the use of the trees, for these and many other uses, is thus vital, especially with rapidly growing households. That control is the responsibility of the land users. Their land space and the resources they draw from it are subject to moral controls or social entitlement (Sen 1981). Coconuts as beverage are just one dimension of social space of a Pacific island society controlled by the collective lineage. Coconuts are not a free drink.

Wells are dug on atoll household sites to tap the fresh water lens sitting on top of heavier salt water. This lens is found approximately one third of the distance across a motu inland from the lagoon shore (Wiens 1962: Chap.4). The well may have to be dug six feet deep or more. The freshness of the water varies with the amount of rainfall and the skill of the person lowering the container to reach the water. Collecting well water is the task of young children, usually girls. They are remarkably skilled at drawing the small band of sweet water. If they should bring back a bucketful of saline water they are sent back to the well to be more careful. The wells in the Marshalls tend not to be covered, so items occasionally fall in, polluting the well. Then it is filled and a new one must be dug, a task requiring the efforts of all the men of the community for the digging, and of the women to obtain the stones to line it.

The well is an important part of the spatial use of land for residential purposes. Not every household has its own well, so must share with another household belonging to the extended family. Rights of accession are thus through lineages. Those households without wells must rely on other sources (NJP Wotje fieldnotes).

Rainwater can be collected in catchments, or from roofs of large structures such as the church or school, or from house roofs. In Majuro the sealed airport runway is the major water catchment for the large urban population. Variations in rainfall mean that even in this urban centre of some 18,000 people, water through the reticulated system is only available a few hours a day, and sometimes, when rains have not come, only for a few days each week. Urban households must therefore also rely on alternative sources, namely soft drinks and bottled water.

Most outer island households today have old oil drums placed strategically to catch rainwater from house roofs. A very few have spouting into a plastic water tank. Formerly in Japanese times (1919–45) concrete tanks were built, one for each household site; some of these have been maintained, but they are liable to leak and to become contaminated with dead rats, etc. Before such systems for retaining rainwater were introduced, people collected a little in old coconuts as the rain dripped into them from the coconut leaves. Downpours, when they occurred, went largely uncontained. Sweet rainwater is thus a luxury on atolls.

Rivers and lakes provide a more readily available source of fresh water on high islands. They too are subject to periodic drought and pollution. Then the population must turn to alternative sources.

Drinking water supplies have thus changed over the last hundred years, as they are drastically affected by population growth. As households have become larger (Pollock 1970 for Marshalls), so there is greater likelihood of groundwater becoming polluted. And those greater numbers draw heavily on the coconut supply, which is also the only source of cash. Thus cement tanks for each household have become a necessary source of both drinking water and, in emergency, for other uses such as washing clothes and bathing. So understanding existing controls of drinking water by the household becomes even more important as population density increases.

In 1985, during the WHO Decade for Water Supply and Sanitation, it was revealed that 69.5 percent of Pacific island people were without an adequate supply of water, but the figure rose to 79.8 percent in rural areas; in Papua New Guinea alone (excluding Irian Jaya), the largest Pacific island population, 75 percent of the population were without adequate water supply. It is all too apparent that improvements in the supply of fresh water are vital (Marjoram 1994:194). The coconut can no longer meet even the needs to quench thirst.

According to WHO and other health monitoring agencies, the standards of drinking water quality are inadequate. A recent overview of these standards for the Kingdom of Tonga revealed water to be generally safe for drinking. The water there includes appreciable amounts of chloride and dissolved calcium carbonates, and care must be exercised in pumping to avoid increased saline intrusion, but drinking water is otherwise safe. The authors suggest that regular monitoring of drinking water throughout Tonga and other Pacific islands must become established practice (Fuavao et al. 1996).

Kava is a local beverage that is made locally out of a local root of the pepper bush (*Piper methysticum*), pounded and mixed with water. It has been widely used in Polynesia, and Vanuatu and Pohnpei (see Pollock 1995; Lebot et al. 1993). It has recently been heavily commercialised so that it is surpassing copra as the major export from Fiji, and also from Pohnpei. The beverage used to be used mainly for ritual purposes, though Futunan chiefs were reported as drinking it first thing in the morning as a preparation for daily activities (Pollock 1995). The narcotic properties of the beverage have been widely discussed (Brunton 1991) and perhaps over emphasised for situations where the ritual surrounding its use has diminished in importance. As Perminow (1995), Crowley (1995), and others have shown, the secular use of kava is increasing as notions of democracy spread amongst the stratified societies of the Pacific. Its use has spread amongst Aboriginal communities of the Northern Territory as a counteractor to overuse of alcohol (d'Abbs 1995). The detailed analysis of the effects of the kavalactones and other ingredients of the root in water that may contain contaminants remains to be provided. The amount of kava that is drunk these days suggests that this is an important area for consideration.

Thus local sources to quench thirst or for cultural enjoyment are very limited. They are limited environmentally, as the geo-ecological-meteorological factors provide a restricted supply. This availability of potable sources must have been a limitation on early settlement of Pacific islands, particularly atolls. Cultural control of the space that allowed access to either a well site or coconuts was vital to the survival of a population. Rights to land use, and hence to establish a residence site were one means by which water usage was controlled spatially. Further rights to ownership of trees, and to disposition of the nuts also developed; for example in Nauru ownership of coconut and other trees was separate from use rights to the land on which those trees grew (NJP Nauru ms).

Commercial Beverages

It is not surprising that water has become a commercial item in its bottled form, as reticulated supplies and other sources are totally inadequate. But whereas access to water and coconuts derived from local sources was circumscribed socially, beverages purchased from a store were/are circumscribed economically. We will discuss five categories of beverage below in terms of the social contexts in which each is appropriate. All of these sources require a drinking water base. For some products the water is imported with the product, such as some Coca-Colas, but by far the greatest quantity of liquids imbibed is derived from the meagre local water sources.

Tea, Coffee, Milo and Cocoa (Koko)

All these beverages are imported, except in the case of local koko in Samoa. They are processed products, leaves, ground beans, etc. to which boiled water is added. That water needs to be untainted, i.e., non saline. Sugar is also a major component of these drinks.

Tea, with much sugar added, is the most ubiquitous drink in the Pacific islands. A pot of tea is extensible to large groups and provides a satisfying beverage for young and old alike. Weak sweet tea over rice is the only weaning food for infants in the Marshalls. Coffee, mainly instant, also made with boiled water, is uncommon because of the expense of the coffee powder, but that makes it more pleasurable, a drink largely confined to men for socialising. Milo, a 'food drink' containing malt extracts, made by mixing powder with milk, is favoured by several religious groups as an alternative to the stimulants in tea and coffee. Cultural groups that must avoid caffeine, such as Seventh Day Adventists and Latter Day Saints members, drink it extensively. Cocoa, a particular favourite in Western Samoa, uses local cocoa beans roasted and processed within the household, and again mixed with boiled water.

A supply of food and drink should be available at all times in case someone stops by the house. Drink, along with food, is thus a social opener. No door is necessary – the language of food and drink communicates welcome. 'Come inside and drink coffee (or tea) with us' is a common call by residents of a house to passers-by; we hear it many times a day as we pass through a village in the Marshalls, or in Wallis and Futuna. The invitation is given to any passer-by, whether a fellow villager, or a stranger. The invitation is to share some talk/gossip, and to socialise. The coffee may or may not be forthcoming – something will be offered, but the invitation is always phrased in terms of an invitation to drink coffee. For rural people and outer islanders coffee is very expensive, but it is considered the marker of sociality.

The invitation to 'come inside and drink coffee' has many cultural boundaries, not the least of which is traversing the spatial bounds of the Other. To enter another's home is considered in many cultures to be a very special invitation. That the inside of the home, the domestic, is set apart from the public, is a dichotomy whose gendered dimensions have been extensively explored (Rosaldo 1974; Ortner 1974). I have argued elsewhere that the public/private opposition is very ethnocentric, and thus not meaningful for universal application (NJP lecture notes 1998–9). Certainly it represents a valued traverse for many Westerners, so an invitation into a house in a Pacific island community takes on those valued inner sanctum connotations. The invitation is a manner of socialising, a part of the warmth of the community's welcome to visitors, I was told in Wallis (NJP and MT fieldnotes 1991).

A visitor would never be offered water. A drinking coconut is now recognised for its worth as appreciated by foreigners – previously people have told me they were ashamed to be seen opening a coconut for me, even though I expressed my desire for one, as it indicated they had nothing better to offer an honoured visitor. Today in Fiji a stranger will be charged one dollar for a drinking coconut bought at the roadside. Such a refreshing drink is now highly appreciated by foreigners, whether because of its uniqueness to them as outsiders, its exotic associations for people from beyond the tropics, or because it is pre-packaged, and can be trusted for its purity. Also the coconut can make a symbolic gift, being a unique cultural item, so the tourist may want to take home a series of photos of the young boy climbing the tree, picking the greennut, opening it with a few deft swishes of the machete, and the tourist's ineptitude in drinking the cool liquid which tends to dribble down the chin wetting the dressfront or shirt. And the nut is likely to be cracked open and thrown aside for the roaming chickens to feast on in their turn. The drinking nut thus opens awareness of a new spatial reality bounded by people, trees, and nature's bounty. This is exotic because it is so different from the cup of tea, which also quenches thirst.

The drink itself represents several dimensions of cultural boundaries. Coffee in many Pacific islands is very expensive in its instant form, and even more so if beans are obtainable (even though many Pacific islands grow coffee as an export crop). So a special sacrifice of sharing a luxury that is barely affordable may or may not enhance the perceptions of the visitor for whom 'instant' is ersatz, not the real thing. The problem of finding a suitable cup and offering milk also serves to widen the gap between the host and the guest. A tin mug or an old coffee jar may be all that is at hand. Milk is only rarely available, in contrast with ever-available sugar.

Coffee, whether instant or ground, tea made with imported tea bags, or leaves, or with local lemon grass, or some local herb, and cocoa (especially in Samoa) are three western-type drinks that are recognised as suitable for a visitor. Tea may be made in a large pot with lots of sugar and milk powder (possibly) added thus giving its drinker a new experience of the local setting, somewhat redolent of billy tea, or a camping experience. The cheerful gossip of the hosts and the interjections of the many children likely to be more or less active all serve to create a picture of which the tea or coffee drinking is just one small part, yet all important as the facilitator of social relations.

Soft drinks, bought from the local store, or drinks made from powders or crystals (Tang or Raro), or juice or milk drinks are uncommon in the outer island communities of the Pacific. They are uncommon for local people as well as items offered to a visitor. A notable exception in my fieldwork experience was when we were celebrating Christmas on an outer island of the Marshall Islands, but had very little food. The party centrepiece of Christmas fare for all fourteen families of the islet, or 230 people in total, was three 10-gallon pots of Hawaiian punch, made from packets of crystals mixed with rainwater and additional sugar (I contributed six packets to this general cause). Hawaiian punch was Christmas dinner for the assembled community. The symbolism of that event was very differently marked for them, as it was also for me. They too remember that Christmas drink twenty-five years later. Its place in their temporal memory sits alongside my memory of it in association with the atoll as place and culture.

Soft drinks are real treats, something very special for many rural Pacific peoples today. While working in a community up the Sigatoka river in Fiji, we took six 14–16 year-old students who had been working for us into the nearby town to buy them drinks and items of food as part of our way of saying thank you. Then (1983) Coke, Fanta, Sprite and some (horrible) strawberry drink were their choices. Individual cans or bottles are expensive for a family to buy for a large number of children, so a large bottle of Coke is more likely to be shared by all the youngsters in the house, and then only on a very special occasion. On this occasion each girl had her own bottle – a special event in itself. The range of bottled soft drinks is increasing rapidly, even in the small stores near a village. Such a cash purchase gives an instant return for the money. For the store owners these drinks represent quick profits. Patel's, a local Fiji merchandiser, now bottles its own brand of coke and other soft drinks to sell them under the firm's own label; they also have large hoardings advertising the familiar product at this store. The same Fiji Indian business packages and advertises tea and Milo. The culture of drinks is commercially very viable. It extends from shore to shore and store to store. No longer are these commercially packaged soft drinks markers of urban living, though they carry a status symbol of use of cash.

Milk is a less popular drink for young and old throughout Pacific island communities, though I have seen a few people in Fiji or Majuro buy a small carton of chocolate-flavoured milk from the refrigerated section of the supermarket, for a lunch snack. Children are breast-fed for two to three years, with only small inroads by the milk powder merchants. Cows' milk is available by reconstituting dried milk with local water. Fresh cows' milk is thus a luxury. The flavour of the reconstituted product is not appealing as a drink itself, though the milk powder may be added to coffee or tea drinks. Yoghurt is available in urban supermarkets. Milk shakes, available only in urban areas, and again using reconstituted milk powder, are a favoured luxury for those who can afford them. So the taste for milk may vary greatly depending on the amount of powder used, the quality of the water, and whether any flavourings have been added. Niuean primary school children were served a mug of milk midmorning in 1976; the value of milk for children was stressed by New Zealand health authorities. This practice has been discontinued, I believe, as it was too costly. UHT milk is also widely available now, but is used mainly in other drinks and foods, rather than as a drink in itself.

Juices are available in supermarkets, mainly in packet form rather than as frozen concentrates. Refrigeration systems are highly susceptible to loss of power, and thus the loss of frozen beverages can be costly. USDA frozen grape juice was delivered to Namu atoll during my field work in the 1960s as a boost to the local nutritional value of their food; however the packets of juice had not been refrigerated for close to two months, as near as I could estimate, so I advised that the whole lot be buried in a garbage pit; that grape juice has a strange flavour for my taste buds even when it is taken straight from the freezer in a mainland supermarket. Packaged juices are opened and used immediately, and may be watered down. Refrigeration space is not used. Today juice is fed mainly to newly weaned young children in urban areas, by those households that consider its added nutritional value.

In our records of household consumption on three atolls in the Marshalls at four points in the annual cycle in 1993–4 we found that tea was the most commonly reported drink. Whether the households did not consider it worthwhile to report drinking water is hard to ascertain. My observations on another atoll in the Marshalls in 1994 also support the finding of tea being the most commonly reported drink on a 24-hour recall of all items consumed. That tea is still heavily laced with sugar, and may or may not be served with milk powder added.

Bottled water has only become available in many Pacific island communities in the last two years. Fiji and Samoa bottle their own water, whereas other island states import the water and bottle it themselves, or import the bottles already filled, e.g., 'H20 to Go'. These are selling well in urban areas, but it is hard to tell who the major clients are without an in-depth study. Certainly Fiji is pushing this product for newly arrived visitors, as a case of bottle water was being offered at 'a special price' at the arrival Duty Free Store in Nadi in early 1998. Attempts at desalinisation plants on both a small and large scale have had varied success. Nauru relies on its desalinisation plant, as a cheaper alternative to back-loading fresh water on ships that return from carrying the phosphate out (Pollock ms). Other islands too are using desalinisation as one answer to their shortage of potable water. The technology needs to be more reliable.

We need better data on just what people in island communities drink, and in what quantities, in order to make better provisions for drinking water supplies. Consumption records of food intake may be unreliable as indicators of how much water is being drunk; future such studies should include key data on what is drunk on a daily basis, and the various sources from which it is provided. As in any household it is not considered important to remember how many times a day any one person, let alone a whole household, has drunk water, if we are just interested in fluid intake to quench thirst, then we are sorely lacking such accurate data. That data could be extremely useful for both health and general social reasons, as well as for planned developments. Contaminated water is a frequent source of disease, and thus must be addressed if populations are to improve their health.

Beverages – New Zealand

Data on what New Zealand people drink in their daily lives is also not well represented in the literature.We know bulk figures on the amounts of soft drinks, coffee, tea etc. that are either manufactured here, or imported, but we must await the results of the recent Nutrition Survey to ascertain just what the sample populations report in terms of their consumption of beverages.

A small pilot study of beverages drunk daily by sixty informants in an urban area (Wellington) ranging in age between six and sixty, of both genders, and from a range of economic backgrounds, attempted to establish some of the key questions for further exploration. We found that tea, coffee and tap water were the most commonly reported beverages. In our attempt to differentiate three social contexts, we found that most people drank water or tea on their own to quench thirst, but a small number (older age group) drank more coffee than carbonated drinks which tended to be consumed by the younger age group when socialising with friends. For the young people aged 6–20 years, several carbonated drinks and tap water were imbibed daily, while for 21–45 year olds the range included several cups of tea or coffee, tap water and orange juice. For the 45 plus age group, tea, coffee and water were drunk frequently each day, while juice was mentioned less often, and only two of this age group mentioned carbonated drinks. Coffee is the beverage people mentioned as likely to be shared with friends. Tea is a more 'solo' drink. At parties or other social events, orange juice was very frequently mentioned as an alternative to alcohol (strong proscriptions against drinking and driving have stressed the necessity for one 'non-drinking' member of the party). For young people, carbonated drinks or energy drinks are 'cool' when out with friends.

Coffee houses, as distinct from cafes, have opened up in the last two or three years attracting a range of city workers and other clientele, and also catering for parents with small children. They are places to meet over a cup of coffee and a muffin, or lunch. A range of types of coffee beans, as well as a range of forms of coffee from latte, to long black, cappuccino, espresso, and moccachino, have further increased the range of choice. The machines to make the latter versions of coffee, and their containers, all serve to underline coffee as a very specialised beverage these days. Coffee has spatially expanded in these many dimensions.

Tea, a more traditional beverage, particularly for those of English heritage, is more restrained socially and spatially. A recent lifestyle item in the local newspaper referred to the limited developments in tea drinking as compared to coffee (Wellington Evening Post 10/98). Many different types of tea, either in bags or loose, are available, but the brewing process requires only hot water and a cup or a teapot. The distinction between a teapot and a coffee pot that used to be very marked in 'polite' circles is diminishing, as coffee is served in so many forms, including instant. Tea bags versus 'a pot of tea' is still a social marker however. Tea is thus every person's drink, no status markers, while coffee has developed a 'luxury' appeal to those with money and urban social values.

In our small sample, hot chocolate and Milo were also mentioned by a few informants, but not nearly as frequently as tea and coffee. Powdered crystals, such as Raro, mixed with water, sometimes boiled, and with added sugar, is a more popular drink than juice or cordials. Fruit juice was mentioned frequently by the 21–45 age group, while the younger age group included both juice and carbonated drinks in their daily consumption. Milk and dairy drinks have diminished in importance. Power drinks are on the increase, but only two informants mentioned having had them in the last week. Media statements about the dangers of these do influence some people's ideas, but on the whole informants said they did not follow media messages.

Water was mentioned by almost every informant, several of whom referred to it as 'healthy'. That is despite several giardia scares in local water supply systems, both here and in Australia. Filtered water has been introduced into some homes, as was mentioned by nine informants. The increasingly common custom amongst university students and some staff to carry their water bottle to drink during classes and meetings was an observation that led to this pilot study.

The urban scene in New Zealand for thirst quenching on a daily basis is thus not that much richer than the island community scene. It is clear that we need a greater focus on this important topic that so far has been overlooked, or down-played. Without base data we can only offer a preliminary analysis.

Analysis

Any analysis of the data provided above must be preliminary as so few studies have been conducted of non-alcoholic beverage intake. Here I have stressed the social context, in contrast with the chapter in Marjoram's book (1994) which approaches water, and sanitation with which it is often coupled, from a technological standpoint. I am more concerned about the cultural pressures and limitations on people drinking non-alcoholic beverages, either individually or in social groups, than in the specifics of economics or technology. Ultimately I am looking at such beverages as they influence health, and are influenced by health criteria.

Generosity with food and drink is a key value for any community in the Pacific Islands, and both should be offered as a form of hospitality. Failure to make such an offer reflects badly on the whole extended family. *Accessibility* is thus a culturally controlled feature of any beverage in the Pacific. Wells, cisterns and coconuts all 'belong' to the lineage on whose land they are found. Wells and cisterns have been constructed by former members of that household, and the coconut trees were likewise planted by ancestors. They are thus part of the household space, and integral to it. They are the means by which drinks (non-alcoholic) are made available to all who reside in that household. No restrictions are imposed of kinship or other status. The household social space thus includes the ability to provide all comers with something to drink to quench thirst, or to meet social prerogatives.

Accessibility is also marked linguistically. Possession is an important means of expressing control. Thus in languages of the central Pacific drinks are marked out as a special cultural category, as is food. A linguistic marker in the form of a possessive pronoun is used to distinguish between drinks and food, and five or eight other items possessed. Thus in Marshallese language to ask 'Have you got some coke?' – '*Eworke limom cola?*', the possessive pronoun *limom* is the special marker of the possessive adjective that refers only to beverages. Another form of possessive pronoun is used when referring to food: '*Eworke kijom pilawa?*' – 'Have you got some bread?' where *kijom* is the possessive marker associated with food. So drinks are conceptualised in Marshallese (and other languages) as a special category of goods whose possession is clearly distinguished linguistically. How such clarity of issues of possession arose is unclear, but it indicates an important distinguishing feature between items drunk and other cultural items.

Also there is a specificity in Marshallese about water, such a vital resource on low-lying atolls. Ren (*dan* in Bender, Abo et al. 1976: 50) is the general term used for water, liquid, fluid, beverage, juice, and sap of coconut tree. *Ren in irak* refers to drinking water, as distinct from *ren in kadek* which is strong liquor or alcohol. *Ren in aiboj* refers specifically to rainwater that is for drinking – the main source of potable water. One explanation for these specific categories is the importance of potable water for human occupation of atolls. Thus the major means of access to such sources is through ownership of wells, catchment cisterns and coconut trees. These fall within the household site, and are thus under the control of the lineage to whom that site (*wato*) belongs (Pollock 1972).

Accessibility to liquids as beverages is closely linked to the means by which that liquid can be carried to the place where it is to be drunk. *Portability* is thus culturally circumscribed. Carrying water in pipes (reticulation) is feasible only in large urban centres. In many of the small Pacific islands and rural communities people still carry water from the well or the river or stream but use buckets; this is often the task of children and women. Before such carrying vessels as buckets were available, the drinker had to go to the water source. On Niue, a raised reef, women used to walk down to caves in the limestone where water collected, and washed clothes there. They carried water up to the household site in banana leaves, I was told (NJP fieldnotes 1976). Elsewhere a hollowed-out coconut was the early means to access well water but there were few means to store water.

The coconut tree thus was highly valued. It not only contained a beverage ready packaged for drinking, but produced it on household land. It was already packaged by nature in units that were easily portable thus making it the most widely accessible beverage, but access was strictly controlled by land use principles, as well as principles of generosity. Though portability made nuts readily accessible, they should not have been taken without asking the land-holders.

Portability of beverages has increased markedly with the availability of a range of different containers for liquids, and with reticulated water supply. Buckets, or pails, and plastic water tanks, as well as recycled tin cans, have eased the former difficulties in accessing water. As the need for water and other beverages has increased with population growth, so the commercial forms of containers in which potable liquids can be carried has increased exponentially. Bottled beverages are much more readily available in urban and peri-urban areas than they are on outer islands, where we can still see the difficulties that portability of water has presented over the early period of settlement of these islands.

Potability has become a major concern, mainly in terms of standards imposed by outsiders. The water available, especially well-water, is not always *potable* due to the high salinity of the water table, and sometimes due to seepage from pit toilets and rubbish pits. Salinity of well water declines as rainfall accumulates, and the fresh water lens increases on top of the heavier salt water. Even young children in the Marshalls are adept at dropping the bucket or can to take only that top layer of water. Salty tea is a source of complaint by household members. Rainwater is the most desirable for potability, but on occasions the rainwater catchments may become polluted. During fieldwork this happened three times, twice with rats dying in the catchment, and once when a child defecated in the cistern. On Ebeye, where water is retained in large plastic catchments, children are a constant source of pollution as they play in these as swimming pools. Cultural restrictions against this are blatantly ignored.

The criteria of potability of water are clearly cultural, but have not been well documented. They will vary with social circumstances, and environmental contexts, and with extra-national standards. More research is needed to increase our understanding of the criteria and threshholds people use to accept or reject the potability of their water supply.

Potability of other substances from tea to carbonated drinks is also strongly culturally circumscribed. Most Marshallese will not drink tea without a very heavy lacing of sugar. Milk is very rarely available. Certain soft drinks appear to be favoured by some sectors of the population over others. In our New Zealand study we found that few adults or people over 45 drank carbonated drinks because they were too sweet, and because they did not consider them appropriate for their lifestyle. Similarly milk used to be drunk by a wider range of the New Zealand population than today, with concerns about the additional calories, especially in full cream milk. An interesting study in Malaysia has undertaken a test of the acidity levels in juice preferred by Malays in order to adjust production accordingly (Abdullah 1997).

Conclusions

Accessibility is thus the major factor for beverages, but associated with portability and potability. In part, access is controlled by social criteria of possession or use rights that limit social groups' access to natural sources, but in part it is also controlled by environmental criteria such as the amount of rainfall, and the non-porosity of the soil. When we consider the introduced beverages, such as tea, or Coca-Cola, or bottled water, we find the packaging is a vital part of the accessibility. A bottle of coke, or a cup of tea, or a plastic water bottle are part of modern urban culture, heavily commercialised under multi-nationals. Thus accessibility of beverages, as well as their portability, is controlled by the politics of international trade, and the economics of the local market. Distribution follows cultural rules.

Potability is largely tied to cultural matters of taste. For some the coconut is the most pure beverage that can be found, for others it cannot replace a cup of tea. Instant coffee is less acceptable to New Zealand Kiwis than 'real' coffee, whether as cappuccino, latte, or espresso. Skimmed milk is considered more healthy than full cream by our New Zealand respondents. Cultural criteria predominate. Thus potability is tied very closely to accessibility. A particular beverage is only selected or accessed if it is culturally acceptable as potable.

Thus drinks are very much tied to cultural space. In the Pacific there is a marked divide between those beverages available in urban areas and those available in outer island and rural areas. On outer islands and in rural areas, potable sources are under the control of the lineage or some equivalent landholding group. Wells and now concrete cisterns or water tanks are an integral part of household space. Drinking vessels are limited to coconut shells, or recycled containers, and carrying water from the well is restricted to buckets.

Urban households are controlled in their access to beverages by finance. Reticulated water systems, or any of the commercial beverages, tea, or Pepsi, must all be paid for. Thus they are community based and controlled by a local authority, whether local government or trade store.

The very liquid nature of beverages requires the use of containers to hold them. Cultural determinants of the range of such containers extend from cups and buckets to coconut shells, and recycled materials such as drums, fishing floats, and tins and bottles found in the local setting.

In SUMMARY, six factors have been highlighted in this paper:

1. Fresh potable water in the Pacific islands is a scarce resource, particularly on outer islands and urban centres of atolls and low lying islands.
2. As demands for more fresh water supplies increase with population growth, so the difficulties of satisfying those demands are becoming more apparent.
3. Thus reliance on imported beverages is increasing, adding a major commodity cost to the import bill.
4. Bottled drinks, including bottled water, are portable, safe and potable, but are only accessible to those with cash to purchase them.
5. The New Zealand pilot study provided some criteria for assessment. Other local cultural criteria must be assessed *in situ* in order to make progress in our assessments of changes in non-alcoholic consumption.
6. Considerations of accessibility, portability and potability must be held pre-eminent for examination in greater depth, as part of both economic and health policies. The social and spatial settings for beverage use are still covert, so need to be examined overtly in context.

Thus though the Pacific Ocean is a very watery environment, drinking water along with other beverages is a scarce resource. Access to it must be controlled locally in order to ensure widespread entitlement. Beverages are thus part of the cultural means of satisfying the need for a drink, whether social or biological, but there is no such thing as a 'free drink'. Each source of beverage is controlled by some agency, whether lineage or local authority. The Pacific as an abundance of water is spatially circumscribed.

A bottle of coke or a cup of coffee each has its appropriate social setting. It may not be culturally appropriate to be seen walking down the street drinking a bottle of coke, but it may be very appropriate to be seen sitting in an outdoor cafe drinking a cup of coffee. There are many cultural dimensions to quenching thirst.

References

Bender, B., Abo et al. (1976) *Marshallese Dictionary*. University of Hawaii Press.

Bindon, J. (1982) Breadfruit, banana, beef and beer, *Ecology of Food and Nutrition* 12 (1): 49–60.

Brunton, R. (1989) The Abandoned Narcotic. Cambridge University Press, Cambridge, London, New York.

Buck, Sir Peter (1938) *Vikings of the Sunrise*. Whitcomb & Tombs, Wellington, NZ.

Crowley, T. (1995) The National Drink and the National Language in Vanuatu, J. *Polynesian society*, 104 (1): 7–72.

Coleridge, Samuel Taylor (1798) *The Rime of the Ancyent Marinere*, in Lyrical Ballads, Woodstock Books 1993, facsimile reprint of first edition of 1798: 17.

d'Abbs, P. (1995) The power of kava or the power of ideas. In, N.J. Pollock (Ed.) The Power of Kava, special volume of *Canberra Anthropology*, vol. 18 (1 & 2), 1995 : 166–83.

Douglas, M. (1987) *Constructive Drinking*. Cambridge University Press, Cambridge.

Drummond, A.C. and Wilbraham, A. (1939) *The Englishman's Food*. Cape, London.

Firth, Rosemary (1963) *Housekeeping among Malay Peasants*. Athlone Press, London.

Fuavao, V., Tuieli, S., Finau, S. and Moala, S. (1996) How safe is the drinking water in Tonga? *Pacific Health Dialog* 3 (2): 47–152.

D. Heath, J.O. Waddell and M. Topper (Eds.) (1981) Cultural Factors in Alcohol Research and Treatment of Drinking Problems. *Journal of Studies on Alcohol* Supplement #9. Smithsonian Institute and J. of Studies on Alcohol.

Intoh, Michiko (1991) *Toddy making in the Western Pacific*. Paper read at Pacific Science Congress, Honolulu.

Lee, Richard B. (1979) The !Kung San. Cambridge University Press, Cambridge.

Marshall, Mac (1979) *Weekend Warriors*. Mayfield, Palo Alto, California.

Marjoram, Tony (1994) Pipes and pits: water supply and sanitation. In, T. Marjoram (Ed.) *Island Technology*. Intermediate Technology Publishers, London.

Miller, R. (1997) *Capitalism – an ethnography*. Berg, New York.

Ortner, S. (1974) Is Female to Male as Nature is to Culture? In, M. Rosaldo and L.Lamphere (Eds), *Women, Culture and Society, an overview*. Stanford University Press, California.

Perminow, A. (1993) *The Long Way Home*. The Institute for Comparative Research in Human Culture, Oslo.

Pollock, Nancy J. (1970) Breadfruit and Breadwinning in Marshallese Society, PhD thesis, University of Hawaii.

Pollock, Nancy J. (1992) *These Roots Remain*. Institute for Polynesian Studies, and University of Hawaii Press, Honolulu.

Pollock, Nancy J. (Ed.) (1995) *The Power of Kava*. Canberra Anthropology, special publication.

Pollock, Nancy J. in press *Three Generations in New Zealand by Gender*.

Rosaldo, M. (1974) *Woman, Culture and Society, an overview*. Stanford University Press, California.

Sen, Amartya (1981) *Poverty and Famine*. Sage, New York.

Sydney Morning Herald (September 1998).

Thornton, M. (1987) Sekt versus Schnapps in an Austrian Village. In, M. Douglas (Ed.) *Constructive Drinking*. Cambridge University Press, Cambridge.

Wiens, H. (1962) *Atoll Environment and Ecology*. Yale University Press, New Haven.

Wilson, C.A. (1993) *Liquid Nourishment*. Edinburgh University Press.

5. DRINKING IN NORTHERN CAMEROON AMONG THE MASA AND MUZEY

Igor de Garine

Introduction

This paper will be centred on various aspects of drinking among the Masa and Muzey who dwell in Cameroon on the flooded plains of the Logone river, 300 kilometres south of Njamena, the capital of Chad. In order to illustrate particular aspects, we shall also refer to other groups we have studied in this area, mostly the Tupuri, Kera and Koma.

We shall consider water, blood, milk, traditional non-alcoholic drinks, home-made sorghum and millet beers, home-made spirits from the distillation of sorghum or millet, and manufactured drinks, mostly beer. For each, we shall deal with the material aspects, the symbolic value, and the social, religious and psychological implications.

Water

The area under consideration is characterised by a tropical climate with a four-month rainy season (irregular annual rainfall ranging from 550 to 1,100 mm). The average temperature is 26.5° Celsius, but the population suffers from heat stress between February and May when the temperature reaches 42°C in the shade and up to 54°C in the sun. Abundant hydration is needed but we have not quantified it.

The villagers are not very particular about the quality of the water they drink. However, whether running or still, water is not drawn too close to the edge to try to avoid pollution. Wells into which animals have fallen are discarded. Ponds located in the village – and around which defecation often takes place – are not used.

Drinking occurs between meals, or at the beginning or the end of them. In order to keep it cool in the compound, water is stored in porous earthenware jars, half buried in the kitchen floor. They are closed by a calabash which also doubles as a drinking cup.

Notwithstanding governmental efforts, a lack of appropriate water supplies still affects a number of villages located on laterite ground. Drinking water

... drinking water may constitute the final episode of religious rituals ...
(Muzey, N. Cameroon).

may have to be carried long distances, a heavy burden for women. Traditional well-digging is very hazardous in light soil. Although wells only represent a small surface of water, they are under the supernatural control of Mununta, the female goddess of all waters, who is responsible for accidents resulting from its use, e.g., suicide by drowning, or death due to inhaling carbonic gas during well-digging. She also chastises with dropsy ('filling them with water') those who have offended her.

Fear of dying of thirst remains vivid. It has occurred three times over the last ten years. Hunters are very careful about carrying a good supply of water during the collective hunts of the dry season. In the oral literature, the theme of the lost hunter, on the verge of dying of thirst, is common. The hero is saved by his foraging dog, returning to him with wet fur. He follows the animal, finds a pond or a calabash, drinks and spills the water, which rushes after him and becomes one of the permanent water courses of the region, such as the Kabia or the Loka rivers.

The Guisey canton was populated by the descendants of a lost hunter coming on horseback from the west side of the Logone and finding at last somewhere to quench his own thirst and that of his horse, and a place to stay. Clan and lineages have fought fiercely to keep their rights and access to permanent water such as that of the Boro and Yirwi lakes in northern Djarao county. Conversely, the two founding heroes of the clan of Gunu, Gaya and Huduk, banished from their home, were offered new land for killing a mythical bird which prevented the original inhabitants from drinking the water of their own river.

The African sorrel drink, which is red in colour, is used as a substitute for wine (Masa, N. Cameroon).

Small lineages have been conspicuously pushed towards the driest parts of the country. A reminder of this is the right they retain to draw water for ritual use from the ponds and streams they originally owned. This is the case, for instance, of the Gobo clan which was expelled from Gamé county in Chad to the south.

Symbolically, water is very important. It is 'cold'. It can be ingested to cool off the bad influences which are often considered 'hot', or the pollution resulting from contact with evil or death. Among the Muzey, drinking water may constitute the final episode of religious rituals performed before returning home, purifying the participants of the polluting contact with the holy world. It also has the property of cleansing malevolent thoughts or spells. Among the Masa if, during a dream, an individual sees the shadow of his neighbour committing an offence (adultery with the dreamer's wife, for instance), he meets the wrongdoer in the early morning, tells him what happened and the potential culprit must give him water to drink in order to wash away symbolically the effects of his nasty deed. Refusal to comply with the offering of water can lead the 'culprit' into the local court.

Water is also used to refresh the body in case of fever. It is used to cure symbolically 'warm' periods and episodes in human life, such as pregnancy or the post-partum period for women, and anger, violence and the consequences of murder among men.

Water is also a main component of paps, gruels, soft drinks and beer.

Blood

In contrast to water, blood is a 'hot' matter. It is the beverage of many supernatural beings, mostly of the spirit of death, Matna, and of Bagaona, the spirit of the dangerous no-man's-land of the bush. Women who are inhabited by these deities drink the blood of slaughtered animals during possession rituals.

Slaughtering animals always involves an offering of blood. By spilling on the ground it will attract the supernatural powers. Left in a broken calabash vessel on the path leading to a house, it will prevent the spirits from coming close to human dwellings. In the divination systems, blood is one of the attributions of the domestic animals which may be slaughtered as a result of the diagnosis during a divination session. Blood is also the drink of the *su dawra,* the cannibal sorcerers. Ingesting the menstrual blood of one's wife is a deadly poison for a husband. It may be used as an ultimate recourse by a woman driven to breaking point.

Traditional Soft Drinks

A number of sour-tasting plants such as tamarind *(Tamarindus indica)* and African sorrel *(Hibiscus sabdariffa)* are macerated in water to obtain refreshing drinks which are consumed between meals. The African sorrel drink, which is red in colour, is used as a substitute for wine during communion services by the abstinent Protestant sects.

A whole range of slightly fermented drinks are used by women. They are made from: (1) a light sorghum pap left to ferment overnight with or without the addition of yeast; (2) *kochett* is a similar beverage made of rice; (3) *kalla* is made from sorghum or millet to which chili and sugar may be added; (4) the crushed fruit of *Grewia villosa* is used in the same way. The Masa and Muzey also know how to make hydromel, and they use infusions made from leaves *(Cassia tora)* or roasted grains from *Cassia occidentalis.*

Tea, very sweet and strong, is becoming a common drink among the elderly and those wishing to demonstrate their Muslim faith.

Milk

The populations we are dealing with are herders. The Masa raise cattle, sheep and goats, so do the Tupuri. The Muzey herd ponies, goats and are progressively adopting sheep and cattle. It would, however, be a mistake to imagine that they consume a large amount of milk. The aim of animal husbandry is to obtain as numerous a herd as possible. According to the climate, the fodder available may be scarce, in which case milk production is low, around two litres per day. The herder has to choose between using the milk for human consumption, thus starving his livestock's offspring, or reserving most of the milk for the young animals.

The milk of sheep and goats is not made use of systematically, and is the privilege of the young shepherds.

We obtained data on the consumption of cows' milk among the Masa. For the ordinary Masa villager it is not very high, only forty-six grammes per day yearly average. Milk is not systematically given to the nutritionally vulnerable groups such as pregnant and lactating women and children as it is believed to induce diarrhoea. Cases of lactose intolerance *(mir galaki* – 'milk bitter') have also been identified.

The traditional viewpoint has nothing to do with nutrition. Cattle are the most valued asset in the community, they constitute the bridewealth. Their use should be seen in terms of prestige. Two institutions allow for the conspicuous consumption of milk. One is informal, the *golla*. It consists of an individual lending a lactating cow to a friend whom he wishes to honour. Milk drinking is a seal of friendship. The second type, the *guru*, is formal (for details, see Garine 1996; Garine and Koppert 1991; Garine and Pollock 1995). This practice enables the male part of the population to gain weight through drinking milk during two kinds of fattening sessions.The first type is collective. At different periods of the year, except during the heart of the rainy season (July, August), men live with the herd, for periods of one to four months, consume mostly cows' milk and sorghum porridge and ingest about 3,500 kilocalories daily (about 1,000 kcal more than the male villagers) and a larger amount of animal proteins (83 gr instead of 46 gr) and lipids, both from milk. In the dry season (January to May) the participants *(gurna)* receive an average of 1,027 gr of milk and the villagers only 66 gr. During the rainy season (June to September) they drink 1,669 gr of milk and the villagers 124 gr. Finally, during the harvest season (October to December) the gurna consume 1,781 gr and the villagers only 46 gr (Garine 1996: 194). The gurna are, on average, 2 kg heavier than the villagers.

The second type of session is individual and more of a conspicuous consumption affair. During a period which lasts for about two months in the middle of the rainy season, which is the shortage period, the participant remains secluded and ingests very large quantities of food, mostly milk and red sorghum porridge. In 1976, the first participant observed consumed over 10,000 kilocalories daily (Garine and Koppert, 1991) and put on 34 kg in three

Tupuri, Kera, Muzey and Masa use the same ritual drink, sorghum beer (Tupuri, Chad).

months, far more than what has been observed among Caucasian volunteers (Sims et al. 1968).

In 1988-89, a detailed energy balance study, including food intake, body weight, body composition and activity, carried out on nine volunteers over a period of sixty-five days, reached slightly lower results than those obtained in 1976 (Pasquet et al. 1992). The average energy intake was around 7,500 kcal. Average body weight increase was 17 kg with two star subjects gaining 20.2 and 23.2 kg respectively.

It should be emphasised that in both kinds of fattening sessions, most of the diet is liquid, consisting of red sorghum loaf, kneaded with milk or water. For example, the feeding schedule over twenty-four hours of a participant in the individual guru in Kogoyna in September 1976 consisted of eleven feeding

Beer is ritually consumed by all categories of individuals, children as well as the elderly (Musey, Chad).

bouts, two of sorghum loaf and relish, and nine of sorghum porridge mixed with water or milk.

It is probably easier to ingest large amounts of food by drinking rather than eating it. Milk is perceived as a privileged commodity, not just an ordinary food, which might be why it was seldom mentioned in the answers to our questionnaires about food preferences. It is a substance which symbolises what is good in life – bliss! It brings happiness and should be consumed in merry circumstances, not during mourning, when only sour milk can be ingested. Milk makes you fat, strong (and courageous as a wrestler). It transforms you into an amiable and peaceful kind of person, so powerful that one does not need to display one's vigour.

This is what is sought through the strict discipline to which the candidates to the individual fattening sessions of the *guru walla* are submitted. The oral literature abundantly documents these aspects. Changing one's personality through the Masa's individual guru sessions is an original function of drinking. If we skim through the myths, we can quote examples concerning beauty and desirability, and others referring to strength and being courteous and reverential to one's parents and the elderly. More prosaically, participating in the fattening sessions shows that you are rich, or at least popular, since someone who is affluent has lent you a cow so that you can drink its milk.

Milk is given to women for two main reasons. The first is biological: skinny girls are sent to the individual guru to make them grow fat and and reach puberty in order to be available for marriage. The second reason is psychological: in order to accustom a recently married girl to her new life and make her lose her inhibitions, her husband may reserve one or two lactating cows for her use.

It should also be pointed out that, unexpectedly, milk is not used in ritual offerings. Its consumption entails something like a feeling of guilt. Drinking milk is so good and the happiness it produces so intense that such a symbolically laden activity is believed to shorten one's life!

Beer

Sorghum beer is the other beverage with high symbolical value. It is used during most rituals. The Masa and Muzey contrast in this respect with the Tupuri and the Kera and with mountain people of Northern Cameroon such as the Koma, where beer drinking is also a profane and much sought-after activity. Many markets cater for it. According to Guillard (1965), among the Tupuri, it represents 23 percent of the domestic income and 4 percent of the expenses. Here, however, we are not reaching the levels of some other populations of Africa. In Burkina Faso, for instance, the consumption is 263 litres per capita per year and represents a real threat to the food supply (Pallier 1972).

We shall only deal briefly here with the technical aspects of brewing. Each population has its own. There are two main kinds of beer. One is thick and opaque, like a thin gruel, for instance, the *balsa* of the Koma. The other is light and transparent, like the *yi* of the Tupuri. Mountain populations use both types. The Masa and Muzey have a beverage which is halfway between the two, opaque but lighter than *balsa*. It is called *suma* among the Masa, *doleyna* among the Muzey. Each population favours specific varieties of sorghum and millet for the preparation. Among the Masa and Muzey, varieties of *Sorghum caudatum* are mainly used.

Ten days are needed for brewing traditional beer. The duration of the process and its various phases are basic to the organisation of the ritual calendar of the plains populations of the area under consideration. Tupuri, Kera, Muzey and Masa are included in the same system and they celebrate their main ritual, the beginning of the annual cycle *(vun tilla* – 'the mouth of the months') according to the order of their settlement in the area. The Tupuri clan of Doré begins, followed by the neighbouring Kera villages, then various Muzey clans, Bogodi, Gunu, Pé, and the Masa from the Guisey clan.

As is the case for most agricultural populations, the Masa, Muzey and Tupuri are aware of seasonal variations in the climate, the ecology and the vegetative cycle of the plants of their land. They master a calendar determining the appropriate time for most of the technical activities, for which an approximate computation of time is sufficient. In the beer-brewing process, the time for the germination of the cereal and for the cooking and the fermentation has to be respected precisely if one is to avoid the public shame of an unsuccessful preparation. Brewing (and distillation) imply a subtle approach to timing.

Fermentation is a mysterious process, as are the inebriating properties of alcohol. A Tupuri legend illustrates this aspect:

In old times, the Tupuri of the Doré clan were living a primitive kind of life and drinking sweet beer only. Bulio, a man from the Peffé area (100 km to the south), lost in Tupuri country, found shelter in a cave in the Doré mountain. At night he would come out to steal food from the autochtones and put yeast in the beer. The Tupuri drank it abundantly and many fell to the ground, completely drunk. The villagers thought they were dead and buried them. This is how death began among the Tupuri.

Beer somehow involves symbolically the people who handle it. Menstruating women cannot brew beer. Ritual beer should be handled only by adults wearing their special ceremonial array and should be drunk from a clean, brand-new calabash reserved for this purpose. In a similar way, women belonging to possession colleges come to sleep in the compound of their ritual chief while he is brewing, guaranteeing by their presence (which symbolises that of the supernatural protection of the community) that everything will go well. Purity and serenity are necessary during the preparation of beer; shouting, arguing, fighting or beating one's wife are forbidden. The fermentation and the drinking of beer are ritualised among the Masa and Muzey and delimit a particular, somewhat holy, interval of time, distinct from the daily routine.

Beer is consumed by all categories of individuals in the society, children as well as the elderly. Beer is the ambrosia of the supernatural beings and the ancestors. Most religious occasions imply libations and drinking of beer. This is done at the end of the offerings and of the preparation of the meal taken in common by the participants. Among the Masa, one of the main sacrifices to the ancestors is called *suma bumba*, 'the beer of the father'. The corresponding prayer is as follows: 'Father, here is your beer. Motherland *(Nagata)*, come and drink. All you spirits of the bush, come and drink. None of you should remain without partaking'.

Beer is powerful magically. For instance, during the celebration concerning the guardian spirit of the Muzey Jarao clan, drops of blood may appear at the surface of the ritual beer. The wort *(sot suma* – 'the excrement of beer') of most ceremonial beer is considered to be loaded with pollution. As such it has to be abandoned at crossroads so that the passer-by will be impregnated with its evil and carry it away.

An order of precedence has to be respected. In the main rituals, the earth chief drinks first, then his assistants, followed by his first wife, the male family heads, their wives, then the children. Among the Muzey, partaking of ritual beer also demonstrates kinship identity. On the first day of the New Year celebrations *(vun tilla)*, beer is reserved for the kinsmen – it would be poison to any reckless outsider who dared to swallow it. Some deities, such as the god of death (Matna), are so dangerous that only the people who belong to the appropriate possession group can drink their beer.

The alcoholic proof of sorghum beer is between 3° and 6°. A fair quantity is needed for an adult to become intoxicated (about five litres). Various barks, such as that of *Khaya senegalensis* (bastard mahogany) are used to make it more bitter and stronger *(galaki)*. Getting drunk on beer is not uncommon. However, among the Masa and Muzey, sorghum beer brings mostly merriment. During intermittent ritual occasions it allows for a mild degree of intoxication, favourable to conviviality. Heavy inebriation is not common. Drunks are not ostracised and carry little responsibility for their deeds whilst under the influence of alcohol, but no brutal behaviour is expected culturally, and only occasionally do fights break out.

What is the nutritional value of beer? Périssé et al. (1969), working in Togo on a light millet beer *(dolo)*, came to the conclusion that, while brewing increases the amount of B-group vitamins, it diminishes the amount of proteins and calcium contained in the grain. In terms of energy, 100 gr of porridge is equivalent to 140 kcal, but 100 gr of beer is equivalent to only 60 kcal. It is more profitable to eat one's cereal than to drink it. Among the Masa and Muzey, however, it is considered to be nourishing. Drinking the beer itself calms hunger, and the residue can be consumed as well. It is also acceptable to women.

Table 5.1   Distillation of *arkina*, home-made alcohol of *Sorghum* and *Pennisetum*, among the Muzey

lst day	The grain is ground, together with dry sorghum or millet porridge. 10 kg of grain will yield about 8 litres of alcohol. It is cooked in water in an iron barrel. The arkina porridge obtained is left to cool in the tightly-closed container for 24 hours.
2nd day	Flour made from the grain of germinated *Pennisetum* or *Sorghum* grain is kneaded with the porridge (2.5 kg for 10 kg of porridge). Water is added. The preparation is carefully mixed, yeast is added. The vessel is tightly closed. The mixture is allowed to ferment for 24 hours.
3rd day	Next morning – tasting of the preparation, to which water may be added. The lid of the barrel is tightly closed.
4th day	The following morning, the still (which consists of an iron pipe coming out of the barrel and transpiercing a vessel full of cold water to condense the alcoholic vapours) is fixed tightly to the barrel. The preparation is boiled. The alcohol drips through a wad of cotton into beer bottles. It is left to cool. The arkina is ready to drink.

However, traditional beer, the 'red drink' *(doley cawna)* is increasingly considered to be too mild to provide rapid intoxication (ending up in loss of consciousness). This role is fulfilled by sorghum alcohol, the 'black drink' *(doley warna – arkina)*, specially distilled for the purpose.

Home-made Alcohol (Arkina)

Arkina is mostly made with sorghum, less often with millet *(Pennisetum)* grain, to which are added germinated seeds of the same cereal and water. 10 kg of cereals plus 2.5 kg of germinated grain and 50 litres of water will yield around 8 litres of alcohol. Its origin can be traced to a few decades ago. It was brought to the Muzey and Masa of Cameroon by a Muzey woman named Badang Vunugu from the Chadic village of Gunu Gaya. The informant adds that 'she should be blessed'.

Distillation takes about four days. The first bottles are considered top quality, and the strongest can reach an alcoholic proof of around 36°. It is sold for 500 CFA (around one American dollar) for a beer bottle of 33 cl. The second quality has an alcoholic level of 20° and costs 300 CFA per bottle (village of Nuldayna, 1989). The third quality costs 150 CFA per bottle, and we have not analysed its alcoholic value. The number of bottles of each quality varies according to the conscientiousness of the brewer. We can estimate that the initial investment will be multiplied by two: 6,000 CFA worth of sorghum and wood will bring in around 12,000 CFA. This is the highest profit one can expect from a traditional product and is a strong incentive to distilling. It constitutes an important asset in the family budget, allowing the husband to be conspicuously drunk most of the time (which is prestigious), and enables women to avoid marriage or escape the overdemanding constraints imposed on housewives (Garine and Koppert 1988).

In the Masa village of Kogoyna (327 inhabitants) in 1976, the weekly production of *arkina* from June to November was the following: June 109 litres, July 83, August 76, September 97, October 116, and November 167, giving a total of 648 litres (Koppert 1981). If we assume that the same quantities were produced during the other six months, the annual consumption for each of the inhabitants would be14.46 litres per capita. This is a sizeable quantity. Since 1976 alcohol consumption and production have increased tremendously, to the extent that some stills are now built with two pipes each, being double-barrelled to produce alcohol more quickly.

Its use is widespread among men (and lately among women also) as a profane drink. It has also replaced sorghum beer in most gatherings. It should not, however, appear as a ritual offering to the supernatural powers but as a necessary encouragement to every ritual or social celebration as well as on religious occasions, creating a rather boisterous general atmosphere. For a long time alcohol – and especially arkina – was prohibited to the guru milk drinkers, which appealed to the missionaries as an alternative to alcoholism.

This is no longer the case. Today, on the contrary, it has become a stimulant for their outstanding performances.

Under previous governments, influenced by a powerful Muslim part of the Establishment (the President of Cameroon being a Fulani), distilling was considered illegal and was a fineable offence; it was even punishable by imprisonment. It is now a perfectly legal activity. Heavy drinking has become a principal marker of wealth and manhood. Arkina plays a major role in the very serious drinking problem Cameroon is facing.

Manufactured Beers

Breweries have existed in Cameroon for several decades and today are operating in most large cities, using imported malt and rice. Beaufort, 33, Guinness, King, and Satzenbrau are the main Cameroonian brands. Gala comes from Chad. Besides its pleasant, thirst-quenching properties in a hot climate, beer allows socio-economic affluence to be demonstrated through the display of cash, a marker of success and wealth. Some canton chiefs never move without their supply of beer.

Local markets and buying sessions for the cash crops (cotton, rice, groundnuts) are the occasions of profuse beer drinking by the farmers. Paying for rounds of beer, accompanied with grilled meat and doughnuts, demonstrates generosity among villagers as well as among blue-and white-collar employees and civil servants in urbanised areas. In town it accompanies snacks of barbecued meat during working hours. It is also consumed after work and during leisure time in bars and 'circuits' (illicit joints) which provide opportunities for romance as well as drunkenness, demonstrating sexual attractiveness at the same time as wealth.

The price of a 33 cl bottle of beer, which shot up from 250 to 350 CFA a few years ago, used to be the standard amount of cash given as a token of friendship, as a preliminary to courtship or as the fine extorted by a thirsty policeman. In order to counteract household sorghum alcohol distillation, the government has moved and now allows distribution of manufactured beer in the countryside. Stands where lukewarm beer is available can be found in the most remote parts of the bush. This dissemination has simply had the effect of offering more opportunities to become drunk. Beer is, by the layman's standards, an expensive drink. It requires about five bottles of beer to begin getting drunk. Two bottles of arkina will achieve a much more spectacular result at half the price and give the drinker the reputation of being a daredevil.

Few manufactured spirits or wines are drunk in Northern Cameroon. Imported whisky and wine are the privilege of the highest non-Muslim politico-economic elite.

In terms of modern progressive scales of values, prestige increases from the consumption of local beer to local alcohol, to manufactured beer, to imported wine and spirits – the more expensive, the stronger, and the more foreign the better. Cameroon ranks high for champagne consumption.

Drunkenness

Alcohol from arkina and beer is mainly utilised to bring about as rapidly and as cheaply as possible serious intoxication rather than pleasure and tipsiness. The Masa distinguish three levels of drunkenness : *surum surum* – 'the wine has come up to his eyes, he sees clearly, speaks without shame, he controls the noises he makes'; *wuyigiya* – 'he walks from the right to the left, falls down, sometimes vomits and fights'; *tofoy ku doleyna* – 'full up with drink'. At this stage, addiction is reached, one gets drunk just by seeing a bottle: 'dead drunk up to loss of consciousness'.

There is little concern about the man who cannot hold his liquor. Offences when drunk are not dealt with harshly, unless they cause severe material or corporal damage, as was the case in 1998, among the Masa. A woman who killed her husband, a notorious drunkard and a brute, with a cereal pounder during a domestic fight was not punished or sent to prison.

Drunkenness has a prestigious image. Random questioning was carried out between 1984 and 1994 among the Masa and Muzey, asking the following questions:

1. What are your preferred drinks? Why?
2. What are the drinks of the poor?
3. What are the drinks of the rich?
4. If you were rich, what would you drink?

The general findings were as follows: Muslims, Protestants and women say they do not use alcohol but consume soft drinks – syrups, Fanta, lemonade, carbonated water. The favourite beverages most often mentioned are the most expensive alcoholic ones, mainly beer. Sorghum beer has a positive connotation as a ritual drink: nourishing and safe to drink but it also reveals lack of money and an obsolete lifestyle. Arkina is in an ambiguous position. Consumers are aware of its negative biological effects: headache, red eyes, tendency towards violence, loss of consciousness, ultimately madness (*hoyna* – 'like a mad dog'). A saying goes 'Arkina cannot kill a poor man, a rich one yes. He has no limit to satisfying his craving'. As a matter of fact, thirty years ago death from alcohol was the privilege of administrative canton chiefs, wealthy enough to gorge on arkina (and taking a long time to die). Today the overall increase in income allows a large amount to be spent on drinking (sometimes 50 percent and more). For example, M., a local extension worker, earns 25,000 francs CFA (about $50.00 U.S.) per month, spends close to 20,000 on arkina, drinking ten bottles per day if he has the necessary cash. He says he cannot stay without it for a day. The Muzey say that addicts have even 'gone to work in other people's fields' in order to earn their necessary daily dose, a highly despised recourse according to cultural standards.

Drink addiction is perceived as having disastrous economic consequences. *Doleyna / arkina / jay / zina* – alcohol / arkina / destroys / the household. 'Arkina / ruins me, it eats up all my money'. However, it is also considered to have positive effects in terms of health and in mustering sufficient motivation to go to work. It is also thought to alleviate hunger. It is said to cure slight sicknesses, diarrhoea, gastric ailments and eye troubles. It fights colds and fever better than 'manufactured drugs sold on the market place by illiterates'. The supposed benefits of arkina and drunkenness are psychological: 'When I drink arkina, I feel strong – I don't get tired easily – I see things clearly – It makes my eyes glitter – I lose my shame – I become bold enough to beat my wife if she needs it – I can stare at a policeman eyeball to eyeball'.

Since 1976 daily life in most of the villages we study has become very difficult in every way. There is little social control and moral rules are no longer respected. Hunger, disease (cholera), theft, revenge, murder as well as prostitution, and administrative and police abuses are constant. In 1997 it was estimated that around 50 percent of the adult population had taken to drinking, much of it heavy, thus dilapidating the meagre resources available.

Drinking alcohol has a cathartic function at both group and individual levels. Among the populations we have studied, villagers are increasingly aware of their inability to integrate the modern lifestyles they are longing for. They have lost their traditional values and have not assimilated the new ones brought in by Christian religions. They are unskilled, are offered few opportunities, and they have lost most of the beliefs which helped social control in traditional life. Intoxication allows hardships to be forgotten and brings on a feeling of superiority, at least for a while. This is similar to what has been abundantly mentioned in the literature about North American Indians: 'Drink addiction is an efficient strategy to cope with acculturation problems due to external intrusion' (MacAndrew and Edgerton 1969). The process we are witnessing in Northern Cameroon is similar to what can be observed elsewhere, especially in Africa. Alcohol is a profitable money-making commodity, consuming it confers prestige, it is a sign of modernity and provides an outlet to the hardships of poverty and the anxiety of acculturation.

Looking at drinking among the Masa and Muzey confronts us with a whole range of liquid products fulfilling biological needs and social wants. They concern satiation (e.g., water) as well as stimulation (e.g., alcohol). They are used to reach biological and psychosocial wellbeing. Together with food, they are pregnant with countless symbols and involve, as we have seen, many material and non-material aspects of each culture. Drinks should, therefore, be systematically studied at the same time as food in order to understand the overt as well as the covert consequences of ingestion in any given society.

In this paper we have tried to consider, from a detached point of view, the use of all types of beverages in two cultures. Our findings in Northern Cameroon compel us to look at the question from a more activist angle.

Alcoholism is rapidly destroying the populations we have known for over forty years. Nothing is done about it and it is difficult to act. In fact, coercion will not bring about much improvement. Combatting the spread of alcoholism implies a total modification of material life as well as of the ethos, locally and in the national society as a whole. Today, among the Masa and Muzey, only religious and moral creeds constitute a very flimsy barrier against 'despair drinking'. Prohibitions on alcohol operate in various Protestant sects such as the Lutheran Brethren of Minnesota and, conspicuously so, among the Muslims. This is the one area in which religious fundamentalism may contribute to the welfare of humanity.

References

Garine, I. de (1995) Cultural aspects of the male fattening sessions among the Massa of Northern Cameroon. In, I. de Garine and N.J. Pollock (Eds.), *Social Aspects of Fatness and Obesity*. Gordon and Breach, Amsterdam: 45-71.

Garine, I. de (1996) Food and the Status Quest in Five African Cultures. In, P. Wiessner and W. Schiefenhövel (Eds.), *Food and the Status Quest: An Interdisciplinary Perspective*. Berghahn Books, Providence, Oxford: 193-218.

Garine, I. de and Koppert, G.J.A. (1988) Coping with Seasonal Fluctuations in Food Supply among Savanna Populations: The Massa and Mussey of Chad and Cameroon. In, I. de Garine and G.A. Harrison (Eds.) *Coping with Uncertainty in Food Supply*. Clarendon Press, Oxford: 210-60.

Garine, I. de and Koppert, G.J.A. (1991) *Guru* – Fattening Sessions among the Massa. *Ecology of Food and Nutrition* 25, 1: 1-28.

Guillard, J. (1965) *Golompui. Analyse des Conditions de Modernisation d'un Village du Nord Cameroun*. Mouton & Co/Ecole Pratique des Hautes Etudes, Paris/La Haye.

Koppert, G. (1981) Kogoyna, Etude Alimentaire, Anthropométrique et Pathologique d'un Village Massa du Nord Cameroun. Diplôme de Fin d'Etudes, Département de Nutrition, Université des Sciences Agronomiques, Wageningen, Pays Bas. Miméo.

MacAndrew, C. and Edgerton, R.B. (1969) *Drunken Comportment: a Social Explanation*. Aldine, Chicago.

Pallier, G. (1972) Les Dolotières de Ouagadougou (Haute Volta). *Travaux et Documents de Géographie Tropicale*, CEGET, Paris, 7.

Pasquet, P., Brigant, L., Froment A., Koppert, G.A., Bard, D., Garine, I. de and Apfelbaum, M. (1992) Massive Overfeeding and Energy Balance in Man: The *Guru walla* Model. *American Journal of Clinical Nutrition* 56: 483-90.

Périssé, J., Adrian, J., Rérat, A. et Le Berre, S. (1969) Bilan Nutritif de la Transformation du Sorgho en Bière. *Annales de Nutrition et Alimentation* 13, 1: 1-15.

Sims, E.A.H., Goldman, R.F., Gluck, C.M., Horton, E.S., Kelleher, P.C. and Rowe, D.W. (1968) Experimental Obesity in Man. *Journal of the Association of American Physicians* 81: 153-70.

6. MILK CONSUMPTION IN AFRICAN PASTORAL PEOPLES

Michael A. Little, Sandra J. Gray, and
Benjamin C. Campbell

Introduction

Milk production as a means of nourishing the young is a remarkable mammalian adaptation. It probably arose sometime during the late Mesozoic Era more than seventy million years ago, but certainly contributed to the adaptive radiation of mammals during the early Cenozoic. Milk glands evolved from simpler apocrine sweat glands, where the function of scent was converted to one of nutrition. For nearly all mammalian species, only the young consume milk from the mother, and it was only with the evolution of our own species, *Homo sapiens*, and the beginnings of animal domestication, that children beyond infancy and adults began to consume milk in a regular fashion as a food.

The origins of dairying as an alternative subsistence method within animal domestication are obscure, but it is estimated that animals were domesticated for food in the Near East as early as 10,000 years ago (Braidwood 1975). Dairying in the Near East, Africa, and Europe almost certainly began between 10,000 and 5,000 years ago. According to Sherratt (1981), there is evidence for the 'Secondary Products Revolution', or the use of domestic animals for more than just slaughter and meat production (e.g., traction, riding, milking, wool production), during the early part of the fourth millennium B.C. in the Near East. Even in Neolithic Europe about 6,000 years ago, there is evidence for milking cattle and ovicaprids (Bogucki 1986; Sherratt 1983). A significant problem that had to be overcome during the cultural evolution of dairying, was the biological evolution of tolerance of milk sugar or *lactose* by children and adults. McCracken (1971) and Simoons (1970) outlined the probable sequence of events leading to the continued production of the digestive enzyme, *lactase*, beyond infancy. This almost certainly occurred via natural selection for the ability to tolerate lactose by breaking down this disaccharide sugar into its digestible monosaccharides. The picture of adult lactose tolerance in adults is a complex one of relationships among genetics, digestive physiology, and digestive enzyme adaptation (Page & Bayless 1981; Scrimshaw and Murray 1988). However, this example of biocultural evolution is one of the best that we have of culture change (pastoralism/dairying) actually producing biological change (in genetics of populations) through natural selection.

In Africa, the first domestic cattle date back to about 6,000 years ago, and savanna pastoralism was well established by 3,000 years ago (Clutton-Brock 1989; Smith 1992 a, b), hence dairying must have been established in northern and eastern Africa sometime between these two dates. Most living populations in Africa that practise pastoralism and milk production have a history of this form of subsistence that is much more recent.

In Africa today, pastoral populations are widely distributed along the belt of sahelian and savanna lands from West Africa to Central Africa and then northward into the Sudan and southward into East Africa (Little 1997). Pastoralists can also be found as far south as Botswana. A herding way of life ranges from a subsistence pattern that almost entirely depends on livestock products to one in which a mixed agro-pastoralism is the norm. Hence, 'pastoralism' as a label need not be reserved only for those wholly dependent on livestock products. In fact, most pastoralists will practise 'multiresource exploitation' of herding, cropping, and hunting/gathering from time-to-time or frequently (Dyson-Hudson & Dyson-Hudson 1980). Moreover, the animals kept may be any number of domestic species (dromedary camels, cattle, donkeys, sheep and goats) and in various herd compositions.

A number of common attributes characterise African pastoralism:

1. In contrast to Western patterns of meat and wool production, African subsistence herding focuses on milk production and dairying. This is clearly indicated by the large proportions of adult animals and, particularly, adult females in most herds, and the importance of milk as a staple food in many pastoral diets (Dahl & Hjort 1976; Dyson-Hudson & Dyson-Hudson 1982; Galvin 1992).
2. African herders exploit arid or semi-arid savanna lands that have distinct seasonality of rainfall with periodic drought, lands that are generally not suitable solely for subsistence agriculture.
3. Because of the African pastoralist's habitation in dry and savanna lands, they are forced to exploit an environment with patchy and limited resources that display marked spatial and temporal variability. Their response to limited resources is a reliance on spatial mobility of people and herds, including nomadism or semi-nomadism (Dyson-Hudson 1972, 1980).
4. Finally, the culture and technology and knowledge of the pastoralist is centred on livestock management and dependence, and is linked to

complex patterns of social organisation and demographic structures, that is, demographic structures of both herds and people (Dyson-Hudson 1989; Leslie et al. 1999).

All of these factors contribute to the pattern of milk consumption on the lives of pastoral peoples, including its production, use, distribution, nutritional significance, and health effects. These can be organised along several themes:

- the marked seasonality in rainfall of savanna lands – that is, the low productivity of the dry season and the high productivity of the wet season (vegetation --> livestock condition --> milk production --> human nutritional status);
- the close demographic relationships between human numbers and livestock numbers, their population growth potentials, age and sex distributions;
- the livestock management practices and human labour requirements vs. productivity of milk and other products of the herds;
- breast-feeding vs. later supplementation by and dietary dependence on animal milk products;
- the unusual nature of a lifelong diet that is high in milk and milk products and its impact on the health of pastoralists vs. the parallel conditions linked to the more traditional diets of African cultivators.

Livestock Management and Milk Production

Much of the following discussion will focus on East African pastoral populations. The locations of several populations discussed here are given in a map of the region (see Map 6.1). These are only a few of the scores of pastoral populations found in Africa. The Ariaal are an amalgam of neighbouring Cushitic-speaking Rendille and Maa-related Samburu populations. Rendille focus on camel subsistence, while Samburu focus on cattle (both keep other livestock, as well) (Fratkin 1991). Karimojong are semi-nomadic, transhumant pastoralists from Uganda, whose pastoral diets are supplemented with cultivated foods (Dyson-Hudson 1966). The Borana (also Boran) live in southern Ethiopia and in population clusters in northeast Kenya. Maasai are distributed widely throughout southern Kenya and northern Tanzania, and are largely cattle-keepers. The Somali can be found in northeast Kenya and Somalia, and engage in considerable trade. The Turkana are closely related to the Karimojong, but are nomadic and practise little or no agriculture. They also inhabit one of the driest regions of northwest Kenya (Little and Leslie 1999). We shall draw most of our detailed observations from this population.

There is considerable inter-ethnic variation in pastoral practices among these selected East African populations. Livestock holdings per person and two indices of combined stock per person are given in Table 6.1. All populations

Map 6.1   A map of Kenya and the surrounding nations of East Africa showing the distribution of several pastoral populations discussed below.

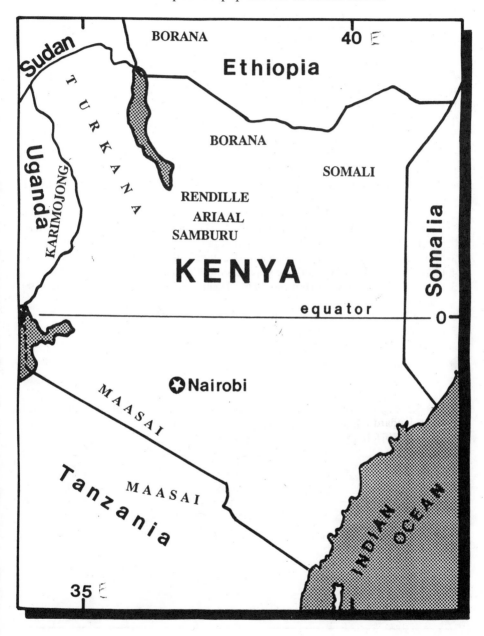

Table 6.1 Camels, cattle, small stock (goats & sheep), TLU (Tropical Livestock Units), and SSU (Standard Stock Units) per person in several East African pastoral populations

Population	Camels	Cattle	Small Stock	TLU[1]	SSU[2]
Ariaal (1976)[3]	1.6	4.6	7.9	7.6	8.1
Ariaal (1985)[3]	2.7	3.6	13.2	8.6	9.5
Rendille (1976–81)[4]	1.4	1.9	8.3	4.7	5.1
Karimojong (1953–55)[5]	0.00	3.6	5.4	4.3	4.1
Turkana (1982)[6]	1.7	2.5	11.4	6.1	6.5
Turkana (early 1980s)[7]	1.0	1.1	8.7	3.4	3.7
Borana (early 1980s)[7]	0.03	2.9	0.9	3.1	3.0

1 TLU (Tropical Livestock Unit) (FAO 1967): 1 cow=1 TLU, 1 camel=1.25 TLU, 1 small stock (goats & sheep)=0.125.
2 SSU (Standard Stock Unit) (Dyson-Hudson & McCabe 1985): 1 cow=1 SSU, 1 camel=1.7 SSU, 1 small stock=0.1 SSU. The SSU values give greater weight to camels, are closely geared to milk production and are more appropriate to drier regions.
3 Fratkin (1991), Kenya Ariaal populations=269 & 239.
4 IPAL (1984:286), Kenya Rendille population=12,900 (survey).
5 Dyson-Hudson & Dyson-Hudson (1970), Uganda Karimojong population=128,700 (survey).
6 Dyson-Hudson (1985), Kenyan Turkana population=1,071 (68 families).
7 Galvin et al. (1994), Kenya Turkana & Ethiopia Borana populations=11,700 & 112,968 (surveys).

Table 6.2 Adult cows and milch cows as a percentage of adult cattle in several East African populations. Data was compiled by Dyson-Hudson and Dyson-Hudson (1970, 1982) and is from Fratkin (1991).

Population	Percent Adult Cows (as percent of adults[1])	Percent Milch Cows (as percent of adults)
Karimojong	61	25–30
Turkana	60	24
Maasai	75	–
Ariaal	55	15–25
Rendille	77	–
Borana	70	–
Somali	92	–

1 Adult males include bulls and steers or bullocks (castrated males). Most pastoral herds have very few bulls. Adult females include adult cows and heifers (heifers are less than 3–3.5 years old and have not yet given birth to a calf).

Figure 6.1 Seasonal variations in milk production in Karimojong cows.

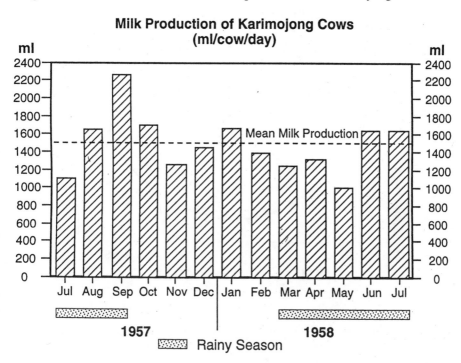

represented in the table, with the exception of the Karimojong, keep camels, cattle, goats, and sheep, although the proportions differ among the groups. What is most striking is the variation in Tropical Livestock Units (TLU) and Standard Stock Units (SSU) per person. Variation among the pastoral populations reflects each population's ability to feed its members; variation within populations indicates the volatility of herd numbers and density according to climate, vegetation, and factors of social conflict. For example, in Turkana District, herds were just beginning to recover from the *Lochuu* drought of 1979–81. The low TLU and SSU values for several of these populations almost certainly result from drought and associated livestock losses. Ariaal and Turkana herds have suffered more than 50 percent losses from drought and associated livestock diseases (Fratkin 1991; McCabe 1987). The species mix of herds is an important variable in combatting drought since camels are more likely to survive limited drought than are cattle. Recovery of herd numbers may take several years, but based on a drought frequency of once each four or five years (for South Turkana), herd numbers and indices of stock holdings are in a constant state of flux, at least, from year-to-year.

Other sources of variation include herd composition by age and by sex of the animals. Most pastoral populations maintain high proportions of adult animals and, specifically, adult females. Adult females as a percentage of all adult animals constitute between 55 and 75 percent of the herd (see Table 6.2).

Figure 6.2   Variations in milk production of four Ngisonyoka Turkana family herds in 1980 and 1981 during and after the *Lochuu* drought. Data is from Wienpahl (1985).

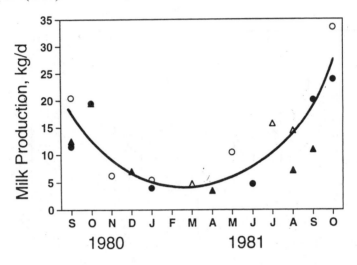

Figure 6.3   Intakes of milk and other food categories in 11 pastoral populations in Africa.

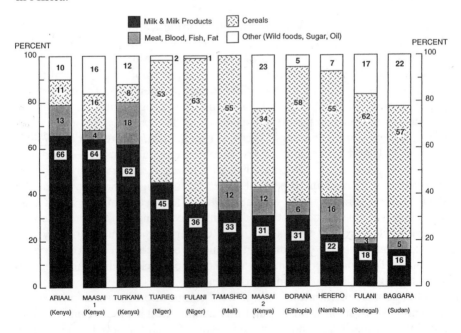

Figure 6.4   Methods of milk processing by the Ngisonyoka Turkana pastoralists.

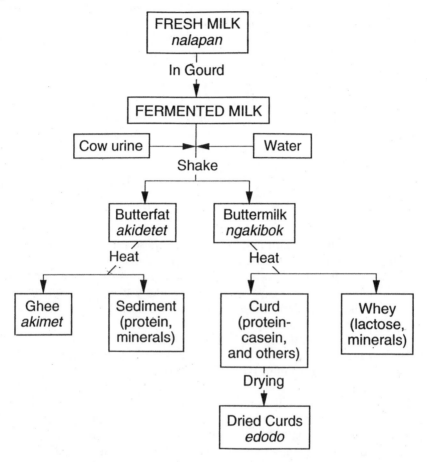

However, at any given time, only a portion of the adult females will be producing milk. Average values of milch cows and other livestock as a percentage of all adult animals appear to fall around 25 percent (Dahl & Hjort 1976; Dyson-Hudson and Dyson-Hudson 1970, 1982; Fratkin 1991). Hence, TLUs or SSUs are not real indicators of milk production, but simply represent livestock resources. Livestock other than lactating females provide meat and blood, and can be traded. There are seasonal- and drought-related variations in milk production, as well. Figure 6.1 illustrates seasonal variations over a 13-month period in Karimojong cows; a good wet season will allow double the milk production of the dry season. Figure 6.2 illustrates the effect of a serious drought on total milk production (all species of livestock) in four Turkana families. Towards the end of the drought, milk production had fallen to about 20–25 percent of the production in an average year.

Milk as a Dietary Staple

Livestock products that have value include milk, blood, meat, hides, and dung. Agro-pastoralists use dung as fertiliser and also to produce hard 'threshing floors'. Turkana use dung to treat hides and also to wean infants by placing a small amount on the mother's nipple. The other products are essential for pastoralists who rely heavily on their livestock. Trading of live animals is always an option, but is usually practised only when livestock products are in short supply. McCabe (1994), for example, has observed, repeatedly, the reluctance of nomadic Turkana to trade livestock for cash or food except during periods of drought. Livestock are the wealth and the invested capital of the pastoralists. The product of the livestock, milk, is life-sustaining. As Galvin (1992: 212) has emphatically noted: 'Milk is the preferred food among all pastoral groups and is the staple when available in sufficient quantity. It is the food of choice'.

An array of pastoral diets by food type is shown in Figure 6.3. Although cereal products predominate in most of the populations, the Ariaal, Turkana, and Maasai take in, on average, more than 50 percent of their food calories in milk or milk products. Smith (1992b) refers to these East African groups as practising *specialised pastoralism*, an adaptation unique to East Africa. There is limited information on other populations, but Karimojong, Rendille, Samburu, Dodos, Jie, and several others are likely to display equally high intakes of milk. These percentages of food items represent the total intakes averaged across all ages, and mask the variability in intakes by age, sex, season, and year. These percentages, also, do not illustrate the variability in caloric intakes. For example, the Ariaal data represents a daily caloric intake of about 2,250 kcal/person/day (Fratkin 1991:53), whereas the Turkana data represents 1,275 kcal/person/day (Galvin 1985).

Seasonal variation in milk consumption is substantial, and associated with the availability of protein- and calorie-rich green forage that flushes during the rainy seasons. As animals regain body weight from the losses experienced during the dry season, they may either conceive, reproduce, or if they are already lactating, increase milk output both in volume (see Figure 6.1 above) and calories. Turkana livestock show increases in the energy value of milk from the late dry season to the wet season of between 25–50 percent (in kcal/100g of milk) (Galvin & Waweru 1987). These differences appear to be largely attributable to seasonal variations in the fat content of milk. The average crude protein content of milk appears to remain fairly constant throughout the year (Galvin & Waweru 1987). In a survey of seasonal variations in diet of several pastoral populations, Galvin (1992) found that wet season milk consumption as a percentage of total calories was almost always twice or more than that consumed during the dry season. This resulted from the dry season pattern, where both the amount of milk available and its caloric content per unit volume decreased. Galvin (1985) also found that milk intake during a particularly good period in Turkana accounted for more than 90 percent of the caloric intake of the people. During periods of drought, milk intakes plummet, and maizemeal

Figure 6.5   The flow of energy from Ngisonyoka Turkana livestock to human food.

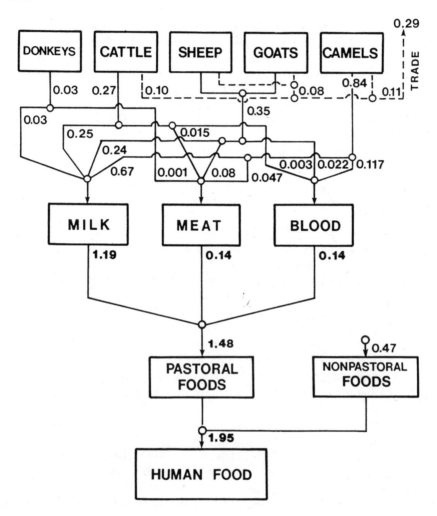

(from trade of animals) usually takes up part of the caloric slack, although wild foods are also hunted and gathered to make up for the depleted milk resources.

The kinds of milk foods consumed by the Turkana are varied (see Figure 6.4: after Galvin 1985). Milk may be consumed fresh or mixed with raw blood. Since in many societies women are responsible for milking animals and keep milk products in the household structure, they probably have access to, and some degree of control over, their own intakes and the intakes of their children. Several milk products can be stored without spoilage, but such products often are prepared only when there is an abundance of milk during especially good years. Ghee, or clarified butter, for example, is easy to prepare, has a high caloric or energy content (9 kcal/g), and can be kept for long periods in tropical heat. Another means of preservation, employed by the Turkana, is to spread fresh milk onto hides, allow it to dry, and then scrape the powdered milk into containers for storage. Dried curds from low-fat milk is a third method of food preservation. Finally, a very important physiological means of energy storage employed and enjoyed by all pastoralists when milk is abundant is simply to drink it all, and store the energy as body fat. Seasonal changes in human bodyweights and skinfolds (fat deposits) have been documented for the Turkana (Galvin 1985).

Milk in the Diets of Turkana

As noted, there are many variables that influence the amount of milk that pastoralists will be able to consume. These are:

1. season of the year;
2. vegetation conditions of the previous year;
3. presence or absence of drought;
4. numbers of Tropical Livestock Units (TLU) or Standard Stock Units (SSU) per person in the household;
5. species, age, and sex composition of the herds, and
6. the management skills of the herd owner.

Herd composition and milk production has been studied for many Turkana families or production units (Dyson-Hudson and McCabe 1985). Detailed studies of dietary intake and nutrition have been conducted on fewer families (Galvin 1985; Gray 1994a).

Based on the livestock holdings and dietary patterns of four Ngisonyoka Turkana families, a model of energy flow through the Turkana ecosystem was prepared by Coughenour and his colleagues (1985). The livestock food production pathways of the model are given in Figure 6.5. The values are in gigajoules of energy (GJ/person/year), where 1 GJ = 2.389 3 10^5 kcal. It must be emphasised that the data for this model was derived from a variety of sources, and that the model represents *average estimates:* variability of any kind is not represented by the model. With this caveat in mind, the model can be very useful to represent how livestock contribute to human diets.

The five species of livestock have different feeding and management needs (not shown) and contribute differentially to the three primary pastoral foods that people eat. Livestock also contribute products that are traded for nonpastoral foods, and the Turkana acquire some nonpastoral food by hunting and gathering. Pastoral food production contributes about 76 percent (1.48 GJ) of energy to the diet, and nonpastoral foods contribute about 24 percent (0.47 GJ). However, incorporating trade of livestock products (0.29 GJ) raises the proportion of livestock contribution to about 91 percent (1.77 GJ) of the total

Figure 6.6 Supplementation of non-breast feeding foods in Turkana infants of less than two years of age.

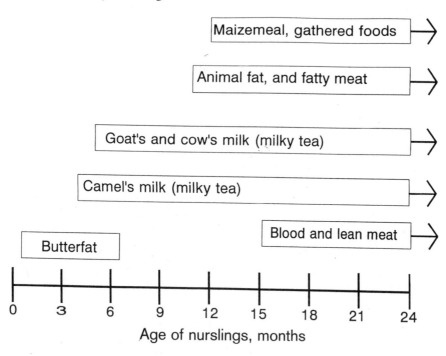

subsistence (1.95 GJ). Milk constitutes about 80 percent of pastoral foods and camels provide about 56 percent of this milk. In fact, excluding trade, camels provide more than half of all pastoral foods consumed by the Turkana, small stock contribute nearly a quarter, and cattle contribute less than a fifth. The value of species diversity in livestock holdings rests with the constant milk productivity of camels throughout the year, the abundant milk production of cattle during the wet season vegetation flush, and the convertibility of small stock by slaughter or trade.

The total average energy intake of 1.95 GJ/person/year translates to 1,276 kcal/person/day determined by a model designed by Leslie et al. (1984) that included resting metabolic rates, body weights and compositions, environmental temperature, pregnancy and lactation adjustments based on fertility rates, activity estimates, and age-sex structure of the population as input variables for the model (Little et al. 1988). The 1,276 kcal/person/day from Figure 6.5 presents about 83 percent of 1,540 kcal/day/person, the food energy requirements predicted by the model of Leslie et al. (1984). The 17 percent difference between the predicted caloric energy requirements and observed caloric intake must result from a number of factors, including: variation in intakes, reduced physical activity, measurement error (foods consumed that were not observed), and cumulative errors in the predictive models.

Table 6.3 Milk consumption as a percentage of total annual food energy intake for children and adolescents. Data is from Galvin (1985)

Age	Females	Combined	Males
2–3 years		74	
4–7 years		66	
8–13 years	67		69
14–21 years	72		65

Milk Consumption by Age and Sex

Milk, as a dietary component, will now be discussed for different age classes of Ngisonyoka Turkana, including infants, children, adolescents, and adults. There is considerable variation in patterns and amounts of milk consumption for each of these age-sex groups.

Infants

From a small sample of nomadic Turkana infants (N=14), full-term birthweight at 3,250 g was within the low normal range of Western populations (Pike 1997). Infants are put to the breast shortly after birth, and breast-feeding patterns are ad libitum throughout infancy, with mothers and infants in close physical contact during the day and night (Gray 1994b). Weaning occurs at 21 months, on average, but the normal range for weaning is between 15 and 24 months (Gray 1996). What is most unusual about Turkana (and other pastoralists), by worldwide standards, is that these infants are weaned from breast milk to animal milk and other animal products, and that the high dietary intakes of milk products will continue for a lifetime. As noted elsewhere: 'The pastoralist system ... provides a nutritious alternative to breast milk in the form of milk from the herds and a complex social network that ensures its availability' (Gray 1996:439).

Non-breastmilk foods are an important part of the diet of breast-feeding Turkana infants from early infancy (Gray 1996). The introduction and duration of specific foods in the nursling diet is shown in Figure 6.6. Butterfat is introduced first, during the neonatal period. By the time of weaning, at approximately twenty-one months, young children are consuming the equivalent of the adult diet. In her study of infant feeding, Gray (1998) argued that butterfat and milk were used not to replace breastmilk in the infant diet but rather to compensate calorically for seasonal variability in the fat and calorie content of human milk. She found that the amounts of non-breastmilk foods and their caloric values were associated with seasonal rainfall, and nurslings' intake of these foods increased between the late-dry and early-wet seasons, when food resources for adults decreased. Butterfat, in particular, contributed an average of 375 kcal/day to infants under the age of six months.

Supplementation of infants who are breast-feeding occurs almost universally before the age of six months. In Turkana infants, supplementation begins quite early within the first postpartum month and continues throughout the period of breast-feeding, until the infant is consuming the equivalent of an adult diet at the age of about twenty-four months (Gray 1996). Figure 6.6 is a diagram of the introduction and duration of supplemented foods. Butterfat supplementation contributed an average of 375 kcal/day to the diets of infants during the first six months of life (Gray 1996). The amounts of supplemental foods and their caloric values were associated with seasonal rainfall, where supplemented foods were increased during the seasons (late dry- and early wet-season) with limited resources (Gray 1998). Anthropometric status of nursling infants during the first two years indicated that length remained at median NCHS levels, but weight tended to falter after the age of six months (Gray 1998; Little et al. 1993).

Children and Adolescents

At ages beyond weaning, children are given special preference for available milk resources. Young children, aged 2 to 5 years, were often offered food by all women in the household – clearly there were strong values for keeping young children well fed (Galvin 1985). Table 6.3 indicates the amount of milk consumed, as a percentage of total calories consumed throughout the year for the period between August 1981 and December 1982. The highest intakes of milk and milk products at nearly 75 percent are in 2- and 3-year-old toddlers. Children beyond these ages consume, roughly, one-third of their calories in the form of milk products. Among adolescents and youths (14- to 21-year-olds), males and females differ: males consume about one-third of their calories as milk, in similar fashion to the children, while females consume more milk as a proportion of the diet.

These patterns indicate variable access to milk and some degree of preferential allocation of milk to different age-sex classes of children and youths. For example, 2- to 3-year-old and 4- to 7-year-old children are given priority to receive milk, particularly when milk is in short supply. Eight- to 13-year-old boys and 14- to 21-year-old male youths who are resident at herding camps will have access to milk and blood from the animals under their care. Girls in the 8- to 13-year-old age category will be in the home camp, and will be responsible for milking animals, along with adult women. The other high-intake group is 14- to 21-year-old females, who also milk animals in the home camp. This latter group constitutes young women who are approaching the age of marriage, and who are given preferences for food energy intake. The evidence for this is indirect, but persuasive, and is based on body composition changes that are apparent in late adolescent girls. Girls in this age category, as in many societies, are provided with beads and elaborate costumes associated with the approach to marriageable age. Beginning around 15 or 16 years of age, these girls begin to put on considerable body fat, which further enhances their appearance of robusticity and attractiveness. Young women reach a peak in fat deposits by about age 20 years (Little et al. 1983), which is close to the mean age at marriage (Gray 1994b).

Adult Men

Young men over age 21 years and the older herd owners consume slightly more than 50 percent of their calories as milk (Galvin 1985). Men also consume larger amounts of high-energy foods such as meat, fat, and sugar than other age-sex groups. However, during the peak dry season or under drought conditions, men will voluntarily reduce their food intake so that women and children may have greater access to the food.

Adult Women

At 56 percent of their energy intake, young and adult women have slightly higher consumption of milk than men (Galvin 1985). They are also more heavily dependent on gathered wild foods and grains (maizemeal) than other age-sex groups. Co-wives will share food, which contributes to a redistribution of resources, and women appear to have a slight dietary advantage because they have responsibility for milking the animals (Gray 1994a). Since women may drink small amounts of milk while milking animals in the morning and early evening, the calculated proportion of milk in the diets of women may be underestimated. Even constant surveillance to record food consumption may overlook a significant intake of food. Milk, buttermilk, and butterfat are stored in vessels hung from the inside framework of the day hut. One of us (M.A.L.) observed a woman, resting in a day hut, consume about a litre of milk in about ten seconds while the observer looked down to take notes! This rapidly consumed drink of milk constituted about 700 kcal of food energy.

Women have high energy requirements from reproduction. For example, nomadic women have a relatively high lifetime fertility of between 6.6 and 7.1 live births (Brainard 1991; Leslie et al. 1999). With a completed fertility of seven live births (5.25 years of cumulative pregnancy) and 21 months of breast-feeding for each of the seven infants (12.25 years of cumulative lactation) (Gray 1994b), this amounts to her food energy needs being substantially elevated for about 17.5 years, or more than half of her reproductive life. Since women also show depletion of body fat between the ages of 20 and 40 years (Little et al. 1983), it is likely that the increased energy needs of pregnancy and lactation are not being entirely met by dietary intakes (Little et al. 1992).

Discussion

Biological interest in milk consumption among pastoral nomads has focussed on genetic changes in lactose absorption as the single most important biological adjustment of pastoral nomads in exploiting this subsistence niche (Holden & Mace 1996). However, as a dietary staple, the impact of milk consumption on pastoral nomads extends beyond the simple availability of calories from the breakdown of lactose to include the impacts of secondary factors. These include the fluctuation of milk availability and the presence of other nutrients, including lipids and protein in milk as discussed above.

As mentioned earlier, milk availability fluctuates substantially with environmental conditions, through both the condition of the animals and the size and composition of the herds. Thus fluctuations in total caloric availability are closely tied to milk availability. Since women are milking the animals and have the potential for first access, changes in milk availability may provide a very direct link between environmental conditions, female nutritional status, and fertility previously outlined by Leslie and Fry (1989).

This may be important in explaining variation in fertility both yearly and over longer-term environmental fluctuations (Leslie et al. 1999). Such fluctuations are likely to be particularly important in the context of maternal depletion of body energy reserves such as found among the Turkana (Little et al. 1992), where differences in food availability are thought to contribute to marginal differences in reproductive ability.

The second consequence of a reliance on milk is its potential contribution to the development of the tall and lean physiques typical of many pastoralists, including the Turkana (Little et al 1983). While it is generally agreed that the thermoregulatory demands of the hot arid climate play a role in adult body shape, dietary intake of East African pastoralists must play a role as well. It has been suggested that the relatively high protein intake of the Turkana promotes linear growth (Little & Johnson 1987; Galvin 1992). Although low caloric intake would appear to account for leanness in this case, Gray (1998) has suggested that the high metabolic cost of converting protein into calories may further contribute to the Turkana's leanness.

It was hypothesised that the high-protein, low-calorie diet limits fat storage in nomadic Turkana via two mechanisms: (1) metabolic costs of gluconeogenesis limit availability of ketogenic amino acids for lipogenesis, and (2) skeletal growth that is supported by high protein and calcium intake increases the overall proportion of fat-free mass, which is more energetically expensive to maintain (Corbett 1998). The metabolic effect again would be to reduce availability of energy-yielding nutrients for lipid synthesis and storage. It was also found that a sample of settled Turkana women were significantly shorter but fatter than their nomadic counterparts (Corbett 1998). He suggested that the agricultural diet of settled women, in which cereals replace milk as the staple food, is higher in calories from carbohydrate but substantially lower in protein. Consequently linear growth is suppressed while the ratio of fat to lean tissue is increased in settled women. Energy demands are reduced both for tissue homeostasis as well as for energy metabolism itself, promoting fat storage among settled women at a caloric intake comparable to or even lower than that of the nomads.

There may be a parallel between patterns of growth and milk consumption with age.While Turkana attain adults' heights that are roughly equivalent to U.S. 50th centiles by ages in the early 20s, they do so despite a very attenuated adolescent growth spurt (Little et al. 1983; Little & Johnson 1987). Final adult height is dependent on continued slow growth throughout the teens and into the 20s. Thus increased consumption of milk among boys and girls throughout the age period of 14 to 21 years may be important in structuring the specific body size and composition of Turkana adults.

More specifically, since the adolescent growth spurt is generally considered to be driven by the effects of gonadal hormones superimposed on continued stimulation by human growth hormone (hGH) (Wootton & Jackson 1996), lack of an adolescent growth spurt suggests only a moderate stimulation of growth in height by gonadal hormones during puberty. Although speculative, access to greater amounts of milk leading to higher protein intake may sustain continued growth through hGH-related processes even in the absence of dramatic increases in gonadal hormone stimulation.

Finally, a broader consideration of milk consumption among pastoral nomads may help us to understand another related and unresolved feature of the Turkana: how they survive, reproduce, and grow on such apparently low caloric intakes. The first possibility is that the amount of milk has simply been consistently underestimated, in part because of the ease with which milk can be consumed surreptitiously, as noted earlier. This would be illuminating for the Turkana and other pastoral nomads, but less interesting in terms of the underlying human biology.

The other possibility is more complex and relevant to discussions of the thrifty genotype. The Turkana are surely an example of the conditions for the thrifty genotype, including marked fluctuations in food supply superimposed on chronic undernutrition. Allen & Cheer (1996), in discussing milk consumption and the non-thrifty genotype, note that milk consumption is a major stimulus for insulin secretion, in part because of the inclusion of protein along with lactose. Thus, in replacing complex starches from cereals with simple sugars and adding protein, the diet of the pastoral nomad may promote the quick clearance of blood glucose leaving little to fuel the use, and hence the development and maintenance, of muscle tissue during both childhood and adulthood (Wootton & Jackson 1996). Not only would this account for the low lean mass of the Turkana (Little & Johnson 1986), despite relatively high protein intake, but it is also consistent with the relatively low work capacity observed by Curran-Everett (1994).

Conclusions

Evidence presented here outlines clearly the importance of milk as a component of Turkana and other East African pastoralists' nutrition and subsistence. Not only is it a dietary staple, constituting up to 90 percent of calories during part of the year, but it is also a culturally preferred food, and animals are seen as milk producers rather than meat producers or as exchange items for grains. This central role as a dietary staple suggests that the impact of milk consumption on the human biology of the Turkana and other East African pastoralists may have been underappreciated. In addition to genetic changes necessary to enable the absorption of lactose, milk consumption may play a key role in the prolonged linear growth of the Turkana, as well as their relatively small muscle mass and associated low work capacity.

References

Allen, J.S. & Cheer, S.M. (1996) The non-thrifty genotype. *Current Anthropology.* 37: 831–42.

Bénéfice, E., Chevassus-Agnes, S. & Barral, H. (1984) Nutritional situation and seasonal variations for pastoralist populations of the Sahel (Senegalese Ferlo). *Ecology of Food and Nutrition.* 14: 229–47.

Bernus, E. (1988) Seasonality, climatic fluctuations, and food supplies. In, I. de Garine & G.A. Harrison (Eds.) *Coping with Uncertainty in Food Supply.* Oxford University Press, Oxford: 318–36.

Bogucki, P. (1986) The antiquity of dairying in temperate Europe. *Expedition* 28: 51–58.

Braidwood, R.J. (1975) *Prehistoric Men, 8th Edition.* Scott, Foresman, Glenview, Illinois.

Brainard, J.M. (1991) *Health and Development in a Rural Kenyan Community.* Peter Lang Publishing, New York.

Clutton-Brock, J. (1989) Cattle in ancient North Africa. In, J. Clutton-Brock (Ed.) *The Walking Larder: Patterns of Domestication, Pastoralism, and Predation.* Unwin Hyman, London: 200–206.

Corbett, S. (1998) Subsistence Effects on Body Composition of Nomadic Pastoral and Settled Agricultural Turkana. M.A. Thesis in Anthropology, Kansas University, Lawrence.

Coughenour, M.B., Ellis, J.E., Swift, D.M., Coppock, D.L., Galvin, K., McCabe, J.T. & Hart, T.C. (1985) Energy extraction and use in a nomadic pastoral population. *Science* 230: 619–25.

Curran-Everett, L.S. (1994) Accordance between VO_2 max and behavior in Ngisonyoka Turkana. *American Journal of Human Biology* 6: 761–71.

Dahl, G. & Hjort, A. (1976) *Having Herds: Pastoral Herd Growth and Household Economy.* Stockholm Studies in Social Anthropology. No.2, University of Stockholm, Sweden.

Dyson-Hudson, N. (1966) *Karimojong Politics.* Oxford University Press, Oxford.

Dyson-Hudson, N. (1972) The study of nomads. In, W. Irons & N. Dyson-Hudson (Eds.) *Perspectives on Nomadism.* Brill, Leiden: 2–29.

Dyson-Hudson, N. (1980) Strategies of resource exploitation among East African savanna pastoralists. In, D.R. Harris (Ed.) *Human Ecology in Savanna Environments.* Academic Press, London: 171–84.

Dyson-Hudson, N. & Dyson-Hudson, R. (1982) The structure of East African herds and the future of East African herders. *Development and Change* 13: 213–38.

Dyson-Hudson, R. (1985) South Turkana herd structures: and livestock/human ratios: report of a survey of 75 South Turkana households: June–August 1982 (Appendix III). In, *South Turkana Nomadism: Coping with an Unpredictably Varying Environment,* by R. Dyson-Hudson & J.T. McCabe, pp. 331–65. Human Relations Area Files, Inc., HRAFlex Books Ethnography Series, New Haven.

Dyson-Hudson, R. (1989) Ecological influences on systems of food production and social organization of South Turkana pastoralists. In, V. Standen & R.A. Foley (Eds.) *Comparative Socioecology: The Behavioral Ecology of Humans and Other Mammals.* Blackwell, Oxford: 165–93.

Dyson-Hudson, R. & Dyson-Hudson, N. (1970) The food production system of the Karimojong. In, P. McLoughlin (Ed.) *African Food Production Systems: Cases and Theory.* Johns Hopkins University Press, Baltimore: 93–123.

Dyson-Hudson, R. & Dyson-Hudson, N. (1980) Nomadic Pastoralism. *Annual Review of Anthropology* 9: 15–61.

Dyson-Hudson, R. and McCabe, J.T. (1985) *South Turkana Nomadism: Coping with an Unpredictably Varying Environment.* Human Relations Area Files, Inc., HRAFlex Books Ethnography Series, New Haven.

FAO (1967) *FAO Production Yearbook.* Food and Agricultural Organisation, Rome.

Fratkin, E. (1991) *Surviving Drought and Development: Ariaal Pastoralists of Northern Kenya.* Westview Press, Boulder.

Galvin, K. (1985) Food Procurement, Diet, Activities and Nutrition of Ngisonyoka, Turkana Pastoralists in an Ecological and Social Context. Ph.D. Dissertation in Anthropology, State University of New York, Binghamton.

Galvin, K.A. (1992) Nutritional ecology of pastoralists in dry tropical Africa. *American Journal of Human Biology* 4: 209–21.

Galvin, K. & Waweru, S.K. (1987) Appendix 3. Variation in the energy and protein content of milk consumed by nomadic pastoralists of northwest Kenya. In, A.A.J. Jansen, H.T. Horelli & V.J. Quinn (Eds.) *Food and Nutrition in Kenya: A Historical Review* : 129–38. Department of Community Health, University of Nairobi, Nairobi.

Galvin, K.A., Coppock, D.L. & Leslie, P.W. (1994) Diet, nutrition, and the pastoral strategy. In, E. Fratkin, K.A. Galvin and E.A. Roth (Eds.) *African Pastoralist Systems: An Integrated Approach.* Rienner, Boulder: 113–31.

Gray, S.J. (1994a) Correlates of dietary intake of lactating women in South Turkana. *American Journal of Human Biology* 6: 369–83.

Gray, S.J. (1994b) Comparison of effects of breast-feeding practices on birth-spacing in three societies: nomadic Turkana, Gainj, and Quechua. *Journal of Biosocial Science* 26: 69–90.

Gray, S.J. (1996) The ecology of weaning among nomadic Turkana pastoralists of Kenya: maternal thinking, maternal behavior, and human adaptive strategies. *Human Biology* 68: 437–65.

Gray, S.J. 1998. Butterfat feeding in early infancy in African populations: new hypotheses. *American Journal of Human Biology* 10: 163–78.

Hamill, P.V.V., Drizd, T.A., Johnson, C.L., Reed, R.B., Roche, A.F. & Moore, W.M. (1979) Physical growth: National Center for Health Statistics percentiles. *American Journal of Clinical Nutrition* 32: 607–29.

Holden, C. & Mace, R. (1996) Phylogenetic analysis of the evolution of lactose digestion in adults. *Human Biology* 69: 605–28.

Holter, U. (1988) Food consumption of camel nomads in the North West Sudan. *Ecology of Food and Nutrition* 21: 95–115.

IPAL. (1984) Integrated Resource Assessment and Management Plan for Western Marsabit District, Northern Kenya. Integrated Project in Arid Lands (IPAL) Technical Report No. A-6. UNESCO, Nairobi.

Leslie, P.W., Bindon, J.R. and Baker, P.T. (1984) Caloric requirements of human populations: a model. *Human Ecology* 12: 137–62.

Leslie, P.W., Campbell, K.L., Campbell, B.C., Kigondu, C.S. & Kirumbi, L.W. (1999) Fecundity and fertility. In, M.A. Little & P.W. Leslie (Eds.) *Turkana Herders of the Dry Savanna: Ecology and Biobehavioral Response of Nomads to an Uncertain Environment.* Oxford University Press, Oxford: 248–78.

Leslie, P.W. & Fry, P.H. (1989) Extreme seasonality of births among nomadic Turkana pastoralists. *American Journal of Physical Anthropology* 79: 103–15.

Little, M.A. (1997) Adaptability of African pastoralists. In, S.J. Ulijaszek & R.A. Huss-Ashmore, *Human Adaptability: Past, Present and Future.* Oxford University Press, Oxford: 29–60.

Little, M.A., Galvin, K. & Leslie, P.W. (1988) Health and energy requirements of nomadic Turkana pastoralists. In, I. de Garine and G.A. Harrison (Eds.) *Coping with Uncertainty in Food Supply.* Oxford University Press, Oxford: 288–315.

Little, M.A., Galvin, K. & Mugambi, M. (1983) Cross-sectional growth of nomadic Turkana pastoralists. *Human Biology* 55: 811–30.

Little, M.A., Gray, S.J. & Leslie, P.W. (1993) Growth of nomadic and settled Turkana infants of northwest Kenya. *American Journal of Physical Anthropology* 92: 273–89.

Little, M.A. & Johnson, B.R., Jr. (1986) Grip strength, muscle fatigue, and body composition in nomadic Turkana pastoralists. *American Journal of Physical Anthropology* 69: 33544.

Little, M.A. & Johnson, B.R., Jr. (1987) Mixed-longitudinal growth of nomadic Turkana pastoralists. *Human Biology* 59: 695–707.

Little M.A., Leslie, P.W. & Campbell, K.L. (1992) Energy reserves and parity of nomadic and settled Turkana women. *American Journal of Human Biology* 4: 729–38.

Little, M.A. & Leslie, P.W. (Eds.) (1999) *Turkana Herders of the Dry Savanna: Ecology and Biobehavioral Response of Nomads to an Uncertain Environment.* Oxford University Press, Oxford.

McCabe, J.T. (1988) Drought and recovery: livestock dynamics among the Ngisonyoka Turkana of Kenya. *Human Ecology* 15: 371–89.

McCabe, J.T. (1994) The failure to encapsulate: resistance to the penetration of capitalism by the Turkana of Kenya. In, C. Chang and H. Koster (Eds.) *Pastoralists at the Periphery: Herders in a Capitalist World.* University of Arizona Press, Tucson.

McCracken, R.D. (1971) Lactase deficiency: an example of dietary evolution. *Current Anthropology* 12: 479–517.

Nestel, P. (1985) Nutrition of Maasai women and children in relation to subsistence food production. Ph.D. Thesis in Nutrition. University of London, London.

Nestel, P. (1986) A society in transition: developmental and seasonal influences on the nutrition of Maasai women and children. *Food and Nutrition Bulletin* 8: 2–18.

O'Keefe, S.J.D., Rund, J.E., Marot, N.R., Symmonds, K.L. & Berger, G.M.B. (1988) Nutritional status, dietary intake and disease patterns in rural Hereros, Kavangos and Bushmen in South West Africa/Namibia. *South African Medical Journal* 73: 643–48.

Paige, D.M. & Bayless, T.M. (Eds.) (1981) *Lactose Digestion: Clinical and Nutritional Implications.* Johns Hopkins University Press, Baltimore.

Pike, I.L. (1996) The Determinants of Pregnancy Outcome for Nomadic Turkana Women of Kenya. Ph.D. Dissertation in Anthropology, State University of New York, Binghamton.

Scrimshaw, N.S. & Murray, E.B. (1988) The acceptability of milk and milk products in populations with a high prevalence of lactose intolerance. *American Journal of Clinical Nutrition,* Supplement 48 (4): 1079–1159.

Sherratt, A. (1981) Plough and pastoralism: aspects of the secondary products revolution. In, I. Hodder, G. Isaac, and N. Hammond (Eds.) *Pattern of the Past: Studies in Honor of David Clarke.* Cambridge University Press, Cambridge: 261–305.

Sherratt, A. (1983) The secondary exploitation of animals in the Old World. *World Archaeology,* 15: 90–104.

Simoons, F.J. (1970) Primary adult lactose intolerance and the milking habit. A problem in biological and cultural interrelations. II. A culture historical hypothesis. *American Journal of Digestive Diseases* 15: 695–710.

Smith, A.B. (1992 a) Origins and spread of pastoralism in Africa. *Annual Review of Anthropology,* 21: 125–41.

Smith, A.B. (1992 b) *Pastoralism in Africa: Origins and Development Ecology.* Hurst & Company, London.

Wagenaar-Brouwer, M. (1985) Preliminary findings on the diet and nutritional status of some Tamasheq and Fulani groups in the Niger Delta of Central Mali. In, A.G. Hill (Ed.) *Population, Health and Nutrition in the Sahel: Issues in the Welfare of Selected West African Communities.* Kegan Paul International, London: 226–52.

Wienpahl, J. (1984) The Role of Women and Small Stock among the Turkana. Ph.D. Dissertation in Anthropology, University of Arizona, Tucson.

Wootton, S.A. & Jackson, A.A. (1996) Influence of under-nutrition in early life on growth, body composition and metabolic competence. In, C.J.K. Henry & S.J. Ulijaszek (Eds.) *Long-Term Consequences of Early Environment: Growth, Development and the Lifespan Developmental Perspective.* Society for the Study of Human Biology Symposium 37, Cambridge University Press, Cambridge: 109–23.

7. THE DRINKING RITUAL AMONG THE MAASAI

Fouad N. Ibrahim

Introduction

This paper deals with the traditional drinking rules and habits of the Maasai, drawing on studies carried out in Naberera area in the Maasai Steppe, Northern Tanzania. There, the drinking 'ritual' varies in form according to the occasion, type of drink, age-group, sex, marital status and social position. While taking traditional food and beverage is usually governed by specific rules, 'modern' drinks have no formal regulations. Some food-drinks, such as milk and honey beer, have spiritual connotations among the Maasai. Other liquid food items, such as blood, soup, fat and ghee also have medical usages. Moreover, infusions made of different plants are taken as medicine.

Drinking manufactured beer and the local 'Swahili' brew is considered by the Maasai as a sign of modern decadence. The *muran* (warriors), being a symbol of Maasai integrity of character, drink milk as their main food and traditionally take no alcohol or tobacco.

The Milk Ceremonial

Milk is not only the main element of the pastoral diet of the Maasai, but also a sacred object. In many rituals, milk is drunk, sprinkled from a gourd or spat from the mouth to give a blessing. It is not astonishing then that the simple act of drinking milk among the Maasai is governed by strict rules of behaviour, especially among the muran who are seen by the Maasai themselves as an incorporation of purity, honesty, solidarity, bravery, sharing, good behaviour and all other social values of which the Maasai are proud. Drinking milk forms a significant Maasai cultural code.

The Milking Ritual

Before a Maasai woman retires to bed at night, she makes sure that her milk gourds are on her bed, clean and ready for the early morning milking. The number and size of the gourds she prepares depends on the amount of milk she expects to get from her cows. The different gourds of different sizes have different names: *esingau, engoti-esoto, oloti-lenkule nairobi, entipi* and *emala*. The latter is the largest and contains about three to four litres. Daily, the gourds in use are meticulously cleaned by the woman and her daughters. They use water and stick-brushes which they have made from the long roots of *olmukatan (Albizia anthelmintica)* or *oiti (Acacia mellifera)*, both of which are also used as medicines for a broad spectrum of diseases. To dry the inside of the gourds, disinfect and give them (and the milk later) a nice smell, glowing embers of *oloirien (Olea africana)*, one of the sacred trees of the Maasai, are put into them, shaken for some time and then poured out. This is done several times.

When the light of day breaks, the Maasai woman gets up, washes her hands with water, and takes with her a few gourds and the calf of the cow to be milked. When she reaches the cattle enclosure she calls the cow by its name and it comes to her. She shakes the remaining *oloirien* charcoal out of the gourds and rinses them with cow urine for further disinfection. The calf starts suckling at one side of the cow and the woman starts milking at the other. Some women still say a traditional prayer at the beginning. The first small quantity of milk drawn is thrown from the gourd into the sky. They pray: 'God give us a good dawn!', 'Let our heads live long!', 'Give us always wet heads!' (dry heads are dead), 'Give us children and cattle!', 'Let blow upon us a good wind which likes cattle and children!' (a wind which carries no diseases).

The Entitlement to Milk

After milking her cows the Maasai woman takes the milk to her house and usually divides it between three gourds: a big one for the children, another large one for the husband who drinks milk two to three times a day, and a gourd for the muran. Then she lays the gourds on her bed and goes to attend other urgent duties, mainly in connection with livestock. Nobody is allowed to go to the woman's bed to take the milk without her permission. This restriction applies particularly to the husband, but, if she leaves the *enkang'* (kraal settlement), she tells the man which gourd is his.

However, the Maasai woman's responsibility for milk does not mean that she is free to do whatever she likes with it. As a matter of fact, the Maasai woman has no share of her own in the milk, she only gets what remains. The Maasai ritual of milk drinking, however, provides a little for the women as it is bad manners for a circumcised man to drink all the milk in the gourd. He has to leave some milk for the children (and their mother). The Maasai believe that if you finish the milk in the gourd, God will finish your cattle. However, as milk is getting scarcer year by year, there is often nothing left for the women to drink.

It is, therefore, doubtful whether, under the present situation of economic decline of the Maasai, Johnson's statement (1998: 170) about the control of the

Maasai women over milk still holds: 'Thus, meat, which is extraordinary food, and blood, are nourishing substances controlled by men, whereas milk, the nourishing substance of daily consumption, is controlled by women. Women have the exclusive right to distribute milk to their family's members as they think appropriate, or sell it, if they wish.'

In our study area, in Naberera/Namalulu, we find that, while Maasai men have the right to sell the family's cattle and get the lion's share of both meat and milk, the Maasai women have practically no right to sell cattle and that their entitlement to both meat and milk is minimal. They are only allowed to sell milk after they have satisfied the needs of husbands, their guests, children and muran. Even if the husband is on a safari for a few days, his wife has to conserve his share by turning it into sour milk and keeping it until he returns home. The vital importance of observing the milk right of a husband is expressed clearly by the newly married Elizabethi, a sixteen-year-old Maasai woman. When asked what a woman can do to make her husband happy, she answered: 'A woman should always take care of her husband's gourd and his cup, and not have children from other men' (Interview by B. Ibrahim, Namalulu, April, 1997). Mentioning the husband's gourd and cup before mentioning 'having children from other men', which is, today, a serious offence among the Christian Maasai, especially if a woman is newly married, illustrates the paramount importance of men's entitlement to milk.

A young elder who has not yet performed the ritual of *enduruj* (see below), is not allowed to drink milk in front of women. When he drinks his milk, the woman has to go out of the hut. When he has finished drinking he calls her back.

After drinking milk, old men pray, saying: 'God, give us more cattle'. Nowadays, some people, especially those belonging to the Pentecostal (Assembly of God) Church say Christian prayers before drinking milk, or milk with tea.

The Muran Rules of Milk Drinking

The muran learn the rules of drinking milk in the *manyatta* where they live alone with other muran. They are governed by the *enduruj* taboo, which forbids them to have sex with circumcised women and to drink or eat in their presence. As a Maasai male informant put it: 'It is bad if women see muran eating. Women are considered unclean. They are always dirty. Muran are considered the purest and most superior members of the Maasai society. Muran do not drink alcoholic drinks. They do not eat the meat of a dead cow, like other Maasai do. They cannot eat with non-Maasai, because these cannot behave in the same way as the Maasai' (Interview in Namalulu, August 1997).

When the muran are with their families in the enkang', they gather to drink milk together alone in one house. Mothers bring milk gourds to that house, or the muran may move from one house to another to drink milk there. One *murani* said: 'We usually drink milk in the house of Helena (the youngest wife of the chief of the enkang'). We have chosen her because she is kind-hearted. Other mothers are supposed to bring milk to her house. But this morning we had only Helena's milk' (Interview in Namalulu, August 1997).

Sharing milk gives the muran a strong feeling of togetherness. It also ensures that every murani, however poor his family may be, is fed. If a murani does not find another age-mate to drink milk with, he joins an elder. Otherwise, he has to take his gourd and look for a vacant isolated house in the bush, where he can drink his milk.

When muran drink milk, any of them may serve it using a small cup *(mamasita)*, or a short gourd with a wide opening *(esiang'au)*. The first to drink milk is the youngest. When he is satisfied, he gives the gourd to the second youngest, and so on. The senior muran age-group drink last.

They drink milk once in the morning and once in the evening. They say: 'We go to drink milk *(emaapeti aok kule)*', even if it is tea with milk, thin porridge or thick porridge. As a rule, the Maasai do not take milk and meat together.

The Rituals of Alcohol Drinking

In the Maasai rites of passage and other personal and collective rituals, whether or not they are ordered or directed by the *laibon* (religious leader, 'prophet' and medicine man), drinking mead plays an important role. Today, other drinks are also served, such as the local brews of the neighbouring ethnic groups, made of sugar, millet or maize, and mixed with certain plants, or else modern bottled drinks, such as soda, *konyagi* (Tanzanian distilled alcoholic drink), whisky and Safari beer. However, these drinks, apart from mead, have no religious function and are not used in connection with the ritual of giving a blessing by an elder.

Traditionally, drinking alcohol (mead) was restricted to elders. Nowadays, a small proportion of women also drink it. A few muran, especially those who go to Merireni for gemstone brokering, have taken to drinking.

In the following, examples of the traditional Maasai ceremonies in which drinking mead plays a vital role are documented.

Circumcision (EMORATA)

The owner of the ceremony (usually the father) chooses a chief of ceremony from among his age-set, a person of good character and a father. The chief of ceremony opens the *ormosori* (mead gourd) and divides the mead among the various age-sets (men), whose members sit in groups according to age-sets and drink together. The higher age-set get their portion first. The oldest member's gourd is filled first (today they use cups). They usually eat meat before drinking. Then they drink, take a break, then drink again. They go on drinking until the mead is finished.

Blessings said by the circumcision ceremony chief before beer drinking:
'Blessings be on this house!', 'Let this house have the smell of cows!', 'Let this house have the smell of goats!', 'All be blessed!', 'God bless you to be rich!', 'Get children!', 'Both girls and boys!, (God give us!)', 'God give us cattle!', 'God give us goats and sheep!', 'Be blessed!', 'God be with you and with us!'[2]

Ngitoropilot Enkang': Ceremony to Bless the Homestead After the Death of a Person

The Maasai have no funeral ceremonies. Traditionally, they used not to bury the dead, but smeared the bodies with fat and lay them in the bush for the hyenas to eat. Nowadays, there is an increasing tendency for burial in the enkang', which, in the past, was only done for the head of the family.

The *ngitoropilot enkang'* is a ritual held for driving evil from the enkang' after the death of one of its members. It is performed one or two weeks after the death. The deceased is not commemorated as the Maasai consider it an evil omen to mention the name of, or even to refer to, a deceased person. In this ritual no animal is sacrificed.

Mead is prepared by the widows of the deceased and by the man who inherits. If the sons are grown-ups, they prepare the beer with their uncle (the eldest brother of the father) who is responsible for the distribution of the wealth and the widows of the deceased. He is the one to bless the sons and make sure that their affairs go smoothly.

In the evening the members of the age-group of the deceased gather to drink the mead. One of them serves. After drinking, they talk about matters concerning the wealth and family of the deceased. At the end, four men of the age-group, including the one serving the beer, say prayers. The Maasai usually perform their prayers after the mead drinking and not before it. The prayer is performed by the first man, then repeated by the second and so on.

Prayer after drinking honey beer for blessing the homestead after the death of a person:

'Let the enkang' be good as usual!	'O God!'
'Rise and continue!'	'O God!'
'Let all be saved and get many cows, goats, sheep and children!	'O God!'
'Let the grass spread!'	'O God!'
'Let be *oreteti*! (holy tree) *(Ficus hochstettere).'*	'O God!'

Suitable additions can be made to the above prayers.

Esiret: Engagement

When the bridegroom has been accepted by the girl's father, he takes to her family a container with twenty litres of honey, a roll of tobacco and a blanket for the girl's father (blankets came with the Germans in the nineteenth century. Originally, the Maasai wore calf hides sewn together).

Some of the honey is distributed among the people of the enkang' and the rest is used to make mead. The girl's mother mixes honey with water and pieces of *osukuroi (Aloe myriacantha)* in a large gourd *(ormosori)* and puts it near, but not too close, to the fire to ferment. This mead is called *'enaisho e siret'*. No animal is sacrificed on this occasion. From the girl's side, the father and persons of his choice take part in the ceremony.

An age-mate of the bridegroom is responsible for the function; he must be a father and a man of good conduct. They drink the mead, but do not finish it. The rest is drunk later at the fireplace (cooking place), after praying. They pray, giving their blessings to the father and the mother of the girl, and to the girl herself.

Blessing given by bridegroom party at the end of the engagement ceremony:

'God give us your blessings!', 'God give us children!', 'God give us cattle!', 'God give us food!', 'God give us daughters (to be able) to drink beer!'.

The girl's father is requested by the other men repeatedly: 'Father of Mosipa give us food' (Mosipa is an example of a girl's name). So, they are then served the rest of the mead. Then they fix a day for negotiating the dowry *(ngishu enkaput* = my daughter's cows). After drinking they disperse. Women do not usually take part in this ceremony.

Negotiating the Dowry

Each party, the bride's father and the bridegroom's, chooses a good negotiator. The bridegroom's party brings mead (nowadays also factory-bottled beer, maize beer or other local brews). The girl's father provides the mead, but it is served by the bridegroom's negotiator. Each age-group receives its portion of beer and each group sits separately. Older age-sets get the lion's share. Elderly women sit together and drink. Younger women get tea instead. This time no blessings are said.

The dowry should be at least five head of cattle, among which there should be two grown-up heifers (two- to three-year-old cows, *ngishu enkaputi).*

Orkiteng lo Nwomonok
(or Enduruj = Haram = Forbidden)

For this occasion, an ox is slaughtered and roasted. An elderly member of the age-group of the owner of the ceremony *(laajijik)* opens the gourd, then, stepping aside, he lets the elders drink. Nowadays even muran drink, in their age-group.

The age-group members and elders say a prayer after drinking. In the praying ritual, they call the owner of the ceremony and his wife using the name of the first-born (boy or girl) and the words 'Father of...' or 'Mother of...' If they do not have a child, the name of a rich person is used, e.g., Ansuer.

Prayer said after honey beer drinking on the occasion of enduruj:[4]

'Father of...!' 'Yes!' 'Mother of...!' 'Rise and continue!' 'O God!'
'Let all be saved and get many cows, goats, sheep and
children!' 'O God!'
'Let the grass spread!' 'O God!'
'Let be *oreteti* (holy tree)!' 'O God!'
Laibon's Blessings, Esujet Oloiboni:

Kerikei Naputi (80), Namalulu, held the last ceremony of this kind in 1995, according to the directions of Lazaru, the *laibon,* so that cattle would not die. Kerikei slaughtered only one goat and bought two boxes of Safari beer of twenty-five bottles each. He did not offer tobacco because the laibon does not like it.

Oseke (Cordia quarensis) branches were laid on the ground of the gate opening so that the cattle passed over it to be blessed. According to tradition, each house must prepare mead for this ceremony. Usually, a number of oxen are slaughtered.

Charms are given by the laibon in the form of stones or pieces of wood. They are covered with leather and made into a necklace, the strings of which are made from the hide of the healthiest ox slaughtered.

Mead is used to bless the charms. It is spat onto them 'so that the charms be as sweet as honey beer'. This blessing is performed by the old men, who have already been blessed by the laibon.

People eat meat first. It is divided among the various groups by two elders, chosen by the owner of the ceremony from among his intimate friends. The meat is distributed according to a strict traditional system. Each group of the society is entitled to certain parts of the slaughtered animal.

After eating meat, the participants drink alcohol. To do so, each age-group goes to a house which belongs to one of their age-set. Each age-group has a person responsible for the drinks assigned by the owner of the ceremony.

After drinking, the blessing is given by the elders. Its wording is the same as the blessing of circumcision.

Drinking Beef Soup at Orpul

Orpul is a bush retreat, mainly for men, which continues for up to a fortnight. Men eat beef and drink beef soup and fresh blood. Drinking alcohol is not allowed at orpul, which has something sacred about it. It is held under a large, shady tree. There, the muran wear waist strings which they weave from the inner bark of the holy tree, *oreteti*. Orpul also serves to strengthen both the muran and the elders. The former gain strength to fight and the latter want to gain sexual potency. A number of plants are added to the beef soup to achieve the highest effect. Orpul is mostly held in the dry season when food (milk) is scarce.

The orpul is originally meant for muran *(orpul: oloikar)*. Elders can participate, but not women. Women's orpul *(orpul le aulo / orpul lo ndomonok)*, which is held near the enkang', is less common.

Orpul Prayers

Morning prayer at orpul, performed individually at dawn:

In the morning, God, I have come to you'. 'I am blessed among the blessed under this tree'. 'Let me live long and give me cattle and children'. 'I love you God and I love cattle'. 'So, bless me to get children and cattle'. 'Take care of me in this orpul until I return home'.

Another Morning Orpul Prayer:

'You muran, let the feast be hot, let the cow help us to get wives, let the curved side of our shield be hard, let the fever be away from us, let us wake up well, the dawn has come'.

Additional prayer in the evening:

'Let us sleep well, the night has come'.

Evening Prayer:

Men close the thorns of the orpul and perform their evening prayer together before supper. One of them prays and the others repeat the refrain: 'O God' *(naai)*.

Evening prayer at orpul, performed collectively 'indoors':

'You muran be blessed and let the orpul become heated'. 'O God!'
'Let God take care of us during the night'.   'O God!'

'Those who are after us let God keep away from us'.   'O God!'
'Let the meat of the cow give us strength'.   'O God!'
'Let us multiply'.   'O God!'
'Let the elders leave the cattle to us warriors'.   'O God!'

Conclusion

Drinking among the Maasai is part and parcel of their social code. Both milk and mead are used for giving a blessing. Blessings are often given by elders whom one tries to please by offering them mead. It is remarkable that, although modern alcoholic drinks and brews of other ethnic groups are growing popular among the Maasai, they have not acquired the sacred value which mead possesses. A serious change, however, is taking place in the behaviour of the muran. Quite a few of them have taken to drinking alcoholic beverages, mostly after contact with urban life. They also recently got permission from the laibon to marry, which previously was the exclusive right of elders. A major change in the drinking habits of the muran, who symbolise all the good qualities of the Maasai, could bring about a serious decadence of that society.

Notes

1. Source for the prayers: Fieldwork, F. Ibrahim, Namalulu, 1997.
2. Source: Fieldwork, F. Ibrahim, Naberera, 1997.
3. Informant: Namolwo Lolpiro (85), at Monee's enkang', Enkarkahi, Namalulu, on 14/8/97.
4. The word means breaking a traditional restriction and refers to the right which a husband has to drink milk in front of his wife.

References

Brenzinger, M., Heine, B. and Heine, I. (1994) *The Mukogodo Maasai, an Ethnobotanical Survey.* Koeln, 314 p.

Ibrahim, F. (1997) The Current Status of Knowledge and Actual Usage of Medical Plants Among the Maasai of Naberera, Northern Tanzania. *Bayreuther Geowissenschaftliche Arbeiten,* Vol. 16. Bayreuth: 88-116.

Johnson, N. (1998) Maasai Medicine – Practising health and therapy in Ngorongoro Conservation Area, Tanzania. Ph.D. Dissertation. Ph.D.-raekke nr. 7. Institut for Antropologi, Copenhagen, 359 p.

8. CHANGING PERCEPTIONS ON MILK AS A DRINK IN WESTERN EUROPE
THE CASE OF THE NETHERLANDS

Adel P. den Hartog

Introduction

The aim of this paper is to give an analysis of how and why milk became an indispensable drink associated with health and a traditional component of the Dutch food culture. Water is most essential to life. However the fluid intake is not only based on water, but likewise on a whole range of beverages, which may include milk as well. The place of milk in the fluid intake varies according to geography, time and culture.

In preindustrial Western Europe the common cattle *(Bos taurus)* has played a dominant role in the food system: supplier of dung for fertilising the arable land, and of meat and dairy products. Milk is a perishable product, so a surplus of milk that is not required for immediate consumption should be preserved in one way or the other, like butter, cheese, curds or yoghurt. At the end of the eighteenth century in the Netherlands, milk was still used more as an ingredient than as a drink. Beverages such as beer, tea and coffee were of more importance.

The rise of milk as a drink in North-West Europe started in the nineteenth century, and is closely associated with the industrial revolution. The diffusion of milk as a drink should be considered as part of a wider process of developing safe and healthy beverages for mass consumption, the spas or mineral waters, fruit juices and later the soft drinks (Burnett 1998).

It will be discussed within the framework of Hobsbawn's theory on the invention of tradition. He points out that traditions which appear or claim to be old are often quite recent in origin and sometimes even 'invented' (Hobsbawn 1983).

Various change agencies with different motives all tried to give milk as a drink a prominent place in the diet. In the study of the modern relationship between man and food, the role of the food industry and sciences, besides the food culture, should be taken into account.

Milk in Western Europe

Western Europe can rightly be classified as a region of lactophiles (Marvin Harris 1985).

Table 8.1   Consumption of liquid milk and fermented products in Western Europe, kg per capita, 1997.

	Liquid milk[1]	Fermented products[2] kg/capita
Finaland	148.8	38.4
Norway	145.6	16.7
Sweden	121.7	28.4
Denmark	96.6	25.9
UK	123.3	–
Ireland	150.9	6.0
Belgium	62.2	25.1
Netherlands	55.9	46.7
Luxembourg	126.2	–
Germany	67.9	23.8
France	75.5	18.5
Spain	101.7	14.5
Portugal	74.9	8.5
Italy	9.6	–

1. 'White' liquid milk, excluding other milk drinks.
2. Milk drinks, fermented products including yoghurt.

Source: International Dairy Federation, Brussels, 1997

Eduard Hahn pointed out already in 1896 that a clear distinction had to be made between milk and non-milk using regions of the world, because of differences in the role of cattle in the food systems. The traditional non-milk using populations are to be found in humid tropical Africa, South-East Asia, but also in the Far East. When the discussion on the question of lactose intolerance broke out, Simoons (1970) took up this matter again. In Western Europe the highest milk consumption is to be found in the Scandinavian countries and Ireland.

The Dutch consider themselves as typical milk drinkers. As a nation with dairy traditions their level of milk consumption is not strikingly high compared with other countries. Italy is the only country of Western Europe where milk consumption is limited. In the Italian food culture milk is regarded mainly as a food and not as a drink. Its use is strictly associated with breakfast and especially for infants (Troiani 1997). Marvin Harris' dichotomy of lactophiles and lactophobes, milk lovers and milk haters, does not hold. The appreciation for milk is very diffuse. Even in populations with a deficiency of the enzyme lactase to make digestion of the milk sugar lactose possible, people generally can drink modest quantities of milk (Scrimshaw 1988).

Dairy and the Early Use of Milk

In the Low Countries (the present Benelux states), with their relatively extensive livestock of cattle, pure milk in the unpreserved form was not a popular ingredient in the medieval kitchen of the gentry (Van Winter 1994). Basically three kinds of milk were used: milk as such, skim milk (from which most of the fat has been removed) and buttermilk (a slightly fermented low-fat content milk), which is a byproduct of butter-making. Milk and buttermilk were mainly used as ingredients for cereal porridges. In the rural areas of the Netherlands, in the period 1900–1925, byproducts such as buttermilk and skim milk were still important ingredients in porridges (Jobse-van Putten 1994).

Buttermilk was, however, also appreciated as a drink in the eighteenth century in the countryside (Burema 1953). Whey, a liquid byproduct of cheese-making, was sometimes used as a drink. Small farmers and rural labourers kept some goats for milk supply. The goat was often called the cow of the poor. In the middle of the nineteenth century, before the industrial revolution in the Netherlands, milk was rarely tasted by the working class households in the cities, a phenomenon which could be found in other cities of Western Europe (Burnett 1979; Teutenberg 1981).

The Rise of Milk as a Drink

In the nineteenth century the supply of fresh milk to the expanding towns and large urban settlements posed many difficulties. Milk of good quality was expensive and out of reach of the working classes.

In England, at that time the main industrialised nation of Europe, not only fresh milk but likewise condensed milk was of importance for the urban consumer. As a relatively cheap milk product its consumption rapidly increased. It was, to a large extent, used for feeding infants and young children (Drummond 1958). In the Netherlands milk supplied to the cities was fresh milk, and condensed milk played hardly any role. As in other European countries, fresh milk was supplied directly from the dairy farm to the consumers in the cities, either by the farmer or by milk traders. The milk maid with her yoke and buckets, selling milk at the doorstep, was a common sight in many Dutch towns until the end of the nineteenth century.

This system was, however, inadequate: milk was often polluted or diluted with water (den Hartog 1998). From the 1870s onwards three factors have played a crucial role in the diffusion of the concept of milk as a diet, namely medical advice from the hygienists, home economics training for girls, and a group of progressive entrepreneurs within the dairy industry.

Milk and Health

The medical profession in the nineteenth century and in particular the group of hygienists were convinced of the importance of milk for the diet. As far as infant feeding was concerned, it was stressed that milk should come from healthy cows. In the second part of that era, concepts of hygiene emerged in the medical sciences and received wide acceptance among the higher classes of society. In the latter part of the nineteenth century the medical profession was beginning to realise that milk could play an important part in the transmission of bovine tuberculosis and diseases caused by the member of the coli-typhoid group of bacteria. In this respect the work of Louis Pasteur on food hygiene and food processing (1865) and that of Robert Koch (1882) on the tubercular bacillus should be mentioned. The hygienists promoted the concept of a sanitary environment as a way to promote public health and to prevent contagious diseases. The general acceptance of new ideas on milk, hygiene and health was a slow process in Europe (Atkins 1992; de Knecht-van Eekelen 1984).

The Role of Home Economics

The concept of milk as a drink was further taken up by home economics training for girls. Various authors have argued that cookery classes and schools of home economics for girls have contributed to a further spread of modern nutritional thinking among the Dutch population (Jobse-van Putten 1987; Van Otterloo 1985). At the end of the nineteenth century, schools of home economics were established for girls, mainly of the upper classes. Later schools of home economics followed for rural girls coming from small-scale farms and agricultural labourer households. These schools were funded from private sources. From 1921 onwards schools of home economics were funded by the state because of the Vocational Training Act. This meant that from then onwards training in home economics became much more accessible to girls from the lower classes. Hygiene and nutrition were major components of the curriculum. The importance for nutrition of the traditional dairy products, butter, cheese and milk, was stressed.

The Dairy Industry, Hygiene and Marketing

In order to satisfy urban demands for good quality milk, some entrepreneurs in various European countries established dairies and model milk farms. Right from the beginning the new concepts of hygiene in handling milk were taken into account by these relatively small groups of progressive entrepreneurs (Pyke 1985). In the Netherlands in 1879 and shortly after, dairies were established in eight major cities. In 1904 a number of dairy producers founded the Netherlands Association for Milk Hygiene (*Nederlandse Melkhygiïnische*

Vereeniging). The aim of the association was not only to promote the material interest of its members, but to promote the profession of milk hygiene.

The dairies introduced a new milk distribution system involving the milkman, milk kiosks and dairy shops. The milkman was dressed in a neat uniform and his milk cart was equipped with big clean copper milk jugs and small jugs to measure the right quantity of milk to be sold at the doorstep of the customers. Concern for hygiene was always stressed by the management of the dairies (Van Lakerveld 1994).

Important for the diffusion of milk as a drink was the subsequent establishment in major cities of dairy shops and tearooms offering the possibility of drinking a glass of milk and eating a small snack. It served as a good lunchtime alternative for office workers and small businessmen who wanted to avoid the temptation of the alcoholic drinks of the pubs and bars. Likewise it was a safe place for housewives when shopping in the city centre.

The arrival of the milk bottle enhanced further milk drinking (den Hartog 1998). The streetside-dispensed milk was raw, had to be put in a container at home and boiled before drinking. However, pasteurised milk in a bottle at home is a safe and healthy drink, ready for immediate consumption. Compared with the United States the general acceptance of milk bottles in the Netherlands, and afterwards in north-west European countries, was a slow process.

A larger use of the glass bottle for milk is most likely connected with the introduction of pasteurisation techniques in the dairy industry. In the 1870s glass bottles were generally used for wine, hard liquor such as *geneva* (juniper gin), not to mention mineral water and related products. Glass was not used for more bulky and less expensive foods such as milk and vegetables. Available sources suggest that in the Netherlands the first bottles containing milk appeared on the market in the 1880s. Some dairies started to produce and sell pasteurised, and also sterilised, milk in bottles (den Hartog 1998).

Originally bottled milk was meant mainly for infant feeding. In 1951 in the Netherlands only 33 percent of the milk distributed to consumers was in bottles. This is in contrast to the United States where already most milk in cities was sold to consumers in wide-mouthed bottles. The price of pasteurised milk in bottles was much higher than the dispensed milk. At the beginning of the twentieth century it was virtually out of reach of the common consumer.

After 1945 the popularity of the milk bottle increased, in the first place by a steady growth in the standard of living. In the 1960s more than 70 percent of the milk consumed came out of a bottle. When later the supermarkets took over the milk trade, cartons started to replace the milk bottles.

Triumph of Milk as an Indispensable Drink

At the end of the 1940s fresh milk consumption in the Netherlands was at its peak, with an average intake of more than half a litre per capita per day. After the miserable period of food shortage during the Second World War people could once again enjoy their glass of milk. Milk was, and mainly still is, consumed at breakfast and at the traditional Dutch sandwich meal *(brood-maaltijd)*, which can be taken at noon or in the evening.

Inspired by the American Food Guide, the Netherlands Bureau of Nutrition Education developed its own Food Guide in 1953. In the illustration of the Dutch Food Guide, dairy food and in particular milk had a central place. Both nutritionists and the dairy industry were in full agreement with each other, that milk was an indispensable component of the diet and its use should be promoted.

Similar development occurred in other countries of north-west Europe. In the UK the Milk Marketing Board had close relations with the nutrition and health sector. In Norway there was for a long time a strong harmony between the interests of the dairy industry and the nutrition and public health sector (Kjaernes 1995).

A Decline in Milk Drinking and Efforts to Reverse the Trend

In the 1950s the living standards in the Netherlands, and in other West European countries, started to rise considerably and caused major changes in food

Figure 8.1 Consumption of milk, milk products and cheese in the Netherlands, 1965–1987.
Source: Netherlands Nutritional Council, CBS, 1992.

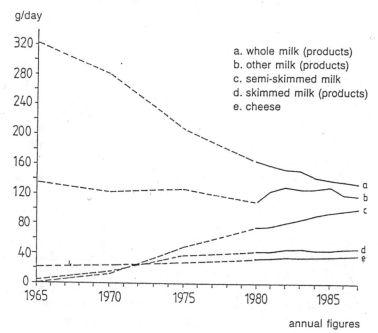

a. whole milk (products)
b. other milk (products)
c. semi-skimmed milk
d. skimmed milk (products)
e. cheese

annual figures

Figure 8.2   Number of schoolchildren participating in the Milk-in-School Programme in the Netherlands.
Source: den Hartog 1994.

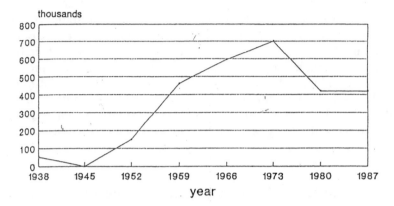

consumption. The amounts of meat and consequently fat, sugar, fruits and vegetables, increased. On the other hand consumption of less expensive foods such as bread, potatoes and milk showed a steady decline. From an average daily intake of 570 g in 1955 the milk consumption declined to 395 g in 1985. The dairy industry, largely a cooperative industry owned by dairy farmers, responded to the process of a diminishing milk consumption in two ways : the 'Milk-in-School Programme', and a collective advertising campaign for the whole dairy sector to promote the use of milk as a drink.

The Milk-in-School Programme began in 1937 during the Depression when the Dutch dairy industry was confronted with milk surpluses (den Hartog 1994). It was an effort by the dairy industry to combine industrial interests with the nutritional needs of primary school children. Parents and teachers were involved in the organisation and distribution of milk. Earlier efforts by local authorities to introduce school meals failed. Family ethics dictated that taking a meal was a family responsibility and should be done at home and not at school (den Hartog 1994). Milk, however, was a healthy drink enjoyed by all classes of the society and could not be considered as a threat to family responsibilities (Figure 8.2).

A central Milk-In-School Committee was created by the dairy industry with the task each morning of coordinating the milk distribution in primary schools in major cities of the country. Each child could receive a bottle with a quarter of a litre of milk and a straw for drinking it. Parents paid a low subsidised price for the milk. When, at the end of the 1950s, it became apparent that milk consumption was on the decline, both the dairy industry and nutritionists were much concerned with this undesirable development. In order to maintain the habits of milk drinking in the future, children should learn at an early age to appreciate milk as a tasty and healthy beverage. As a result the Dutch Dairy Bureau, a joint marketing organisation of the dairy industry, tried to stimulate the use of milk

Table 8.2 Consumption of drinks per head per year in Western Europe, 1985–1995.

	1985	1995
Total	487 litres percentage of volume	552 litres
Milk	20%	17%
Tea, coffee	30%	26%
Soft drinks	23%	34%
Alcohol containing drinks	27%	23%

Source: based on Lemoine, 1996.

among children and adults by means of radio programmes, articles in newspapers and magazines, and distribution of folders to parents and teachers.

New was the introduction of collective food advertising, advertisements of a food product and not a brand as such, paid for by most of the industry concerned. In the Netherlands a major collective advertising campaign was already initiated by the brewery sector in 1948. The beer brewers were facing a decline in beer drinking and feared that the soft drinks coming from the United States, such as the colas, were gradually replacing beer, so they started a nationwide campaign with the slogan 'beer is best' (or in Dutch *het bier is weer best*). The brewery sector was inspired by a British collective advertising campaign which started before the Second World War (Scheurs 1991). It is of interest to note that the collective advertisements for milk were mainly directed at young people. Well-known campaigns were, among others: the 'Milk Brigade of the Milkway', a little boy called 'George the milk drinker' and 'Milk the White Engine'.

How successful were these campaigns? This is difficult to say. The promotion activities could not in any case reverse the trend. In the 1990s milk consumption reached a more or less stable level of 370g a day. The promotion activities have most likely contributed to the preservation of milk as a drink in the food pattern. In this respect the collective advertising of beer was more successful. In 1948, the first year of the campaign, the average beer consumption per capita per year was 13.4 litres, ten years later in 1958 a level of 20.2 litres was reached. Despite massive promotion activities of the soft drink industry, beer consumption rose steadily. It was, to put it in modern marketing language, an early example of the struggle for 'the share of the throat'.

In the European Union the per capita consumption of all drinks increased from 487 litres in 1985 to 552 in 1995. While the consumption of soft drinks increased by 75 percent during this period, consumption of all other drinks decreased such as tea, coffee, alcohol-containing beverages and milk (Table 8.2).

Milk and the Changing Position of Nutritional Thinking

In the 1970s the so far unchallenged position of milk as a healthy drink came under serious attack as one of the contributors to the high intake of unsaturated fat of the Dutch population. Consumers demanded a low-fat content milk. The dairy industry was slow to respond. In their way of thinking fat was the best component of milk and they were reluctant to reduce it. However a private dairy firm introduced a low-fat content milk (1.5g fat per 100 g instead of 3.5 g) which became very successful, and other firms followed suit. In the Scandinavian countries during the period 1975–1995, the intake of milk fat was reduced because of a decrease of full cream milk consumption. The total milk consumption was not fully counteracted by an increase in low-fat content milk (Berge 1997).

In 1977 the Dutch Milk-in-School Programme celebrated its 40 years with a conference on milk and schoolchildren. One of the invited speakers, a nutritionist, stated that he was not convinced that milk in school was essential from a nutritional point of view. Most nutrients were already covered, so there was no direct need for a supplement at school (Hermus 1977).

The loosening of the ties between the dairy industry and nutritionists became more apparent when in 1981 the Bureau of Nutrition Education changed the Food Guide. In the new Food Guide milk was no longer depicted as a separate item. Now it was lumped together with meat, fish and eggs as one group. The dairy industry was very upset and worried about the new and rather obscure place of milk in nutrition education. The Dutch Dairy Bureau therefore changed its marketing philosophy at the end of the 1970s. Milk should be seen as a cool refreshing drink, alongside other beverages, and not so much only as a health drink. Efforts to introduce flavoured milk drinks were not very successful, with the exception of chocolate flavour. The yoghurt kind of milk drinks, flavoured with fruit, were more successful.

However, new changes occurred in the relationship between the dairy industry and the nutritional sciences in Europe, which had an impact on milk. It started, strangely enough, a long time ago in Japan, a country without a dairy tradition, with the tiny bottle of Yakult, a fermented milk product. In Japan the idea emerged that instead of changing food habits, nutrition-related health problems could be better solved with the development of these so-called functional and new foods. A functional food is a food with a substance, with a specific nutritional property to contribute to health or to prevent nutrition-related diseases.

There is some evidence that lactic-acid bacteria can give a valuable contribution to the protection of the digestive tract. Not much is known of the mechanisms of protection. It is known that in the food culture of the Balkans, Asia Minor and the Caucasus, yoghurt and related kind of products have been hailed for their health effects (Akiyoshi 1988; Michio Kanbe 1988).

As a result of Japan's interest in the possible healthy role of lactic-acid bacteria, European dairy firms have introduced a variety of new yoghurt-type products and fermented milk drinks. Various studies indicate that milk is not only a source of nutrients such as protein, calcium and the vitamins A and D, but is also a carrier of numerous bioactive compounds (Ruo-Jun Xu 1998).

Conclusion

Milk is an age-old food, part of the food culture of north-west Europe. In the food culture of the Netherlands the role of milk as a generally accepted drink at breakfast, lunch or just as a refreshment is relatively new. Far into the nineteenth century milk was more an ingredient in dishes, such as porridges, than just a drink. After the 1950s milk drinking declined and faced fierce competition from the soft drink industry.

The rise of milk as a drink was stimulated and promoted by change agencies, the dairy industry, home economics and the nutritional sciences.

Milk as a drink in the dietary pattern is not the result of autonomous processes. With Hobsbawn we may speak of an invention of tradition. The paper also indicates that the food industry and the nutrition and health sector are mighty agencies in influencing and shaping a food culture.

References

Akiyoshi Hosono (1988) Fermented milk in the orient. In, Yuji Nakazawa and Akiyoshi Hosono (Eds.), *Functions of fermented milk, challenges for the health sciences.* Elsevier Applied Science, London: 61–78.

Atkins, P.J. (1992) White poison? The social consequences of milk consumption, 1850–1930. *Social History of Medicine,* 5: 207–27.

Berge, S. (1997) Trends in consumption of milk products and milk fat in the Nordic Countries. *Scandinavian Journal of Nutrition,* 41: 121–4.

Burema, L. (1953) *De voeding in Nederland van de middeleeuwen tot de twintigste eeuw* [Nutrition in the Netherlands from the middle ages until the twentieth century]. Van Gorcum, Assen.

Burnett, J. (1979) *Plenty and Want. A social history of the present day.* Scolar Press, London.

Burnett, J. (in press) From cordial waters to Coca-Cola: soft drinks and health in Britain. In, A. Fenton (Ed.), *Health implications of eating and drinking in the nineteenth and twentieth centuries.* Tuckwell Press, East Lothian.

CMC/Melkunie. (1979) *De geschiedenis ener melkinrichting, een eeuw consumptiemelk 1879–1979* [The history of a dairy, a century of liquid milk]. J&T Publicity, Amsterdam.

Drummond, J.C., Wilbraham, A. and Hollingworth, D.F. (1958, rev. ed.) *The Englishman's food: a history of five centuries of English diet.* Jonathan Cape, London.

Harris, M. (1985) *Good to eat, riddles of food and culture.* Simon and Schuster, New York.

Hartog, den, A.P. (1994) Feeding schoolchildren in the Netherlands: conflict between state and family responsibilities. In, J. Burnett and D.J. Oddy (Eds.), *The origins and development of food policies in Europe.* Leicester University Press, London: 70–89.

Hartog, den, A.P. (1998) Serving the urban consumer: the development of modern foodpackaging with special reference to the milk bottle. In, A. Fenton (Ed.), *Food and Material Culture*. Tuckwell Press, East Lothian.

Hermus, R.J.J. (1977) De voeding van de schoolgaande jeugd: gezonde voeding ofgezondheidsopvoeding [Nutrition of school children: a healthy nutrition or health education]. *Melk in relatie tot de gezondheid*, 4, no.4: 35–62.

Hobsbawn, E.J. (1983) Introduction: inventions of traditions. In, E.J. Hobsbawn and T. Ranger (Eds.), *The invention of tradition*. Cambridge University Press, Cambridge: 1–14.

International Dairy Federation (1997) World dairy situation 1997. *Bulletin of the International Dairy Federation*, no. 323.

Jobse-van Putten, J. (1987) Met nieuwe tijd nieuw (w)eten. Invloed van voedingsonderrichtop de Nederlandse voedingsgewoonten, ca. 1880–1940 [The influence of home economic teaching on Dutch food habits]. *Volkskundig Bulletin*, 13: 1–29.

Jobse-van Putten, J. (1994) Porridge consumption in the Netherlands: changes in function and significance. In, P. Lysaght, P. (Ed.), *Milk and milk products from medieval to modern times*. Canongate Press, Edinburgh: 151–62.

Kjaerres, U. (1995) Milk: nutritional science and agricultural development in Norway, 1890–1900. In, A.P. den Hartog (Ed.), *Food technology and marketing: European diet in the 20th century*. Tuckwell Press, East Lothian: 103–16.

Knecht, de -van Eekelen, A. (1984) *Naar een rationele zuigelingen voeding* [Towards a rational infant feeding]. Thieme, Nijmegen.

Lakerveld, P. van (1994) RMI en De Sierkan, Bloei en ondergang van twee melkinrichtingen [Rise and fall of two dairies], *NEHA Jaarboek voor economische, bedrijfs- entechniekgeschiedenis*. 57: 417–43.

Lemoine, R.(1996) Le lait boisson: un marché à dynamiser. *Revue Laitière Francaise*, no. 564: 14–15.

Michio Kanbe (1988) Traditional fermented milks of the world. In, Yuji Nakazawa and Akiyoshi Hosono (Eds.), *Functions of fermented milk, challenges for the health sciences*. Elsevier Applied Science, London: 41–60.

Otterloo, van, A.H. (1985) Voedzaam, smakelijk en gezond. Kookleraressen en pogingen totverbetering van eetgewoonten tussen 1880 en 1940 [Home economics teachers and efforts to improve food habits]. *Sociologisch Tijdschrift*, 12: 495–542.

Pyke, M. (1985) The impact of modern food technology on nutrition in the twentieth century. In, D.J. Oddy and D.S. Miller (Eds.), *Diet and health in modern Britain*. Croom Helm, London: 32–45.

Ruo-Jun Xu (1998) Bioactive peptides in milk and their biological and health implications. *Food Review International*, 14: 1–16.

Schreurs, W. (1991) *Collectieve reclame in Nederland* [Collective advertising in the Netherlands]. Stenfert Kroese, Leiden.

Scrimshaw, N.S. and Murray, E.B. (1988) The acceptability of milk and milk products in populations with a high prevalence of lactose intolerance. *American Journal of Clinical Nutrition*, 48: 1083–1159.

Simoons, F.J. (1970) Primary adult lactose intolerance and the milking habit: a problem in biologic and cultural interrelations, a cultural historical hypothesis. *American Journal of Digestive Diseases*, 15: 695–710.

Simoons, F.J. (1973) The determinants of dairying and milk use in the old world: ecological, physiological, and cultural. *Ecology of Food and Nutrition*, 2: 83–90.

Teuteberg, H.J. (1981) The beginnings of the modern milk age in Germany. In, A. Fenton, *Food in perspective. Proceedings of the third international conference of ethnological food research*. John Donald, Edinburgh: 283–311.

Troiani, C. (1997) Il latte bevanda: un mercato da sviluppare [Milk as a beverage: a market to be developed]. *Latte*, 22, no. 5: 42–43.

Whetham, E. (1976) The London milk trade, 1900–1930. In, D.J. Oddy and D.S. Miller (Eds.), *The making of the modern British diet.* Croom Helm, London: 65-76.

Winter, van, J. M. (1994) The consumption of dairy products in the Netherlands in the fifteenth and sixteenth centuries. In, P. Lysaght, *Milk and milk products from medieval to modern times.* Canongate Academic, Edinburgh: 3–13.

9. MILK IN THE MOUNTAINS

Helen M. Macbeth

Information about a population where children and adults drink at least one large bowl of fresh milk daily might make one think of the United States, Scandinavia or Holland. However, in these countries attitudes have been changing (see den Hartog, this volume). His chapter relates changes in public health policies in the Netherlands to progress in biochemical research. The fall in consumption of full fat milk in Northern Europe, U.S. and Australia results particularly from concerns with slimming and more recently with greater public awareness of the findings in the medical literature on cardiovascular risks (e.g., Keys 1980; Denke and Grundy 1991). On the other hand, medical literature has, for three decades, been promoting the benefits of a 'Mediterranean Diet' for lowering cardiovascular risks as well as reducing risks of cancer (for useful summaries of these see Kushi et al. 1995 and other papers in the 1995 supplement to volume 61 of the American Journal of Clinical Nutrition). It may, therefore, surprise some readers that the milk-drinking population referred to in the first sentence is found on the Franco-Spanish border in a valley approximately one hundred kilometres from the Mediterranean Sea. One does not generally associate high milk consumption with southern Europe, although conversion of the milk of different domestic animals to cheese is well known in these regions.

I have argued elsewhere (Macbeth 1998) that the phrase 'Mediterranean Diet' reflects an Anglo-American concept, and to identify such a 'diet' is not possible since there are nineteen nation states in and around the Mediterranean, and well-known regional differences within some of these countries. My research has demonstrated significant micro-regional differences (Macbeth 1997) in food intake frequencies in the 1990s between adjacent population samples either side of the Franco-Spanish border. Such diversity throws the idea of one 'Mediterranean Diet' into some doubt. Nutritionally it is a question of whether the few items of traditional communality around the Mediterranean, for example olives, olive oil, certain pulses and wheat products, are indeed more significant to health than the diversity in other items, in relative quantities or frequencies, in cuisine and in attitude to food and cooking. The biochemical evidence linking components of the traditional foods of southern Europe to health benefits is now impressive (for useful summaries see Ferro-Luzzi et al. 1994; Willett 1994; Kushi et al. 1995a and 1995b).

Troncoso et al. (this volume) write persuasively about red wine and the health value of moderate consumption, although the evidence in regard to cancer is more controversial than portrayed here, especially with regard to breast cancer in women (Rimm and Ellison 1995). Since my research has been in Catalonia, where many excellent red wines are produced among both the Spanish and the French foothills of the eastern Pyrenees, I might have been expected to discuss these in a volume devoted to the anthropological perspectives on drinking, especially as I have a personal connection with the Domaine Sainte Hélène.

However, I shall discuss the other significant element in the 'French paradox' (Renaud and de Lorgeril 1992; Artaud-Wild et al. 1993). Milk is another fluid much discussed now in regard to cardiovascular risks. One reason for this is the effect of dairy fat on low-density lipoprotein cholesterol (Denke and Grundy 1991), which may be greater even than beef fat. Unlike some earlier authors with their monocausal explanations, Kushi et al. (1995a) linked the low consumption of full fat dairy products *and* the high intake of fruit, vegetables and whole grains in the Mediterranean area with the lower rates of numerous chronic degenerative diseases.

Low milk consumption is certainly part of the concept that northern Europeans have of the diet of southern Europeans. Yet, this is contrary to my own impressions following fieldwork since 1990 in an eastern Pyrenean valley. This valley, called Cerdanya in the Catalan language, is surrounded by mountains which give it a physical unity. It is, however, divided by the Franco-Spanish

Table 9.1   Milk as a percentage of breakfast drinks[1]

	Cerdanya Valley		Costal region		Mallorca[2]	
	Milk	Other	Milk	Other	Milk	Other
SPAIN						
Teenagers[3]	87.8	12.2	76.8	23.2	80.0	20.0
Adults	64.1	35.9	59.2	40.8	52.8	47.2
FRANCE						
Teenagers[3]	79.5	20.5	66.1	33.9	–	–
Adults	41.0	59.0	34.6	65.4	–	–

1 Drinks considered as 'milk drinks' were drinks of milk and of 'flavoured milk', eg. chocolate. These can be futher broken down by full-fat, semi-skimmed and skimmed. Included under 'other' drinks were those drinks where the respondent had recorded 'added milk', in which case the milk was considered a minor part of the drink.

2 Data collected in Mallorca did not distinguish time of day. This figure, therefore, is an over-representation as it includes milk drinks at other times of day. In Cerdanya, for example, many further drinks of milk occurred before going to bed.

3 Teenagers here aged 11–14 in schools in the adjacent towns of Bourg Madame (France) and Puigcerdá· (Spain).

border, which has increasingly caused differences between the populations of the two sectors in many aspects of lifestyle. It was during 1991 food intake frequency studies (Macbeth 1997) that the high level of milk consumption first came to my attention. The majority of teenage children, aged 11–14, recorded a milk drink for breakfast (Table 9.1). For many it was all they recorded. This was sometimes with sugar, and sometimes with chocolate or other flavouring, but coffee or tea was not often recorded by them. A recent secular change, found more frequently in the French than the Spanish sector, but still only occasionally recorded, even by teenagers, was breakfast cereal. Teenagers may be presumed in many places to drink more milk than adults, but as Table 9.1 shows, well over half (64 percent) of the Spanish adults were also drinking milk for breakfast, as were over 40 percent of the French adults. Further study of the data from Cerdanya showed that a bowl of milk was also frequently consumed for supper or before going to bed. An equivalent food intake study on the Mediterranean coast, also either side of the Franco-Spanish border and still in Catalonia, showed the lower milk consumption expected along the Mediterranean shores but, I suggest, even these frequencies are higher than would accord well with northern European concepts of the South. More recent work on the Island of Mallorca confirms the lower milk consumption at sea level (Table 9.1). However, for the Mallorca study the intake was not subdivided by time of day and the figures given refer to milk drinks at all times of day and not just at breakfast; these sets of data, therefore, are indicative, but not directly comparable.

Local Production in Cerdanya

The fertile pastures of Cerdanya used to feed horses until the tractor replaced them on farms. Then when refrigeration allowed milk transportation to the coastal area and more distant towns and cities, dairy cattle replaced the horses on Cerdan pastures. Currently dairy cattle are being replaced by beef cattle and there is a return to horses reared for trekking holidays and the tourist trade. In the late 1950s there were 301 dairy farmers in French Cerdanya (Delmas, 1966). In 1998 there were only 27, although a few other farmsteads retained one cow for family milk. Low economic return for small-scale milk production is said to be the cause. In Spanish Cerdanya, the decrease in dairy farmers has been more recent, and so more dramatic. The legislation of the European Union is primarily blamed; Spanish farmers say that quotas, health controls, required fat and vitamin levels, etc. have all caused them problems. This concurs with disparaging comments about Spanish milk production in regard to these points, as reported on the French side in 1991 before full Spanish entry into the European Union. It might be expected, too, that opening markets to milk from northern European pastures would have caused irresistible competition. However, even though most milk in the Spanish supermarkets is ultra-heat treated and so transportation is not an issue, in 1998 all was labelled as having a Spanish origin, primarily Galicia and Asturias, but some was from Ripoll, in Catalonia.

Cattle were traditionally pasture fed in the Cerdanya valley as elsewhere, but now there are feed differences either side of the border. In France most cattle are still put out to pasture, mountain pastures in summer and, when weather allows, valley pastures in winter. Their nutrition is supplemented mainly with maize. Meanwhile the Spanish farmers use more concentrates which include leftovers from the food and beer industries, and many cattle never leave their stalls. The overgrown hoof deformities of some stall cattle horrified this author.

The Past

From interviews in the Cerdanya it is clear that locals of all ages from throughout the valley have always drunk a large bowl of milk, not only at every breakfast but most evenings as well. The intake frequency studies made no attempt to record quantities.Yet, the traditional breakfast bowls, which are still common, contain about a third of a litre, but the ubiquitous mugs, containing about a quarter of a litre, are increasing in popularity. While the study in the 1990s showed that many of the teenagers had nothing with their breakfast milk, elderly informants said that unless there were leftovers from a previous meal nothing was traditionally eaten, and that in many homes little would have been eaten with the evening drink either. Milk drinking is therefore not a recent change, as it is said to be in many other parts of southern Europe. In fact, in the French Cerdanya, informants said that milk drinking had lessened over the last 20 years. This is in contrast to the reported increase in milk drinking by children in Perpignan and the coastal area. As shown above (Table 9.1), the amount of milk drinking at breakfast in the valley is considerably greater for teenagers than for adults, but this does not throw light on what the adults drank when they were teenagers. What is interesting, however, is that Table 9.1 shows that for both France and Spain more is drunk in the mountain valley than on the coast and that milk drinking is greater in Spain than in France, and that the differences between teenagers and adults in both ecological regions is far greater in France than in Spain.

I have personal experience of urban Barcelona in the late 1950s where milk was given to children but was seldom drunk by adults. I recall it as thin and relatively blue-grey. It is evident that the children of my contemporaries have had more milk to drink than their parents had, whose grandchildren now receive even more. One might presume that this pattern of generational increase in milk consumption in Barcelona, Perpignan and on the coast is common for much of the Mediterranean area. However, in the Cerdanya the drinking of milk has long been an important part of the diet. This is not necessarily true of other parts of the Pyrenees, for example among the

Basques (Ott: personal communication) where cheese-making is important
(Ott 1981).

Fat Content

It is the dairy fat, however, rather than the fluid milk, which is much mentioned
in regard to the chronic degenerative diseases, and the fat content of milk is
not constant. To find out the fat content of supermarket milk is a simple task
today as it is marked on the cartons. European Union legislation has now
ensured homogeneity of milk sold with full cream at 3.6 percent fat and semi-
skimmed at 1.55 percent fat, although even in 1998 some Spanish milk was
marked at 3.5 percent. In 1991 Spain had not entered full EU legislation and
fat content was lower than in French supermarkets (Table 9.2). However, it is
impossible to know the fat content of milk drunk or purchased on the local
farms.

In the food intake frequency studies, respondents were asked to distinguish
between full-fat, semi-skimmed, skimmed and flavoured milk. Table 9.3 shows
mean frequencies as a comparison between the valley (both sides) and the
coast. Only the figure for semi-skimmed is higher for the coastal region.

It should be clarified that there was also a place to mark when milk had been
added to another drink, for example coffee, and this item has not been
included in any of the calculations of milk drinks in this paper.

Cardiovascular Risk

Subirats et al. (1997) have shown that ischaemic heart diseases and cerebrovas-
cular diseases are higher in Spanish Cerdanya than in the rest of the Spanish
state of Catalonia. Mortality data for 1988–92 for the Languedoc–Roussillon
department of France show that of all deaths, the proportion due to circulatory

Table 9.2   Diversity in fat content in supermarket milk in two periods

	France	Spain
1991 Supermarket milk		
Full cream	3.6%	3.2–3.3%
		(but often not marked)
Semi-skimmed	1.55%	1.5%
1998 Supermarket milk		
Full cream	3.6%	3.6%
Semi-skimmed	1.55%	1.55%

Table 9.3 Cerdanya valley and Mediterranean coastal differences in average frequency of milk drinks in seven-day intake studies – all ages

		Full fat	Semi-skimmed	Skimmed	Flavoured	Total Milk Drinks
Cerdanya Valley (French and Spanish sectors) n=648	mean	2.46	1.60	0.74	1.21	6.01
	sd	4.28	3.55	2.55	2.80	–
Mediterranean Coast (French and Spanish populations) n=526	mean	1.09	1.92	0.49	1.09	4.59
	sd	2.79	3.62	1.93	2.68	–

diseases in French Cerdanya and neighbouring Capcir together was slightly higher than for the whole of the Languedoc–Roussillon (Information obtained from mortality data 1988–92 provided by INSERM). There is also some indication that mortality from ischaemic heart disease alone is considerably higher in the mountains than in the coastal regions.

There may be many reasons for these mortality differences. Subirats et al. found lower rates of smoking but higher obesity in Cerdanya. Macbeth (1998) was able to show from the seven-day food intake studies how little the diet in the Pyrenean valley resembled the Anglo–American concept of a 'Mediterranean Diet'. Furthermore, the comparable studies in the coastal regions around Port Vendres, France, and Llansa, Spain, still did not accord well with this conceptual 'diet' in that, for example, meat consumption was far higher than fish consumption, etc. However, since there are milk drinking differences and dairy fats have been shown to have even more harmful effects in regard to cardiovascular risk (Denke and Grundy 1991), the lower consumption of milk in the coastal regions just might be a significant factor in the difference in mortality. The question remains, however, whether this will now change. In the context of the chapter by Troncoso and reference to the 'French Paradox', it should be noted that the intake of red wine between the regions has not been analysed.

As a final note, the nutritional benefits of milk in regard to calcium and protein, especially in diets that might be deficient in plant or other sources of calcium, should not be ignored. It should be realised that the proportion of deaths from the chronic degenerative diseases increases when causes of earlier deaths are eliminated. For example, the classic problems of calcium deficiency, such as rickets and osteomalacia, can have significant effects on the proportions of maternal and perinatal mortality.

Acknowledgements

The author wishes to record the friendly assistance of head teachers and other staff at the secondary schools of Bourg Madame and Puigcerda in the Cerdanya Valley, Port Vendres, Llansa and Port Bou on the coast and Andratx on the Island of Mallorca, and to thank all those who filled in the dietary intake forms.

The financial assistance of the Economic and Social Research Council (grant no R-000–232816) and of Oxford Brookes University research funds are acknowledged.

Aleks Collingwood, Alex Green and Eleanor McDonald are all thanked for attempts to keep my data and paperwork organised. Francesco Grippo and Fernanda Marques Quinta have assisted with Mallorca analysis. Finally I want to thank Igor and Valerie de Garine for organisation of the conference and this volume.

References

Artaud-Wild, S.M., Conners, S.L., Sexton, G. and Connor, W.E. (1993) Differences in coronary mortality can be explained by differences in cholesterol and saturated fat intakes in 40 countries but not in France and Finland. A paradox. *Circulation* 88: 2271–9.

Delmas, C., (1966) L'Economie de la Cerdagne française. Thèse pour Diplôme d'Etudes supérieures, Université de Montpellier, Faculté des Lettres et des Sciences Humaines.

Denke, M.A. and Grundy, S.M. (1991) Effects of fats high in stearic acid on lipid and lipoprotein concentrations in men. *American Journal of Clinical Nutrition* 54: 1036–40.

Ferro-Luzzi, A., Cialfa, E., Leclercq, C. and Toti, E. (1994) The Mediterranean diet revisited. Focus on fruit and vegetables. *International Journal of Food Sciences and Nutrition* 45: 291–300.

Keys, A. (1980) *Seven Countries: A Multivariate Analysis of death and coronary Heart Disease.* Harvard University Press, Cambridge, Mass.

Kushi, L.H., Lenart, E.B. and Willett, W.C. (1995 a) Health implications of Mediterranean diets in light of contemporary knowledge. 1. Plant foods and dairy products. *American Journal of Clinical Nutrition* 61 (Supplement): 14075–155.

Kushi, L.H., Lenart, E.B. and Willett, W.C. (1995 b) Health implications of Mediterranean diets in light of contemporary knowledge. 2. Meats, wine, fats and oils. *American Journal of Clinical Nutrition* 61 (Supplement): 14165–275.

Macbeth, H.M. (1997) The Cerdanya, a valley divided: biosocial anthropology in a research project. In, A.J. Boyce and V. Reynolds (Eds.) *Human Populations: Diversity and Adaptation.* Oxford University Press, Oxford.

Macbeth, H.M. (1998) Concepts of 'The Mediterranean Diet' in U.K. and Australia compared to food intake studies on the Catalan coast of the Mediterranean. *Rivista di Antropologia* Vol. 76 (Supplement): 307–13.

Ott, S. (1981) *The Circle of Mountains: A Basque Shepherding Community.* Oxford University Press, New York.

Renaud, S. and de Lorgueril, M. (1992) Wine, alcohol, platelets and the French paradox for coronary heart disease. *The Lancet* 339: 1523–6.

Subirats i Bayego, E., Vila i Ballester, L., Vila i Subirana, T. & Vallescar i Piñana, R. (1997) Prevalencia de factores de riesgo cardiovascular en una población rural del norte de Cataluña: La Cerdaña. *Anales de Medicina Interna* 14 (1): 1–7.

10. WINE AND HEALTH
THE PROTECTIVE ROLE OF MODERATE CONSUMPTION

....

A.M. Troncoso, M.C. Garcia-Parrilla, and
M.V. Martinez-Ortega

General Aspects

How can wine be defined? Louis Pasteur the famous French scientist (1822–1895) described it as: 'The most healthy and hygienic of all drinks'. In fact, the academic definition, accepted by the OIV (Office International du Vin), an international organisation constituted by forty-five producing countries, defines wine as: 'The drink resulting from the total or partial alcoholic fermentation of the matured grape or must'. Wine is, then, a natural product coming from a fruit and converted into a delicious drink by the activity of micro-organisms (yeasts). During alcoholic fermentation, grape sugar is transformed into alcohol and other substances, but many of the compounds present in low amounts in grapes remain in the resulting wine.

Considered from the food regulations point of view, wine is thus a food, resulting from a fermentation and it has a certain nutritional value. Wine has been included in the human diet since the beginning of history. Popular intuition has traditionally attributed to it beneficial healthy effects. Since the Babylonian civilisation (2,000 years BC), it was used in therapeutic practice in order to provide a vehicle for the administration of drugs. Grapevines grew spontaneously in Mediterranean countries. In the sixth century BC, Greeks introduced it as a cultivated plant in the west Mediterranean area. The Romans developed intensive exploitation. Greeks and Romans made extensive use of wine and in fact these 'medicinal wines' have been used until recent times in medicine. North Americans are relatively latecomers to viticulture. Franciscan missionaries planted the first large-scale vineyards in California two hundred years ago. Wine, particularly red wine, has traditionally been considered by the population as a healthy and therapeutical product (Castro 1993). Wine was used for sacramental purposes in Egypt no later than the beginning of the third millennium BC, although evidence indicates that it was not produced there for general consumption for another two thousand years. This fact seems to be strongly related to the occidental cultural paradigm in which wine and the grape represent Christ's blood. Moreover, ingesting red wine was supposed to promote blood production. One of the consequences of linking wine to religion is that vineyards have a widespread distribution all over the world.

However, wine has gradually been brought into discredit due to the social problem of alcoholism, especially in developed countries. Public health authorities and governments are concerned with the question of excessive alcohol intake, and we are faced with a controversy about wine consumption. Is it really dangerous? Is it beneficial? At this point, Paracelsus' statement should be remembered: *dosis sola facit venenum* – it is the dose which makes the poison. This supposes that a single product may be beneficial or dangerous, depending on the quantity.

French Paradox

More recently, in the 1970s, the Mediterranean diet was recognised as a healthy model to follow. Epidemiological studies have revealed that countries where this kind of diet is consumed have a lower mortality due to cardiovascular diseases. This fact was explained by the level of fat intake in the different populations. Olive oil, the culinary fat traditionally used in Mediterranean cooking, was mainly responsible for this beneficial aspect, but the so-called *Mediterranean trilogy* (Medina 1996) includes, together with olive oil, wine and wheat.

Highly-saturated fatty acids, mainly present in foods of animal origin, are supposed to be related with a high mortality from coronary heart disease. This fact was clearly pointed out by the World Health Organisation through epidemiological studies carried out in many developed countries. In 1991 a high-audience television programme in the United States showed the results of an interesting epidemiological and clinical study, which was later known as the 'French Paradox' (Figure 10.1) (Renaud and Lorgeril 1992). In this study it was demonstrated that in some French regions, such as Toulouse, in spite of a high consumption of dairy fat (saturated fat), the mortality from coronary heart

Figure 10.1   (a) Relation between age-standardised death rate from CHD and consumption of dairy fat in countries reporting wine consumption (b) Relation between age-standardised death rate from CHD and consumption of dairy fat and of wine in countries reporting wine consumption.

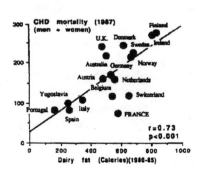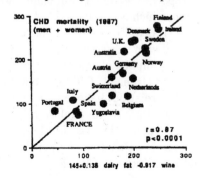

disease was very low, as low as that of those populations with lower fat intakes. Once the diet of this French population was studied, the conclusion was that the only differential food was red wine, which is included in French meals in moderate, but frequent, intakes. Though some time earlier the relation between moderate wine consumption and cardioprotective effect had been established (Marmot et al. 1981; Moore and Pearson 1986), the so-called French Paradox was really a revolution, and French red wines increased their sales in the United States. We can truly speak about the before and after of the French Paradox.

Once the French Paradox was postulated, more than twenty-five epidemiological studies were performed in different countries, and the conclusion of all of them was that a frequent but moderate consumption, one or two glasses a day, provided a cardio-protective effect (Stockley 1995; Ticca 1995). Mortality from coronary heart disease is lower among moderate wine drinkers than among people who never drink or those who drink in excess (Klatsky et al. 1990).

Soon after, it was stated that populations with regular consumption of beer, or another alcoholic drink, did not display the healthy effects observed in populations with moderate intakes of wine (Klatsky and Armstrong 1993). Epidemiological data leads us to conclude that alcohol was not the only factor responsible for the cardioprotective effects observed in wine consumers. This fact was the starting point of a series of studies concerning all wine components which are not present in other alcoholic beverages and could account for the beneficial effects. A study carried out with healthy volunteers drinking red wine or vodka provided evidence that long-term consumption of red wine, but not ethanol, inhibited LDL (low density lipoprotein) oxidation *in vivo* (Kondo et al. 1994).

Effects of Alcohol Drinking

Excessive alcohol consumption has very negative effects on human health and this point should never be forgotten. Alcohol is known to possess euphorising properties as well as stimulant and tonic actions. Alcohol inhibits LDL oxidation, which is considered to be the first step towards atherosclerosis (Stockley 1995). Oxidised LDL is rejected by the liver and continues circulating in the blood with subsequent damage to the artery walls. In addition, alcohol significantly inhibits platelet aggregation, which is directly related to coronary heart disease (Renaud et al. 1992) and thrombosis (Meade et al. 1979; Stockley 1995).

The relations between moderate alcohol consumption, concentration of low density lipoprotein cholesterol, and risk of ischaemic heart disease, have also been studied (Hein et al. 1996). There is now evidence that a moderate intake of alcohol (less than 5 g per day) always presents a cardiovascular protective effect (Criqui and Ringel 1994).

Oxidative Damage

The effects of red wine consumption have also been studied *in vivo*; a significative reduction of the oxidisability of whole plasma was achieved. These results were attributed to the polyphenols present in wine.

Recent research concerning health and ageing accepts that, in general, human health is subject to oxidative damage. Many of the diseases of modern life, e.g., cardiovascular disease, cancer, macular degeneration (blindness of the elderly), senile dementia ... are caused or promoted by oxidative damage. There is increasing evidence that oxidised lower density lipoprotein (LDL), found in blood as cholesterol carriers, may be involved in the pathogenesis of atherosclerosis and cancer.

Consequently, it may be assumed that longevity is the body's resistance to oxidation. In a certain way, to live is to get self-oxidised. We are provided with a defensive system against oxidation (Cutler 1984), but it has limited efficiency; it is the so-called endogenous antioxidant system. As a person gets older, and the value of this defensive system decreases, it is essential to have an exogenous contribution of antioxidants. These are present in foods, mainly in vegetables (Table 10.1) in very low quantities. They are antioxidant molecules with two different functions, as follows. One group of them has protective actions against oxidation; they get oxidised themselves, preventing the oxidation of essential biomolecules. This is the case of ascorbic acid (Vitamin C), alpha tocopherol (Vitamin E) or carotenoid. The other group protects the body against oxidative damage by quenching free radicals; among them are polyphenols, present to a great extent in grapes, wine and vegetables. As it has been pointed out recently (Frankel et al. 1993), they are responsible for the cardioprotective effect of wine.

Besides their vitamin and fibre content, phenolic compounds are one reason why fruit and vegetables are deemed to protect against cancer and other chronic and inflammatory diseases as well as coronary heart disease (CHD). A major advantage of the wine matrix for dietary polyphenols is that they are soluble and bioavailable in wine, in contrast to foodstuffs which contain their phenolic components in polymeric, insoluble or tightly-bound and compartementalised forms that render them unavailable for absorption. Indeed, very little is known about the extent or amount of uptake of these dietary constituents in the human alimentary system (Soleas et al. 1997 a).

LDL is a lipoprotein whose origin is the circulation. It is formed by remodelling of VLDL through the mechanisms of lipolysis and the exchange of lipids and proteins with HDL. While LDL itself presents no risk, oxidated LDL is thought to play an important role in the current concept of atherogenesis as it is related to the initial stages of the formation of the atherosclerotic plaque. When this lipoprotein has suffered a modification by an oxidation process, oxidised LDL suffers an endocytosis process by monocyte-derived macrophage. These cells, filled with lipids, are known as foam cells and they are related with the accumulation of cholesterol in the intima subendothelial cells and finally the atherosclerotic plaque is formed.

Table 10.1 Gross estimated phenol content for typical young, light table wines (mgL^{-1})

	White	Red
NON FLAVONOIDS, total	165	200
Volatile phenols	1	5
Tyrosol	14	15
Gallic and other C6C1 acids	10	40
Caffeic acid and related cpds.	140	140
Hydrolysable tannins	0 (no oak)	variable
FLAVONOIDS, total	35	1000
Catechins (flavan-3-ols)	25	75
Anthocyanins and derivate	0	400
Other monomeric flavonoids	trace	25
Oligomeric flavonoids	5	500
TOTAL PHENOLS	200	1200

(Source: V. L. Singleton)

Moreover, oxidised-LDL stimulates inflammatory reactions, blocks reverse cholesterol transport by HDL, and promotes the adhesion of platelets to the superficial endothelium. An excess of free radicals can be the beginning of uncontrolled chain reactions which are going to produce oxidative damage, i.e., lipid peroxidation. Free radicals abstract hydrogen from the polyunsatured fatty acids present in cell membranes to form a lipid radical. Then, this lipid radical reacts with molecular oxygen to form the lipid peroxy radical which is going to generate more free radicals. In pathological conditions, lipid peroxidation of polyunsaturated fatty acids is also related with atherosclerosis and cancer (Cook and Samman 1996).

Polyphenolic Compounds of Wine

Phenolic compounds are organic substances from the vegetal kingdom that may present more than one phenol group (aromatic ring and hydroxyl substituent), so they are often called polyphenolics. They occur naturally in plant tissues, often produced as secondary metabolites, with defensive functions against infection, environmental stress or pathogenic attack. In that case they are called phytoalexins. Phenolic compounds present in grapes and wines, as well as in other vegetable foods and fruits, are exogenous antioxidants. Known as phytochemicals (Kinsella et al. 1993), they are located in the solid parts of the grape: skins, seeds and stalks.

These compounds have been known for a long time and the crucial role they play in wine has been studied extensively because they are responsible for important properties (colour, astringency, flavour ...) (Singleton and Essau 1969). In the 1950s Professor Masquelier, in France, began to study a series of polyphenolic compounds called proanthocyanidols, responsible for the astringency sensation, since they have a great affinity towards proteins and can coagulate the saliva's protein; moreover they have an anti-oxygen effect, at least demonstrated in vitro.

During red wine production, the pressed grape is submitted to fermentation in contact with solids, and polyphenols are extensively extracted. In addition, these compounds are better solubilised in hydroalcoholic solutions, like wine. As a consequence, red wines contain far higher quantities of polyphenols than white wines, in which no contact with solid parts takes place. Phenolic compounds present in wine are classified according to their chemical structure into flavonoids and non-flavonoids. Non-flavonoids are derived from hydroxy benzoic and hydroxy cinnamic acids, and they are often found conjugated with alcohol, sugar or organic acids.

Flavonoids often occur as oligomeric and glycosides (Rice-Evans et al. 1996). Epidemiological studies have pointed out the relation between flavonoids intake in the diet and the incidence of cardiovascular diseases and cancer (Hertog et al. 1993; 1995). Physiological properties of flavonoids are also studied in vitro and in vivo, as explained below. They are lipophilic molecules so they can pass biological membranes and act as antioxidants *in situ*. Flavonoids promote relaxation of cardiovascular smooth muscle and their antiviral and carcinostatic potential has recently been shown (Formica and Regelson 1995).

Figure 10.2   Flavonoids basic structure

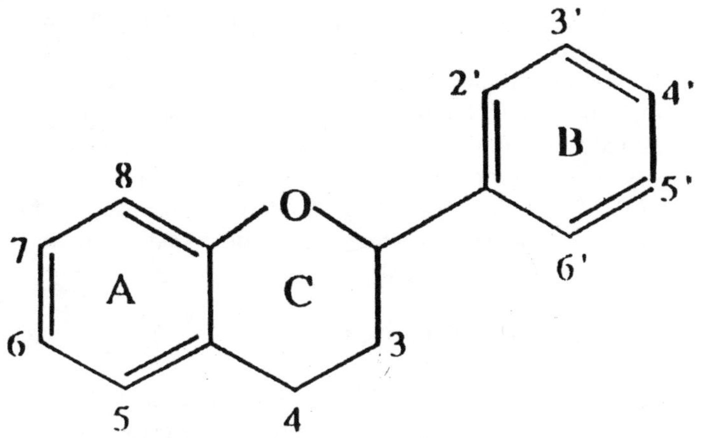

Physiological Properties of Phenolic Compunds

Cancer and cardiovascular disease (CD) are recognised as the two main causes of human death in developed countries. In both of them there is not just a single factor responsible for the appearance of the disease so they are considered multifactorial. In the case of CD there is epidemiological evidence that excessive blood pressure, tobacco, diabetes, high LDL cholesterol levels, diet, as well as a genetic component, are risk factors.

Whatever the cause, it seems clear that it starts with the damage of the endothelial cells to the inner surface of the arteries (hypertension or a lipid deposition and possibly lipid oxidation in the subendothelium of the arteries). As a consequence, a cascade of inflammatory reactions occurs, resulting in the development of the atherosclerotic plaque which narrows the lumen of the vase. The subsequent reduction of blood damages the muscle as it stops receiving the necessary oxygen and nutrients, which leads to infarct. The supposed mechanism to prevent cardiovascular disease and cancer can be explained by the antioxidant power of phenolic compounds. Most of those present in wine have demonstrated beneficial physiological properties. As phenolic compounds possess the ideal structural chemistry for free radical-scavenging activities, they are going to protect human health against oxidative damage. They are able to inhibit LDL oxidation and lipid peroxidation when they are present in adequate intake in the diet.

1. Inhibition of LDL Oxidation

The oxidation in the artery wall starts the establishment of atherosclerotic plaques and the supposed mechanism to prevent CD is that an adequate intake of antioxidants avoids LDL oxidation.

The enhancement of the resistance of LDL to oxidation is a model used to evaluate the efficacy of polyphenols as antioxidants against radicals generated in the lipophilic phase. This model consists of the exposition of human LDL to oxidation in the presence of catalysers and the measure of hexanal (a volatile compound formed by oxidation of n-6 polyunsaturated lipids). Inhibition of LDL oxidation depends upon entry of the antioxidant into the lipid core. Many studies have proved that phenolic substances in wine inhibit LDL oxidation in vitro (Frankel et al. 1993; 1995; Teissedre et al. 1996). Furthermore, most phenols tested showed higher antioxidant activity than tocopherol.

2. Inhibition of Lipid Peroxidation

It has been demonstrated that wine phenolics are able to block lipid peroxidation in vitro catalysed by myoglobin or cytochrome c (Kanner et al. 1994).

Phenolics can intercept the peroxidation process by reducing the alkoxiloperoyl radicals. Gallic acid is more hydrophilic and therefore has less access to the lipid peroxyl radicals than others like cholorogenic and caffeic acids (Rice-Evans et al. 1996).

Flavonoids can inhibit lipid peroxidation in vitro by acting as scavengers of superoxide anions and hydroxyl radicals. Also, some flavonoids, such as quercetin and its glycoside, rutin, may act as metal-chelating agents in vitro, inhibiting the formation of active oxygen radicals by Fenton reactions (Afanas'ev et al. 1989; Cook and Samman 1996).

3. Inhibition of Platelet Aggregation

Platelets are involved in thrombus formation as they adhere to the endothelial surface of the arteries provoking occlusion which leads to infarct. Therefore, resistance to aggregation measured in vitro in presence of a determined substance, offers a measure of the extent to which a compound may protect from CD. As there are varied pathways involved in platelet aggregation, research has been undertaken to test the role that phenols play in each different step.

Flavonoids also present anti-aggregating activity due to several biochemical mechanisms in the eicosanoid pathway: inhibition of the enzymes cyclo-oxygenase and lipoxygenase, antagonising thromboxane formation, blocking thromboxane receptors and increasing platelet cyclic AMP (Cook and Samman 1996; Formica and Regelson 1995).

4. Antioxidant Activity

There must be an equilibrium between the reactive oxygen species formed during respiration and the repair mechanisms. Humans have to defend themselves from oxidative stress. Antioxidants account for these mechanisms. In order to evaluate their antioxidant activity, radicals formed during lipid peroxidation are measured by spectrophotometric means in presence and absence of the antioxidant compound. Direct relationship has been demonstrated between the antioxidant activity of wine and its total phenol content. Most phenols tested showed higher antioxidant activity in vitro than other well-known antioxidants, such as -tocopherol or vitamin C on a molar basis (Rice-Evans et al. 1996). Red wines were more efficient in inhibiting oxidation than white wines (Frankel et al. 1995; Hurtado et al. 1997; Rice-Evans et al. 1996, 1997; Sato et al. 1996; Simonetti et al. 1997), proving that total antioxidant activities are well correlated with total phenols and flavonols. This parameter is known as Total Antioxidant Status or Total Antioxidant Activity and it is determined by a spectrophotometric technique that measures the relative abilities of antioxidants to scavenge free radicals (Simonetti et al. 1997).

Extensive production of peroxynitrite is related with coronary heart disease, as it has been found present at high levels in atherosclerotic lesions (Bekman et al. 1994) and it is known to oxidise LDL (Graham et al. 1993). Peroxynitrite is formed by the reaction between nitric oxide (NO) and superoxide radicals. Wine has been proved to scavenge peroxynitrite very efficiently, red wine being better than rosé and white wine in this respect (Paquay et al. 1997). This effect can be attributed to wine phenolics since, when these compounds are absent, the peroxynitrite scavenging activity drastically diminishes. A correlation between this activity and the polyphenol index can be established (Paquay et al. 1997). Polyphenols in wine are capable of scavenging superoxide anion radicals (Sato et al. 1996) and wine flavonoids effectively scavenge nitric oxide radicals (Verhagen et al. 1996).

5. Vasorelaxing Effect

Prostacyclin and nitric oxide are cell-signalling molecules that have been described as inhibitors of vasoconstriction, platelet aggregation and thrombosis. Cabernet-Sauvignon alcoholised and dealcoholised musts were tested in vivo and results proved that they stimulated endothelial cell release of prostacyclin but not of nitric acid (Schramm et al. 1997).

6. Anticancer Activity

Oxygen radicals produced by cells' metabolism may accumulate and initiate inflammatory reactions leading to chronic disease process, and finally DNA damage resulting in cancer. So, antioxidant powers of phenolic compounds in an aqueous environment are very important because they protect the protein component of LDL and scavenge oxygen-free radicals.

   This antioxidant function is measured in a recent paper using multiple regression techniques for the development of a predictive model (Soleas et al. 1997b). They show that isolated compounds may present different, antioxidant activity when they are in combination, as in wines. In this sense, vanillic and gallic acids of wines proved to be very effective.

Resveratrol: A Vine Phytoalexin

Resveratrol (Fig. 10.3) is a phenolic compound present in berry grape skins and synthesised by the plant in response to the infection produced by a mould: *Botrytis cinerea*. The physiological function of resveratrol in plants is not well defined. It is thought to be a phytoalexin, one of a group of compounds that are produced during times of environmental stress or pathogenic attack. This polyphenol, present in wines, was considered as the answer to the French Paradox since it presents an important cardioprotective effect due to its potent antioxidant power (Siemann and Creasy 1992). The term resveratrol is often applied to the trans-isomer. However, when trans-resveratrol is under ultraviolet exposure, as in sunlight, it becomes the cis-resveratrol isomer (Roggero and García-Parrilla 1995), so it is important to quantify both isomers. In addition, resveratrol glycosidated forms for both isomers are also found in grapes and wines (Lamuela-Raventós et al. 1995). Physiological properties of trans-resveratrol have been studied to a greater extent than the cis-isomer. Resveratrol has proved to have three types of physiological properties: cardioprotective, anticancer and anti-inflammatory activities.

The cardioprotective activity of resveratrol can be explained by its antioxidant activity. The antioxidant effect of trans-resveratrol has been compared in vitro with other well-known antioxidant substances such as quercetin, butylhydroxytoluene (BHT) and -tocopherol (Blond et al. 1995). In all the systems tested, resveratrol was demonstrated to be the more effective antioxidant in peroxidation induced by Fe2+. The authors proposed that resveratrol can react with oxidised free radicals to protect lipids against peroxidation, proving that resveratrol possesses strong antioxidant capacity (Blond et al. 1995).

Moreover, resveratrol can prevent platelet aggregation and promote a positive effect in lipid balance in serum. It has been observed in vivo in rats with high cholesterol serum levels that resveratrol promoted the healthy ratio HDL/LDL in the serum lipid balance. It increases the HDL cholesterol while it decreases the LDL (Arichi et al. 1982; Kimura et al. 1983).

Studies about the antiaggregating activity of resveratrol were performed in vitro at different concentrations for both resveratrol isomers, verifying that both possess antiaggregating activity (Bertelli et al. 1996). Also, resveratrol 3-O- B-D-glucopyranoside has been tested in vitro, showing a significant inhibitory effect on platelet aggregation induced either by collagen, or by adrenalin (Orsini et al. 1997).

In popular medicine, extracts of the *Polygonum cuspidatum* plant, rich in stilbenic compounds, have been used for anti-inflammatory purposes (Kimura et al. 1983). Resveratrol inhibits the hydroperoxidase activity of COX-1, which catalyses the conversion of arachidonic acid to pro-inflammatory prostaglandins (Jang et al. 1997). This anti-inflammatory activity of resveratrol

Figure 10.3   Resveratrol isomers

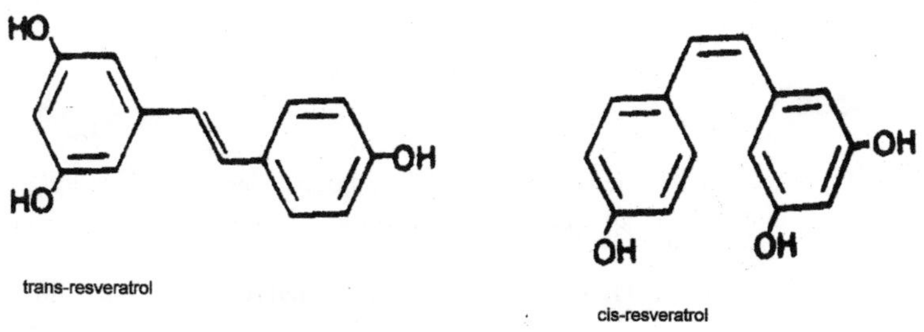

trans-resveratrol

cis-resveratrol

was studied in rats, and it was capable of reducing pedal edema in both the acute and the chronic phase (Jang et al. 1997).

Recently, cancer chemopreventive effects of resveratrol have been pointed out and a great interest has been focussed towards this compound. University of Illinois researchers (Jang et al. 1997) have studied the special characteristics of resveratrol as a chemopreventive agent in human cancer. It inhibits cellular events associated with tumor initiation, promotion and progression. Resveratrol possesses anti-initiation activity while it acts as antioxidant and antimutagen and induces phase II drug-metabolising enzymes. It stops cancer promotion inhibiting cyclooxygenase (being specific for COX-1) and hydroperoxidase. Finally, resveratrol inhibits progression because it is capable of inducing human promyelocytic leukemia cell differentiation. Also, it was demonstrated that resveratrol was able to inhibit the development of preneoplastic lesions in carcinogen-treated mouse mammary glands in culture and tumorigenesis in a mouse skin cancer model (Jang et al. 1997). Physiological activity of cis-resveratrol is unclear yet. It has been pointed out that cis-resveratrol may inhibit kinase enzyme, so an anticancer action can be attributed to it (Jayatilake et al. 1993).

Final Considerations

The human organism is not provided with antioxidants in excess; increases in free radicals may take place as a result of oxidative damage. Diet must provide antioxidants capable of avoiding these injuries. Wine provides antioxidants and wine producers are very interested in these studies. The quality of a given wine is beginning to be measured in terms of its beneficial potential: quantity of polyphenols, especially resveratrol and quercetin. Wine consumption is slowly increasing in developed countries.

The experiments we are now carrying out in the University of Seville are focussed on the study of potential modifications of phenolic compounds through the gastrointestinal tract. We can now say that the discovery of the properties of resveratrol has been revolutionary and that many studies in laboratories all over the world are being developed. More evidence is needed concerning the beneficial aspects of polyphenolic compounds. The protective benefits of a diet rich in phytochemicals are best obtained from frequent and moderate consumption of wine, fruits and vegetables.

References

Afanas'ev, I.B., Dorozhko, A.I. and Bordskii, A.V. (1989) Chelating and free radical scavenging mechanisms of inhibitory action of rutin and quercetin in lipid peroxidation. *Biochem. Pharmacol.* 38: 1763–69.

Arichi, H., Kimura, Y., Okuda, H., Baba, K., Kozawa, A.M. and Arichi, S. (1982) Effects of stilbene components of the roots of Polygonum cuspidatum Sieb. Et Zucc. on Lipid Metabolism. *Chem. Pharm. Bull.* 30: 1766–70.

Beckman, J.S., Ye, Y.Z., Anderson, P.G., Chen, J., Accavitti, M.A., Tarpey, M.M. and White, R. (1994) Extensive nitration of protein tyrosines in human arterosclerosis detected by inmunohistochemistry. *Biol. Chem. Hoppe-Seyler* 375: 81–88.

Bertelli, A.A.E., Giovannini, L., De Caterina, R., Bernini, W., Migliori, M., Fegoni, M., Bavaresco, L. and Bertelli, A. (1996) Antiplatelet activity of cis-resveratrol. *Drugs Exptl. Clin. Res.* XXII, 2: 61–63.

Blond, J.P., Denis, M.P. et Bezard, J. (1995) Action antioxydante du resvératrol sur la lipoperoxydation. *Sciences des Aliments* 15: 347–58.

Castro, X. (1993) Historia da dieta popular na sociedade galega. O viño como nutriente e axente terapéutico. In, X.A. Fidalgo & X. Simal (Eds.) *Alimentación e cultura*. Laboratorio Ourensán d'Antropoloxia Social, Vigo.

Cook, N.C. and Samman, S. (1996) Flavonoids-Chemistry, metabolism, cardioprotective effects and dietary sources. *Nutritional Biochemistry* 7: 66–76.

Criqui, M.H. and Rinel, B.L. (1994) Does diet or alcohol explain the French paradox? *The Lancet* 344, December 24/31: 1719–23.

Cutler, R.G. (1984) Antioxidants, aging, and longevity. In, W.A. Pryor (Ed.) *Free Radicals in Biology*. Academic Press, New York: 371–428.

Formica, J.V. and Regelson, W. (1995) Review of the biology of quercetin and related bioflavonoids. *Fd. Chem. Toxic* 33, 12: 1061–80.

Frankel, E. N., Kanner, J., German, J. B., Parks, E. and Kinsella, J. E. (1993) Inhibition of oxidation of human low-density lipoprotein by phenolic substances in red wine. *The Lancet* 341, February 20: 454–7.

Frankel, E.N., Waterhouse, A.L., Teissedre, P.L. (1995) Principal phenolic phytochemicals in selected California wines and their antioxidant activity in inhibiting oxidation of human low-density lipoproteins. *J. Agric. Food Chem.* 43: 890–4.

Graham, A., Hogg, N., Kalyanaraman, B., O'Leary, V.J., Darley-Usmar, V. and Moncada, S. (1993) Peroxinitrite modification of low-density lipoprotein leads to recognition by macrophage scavenger receptor. *FEBS Lett.* 330: 181–5.

Hein, H.O., Suadicani, P. and Gyntelberg, F. (1996) Alcohol consumption, serum low density lipoprotein cholesterol concentration, and risk of ischaemic heart disease: six-year follow up in the Copenhagen male study. *British Medical Journal* 312, 23 March 1996: 736–41.

Hertog, M.G., Feskens, E.J.M., Hollman, P.C.H., Katan, M.B. and Kromhout, D. (1993) Dietary antioxidant flavonoids and the risk of coronary heart disease: the Zupthen elderly study. *The Lancet* 342: 1007–11.

Hertog, M.G., Kromhout, D., Aravanis, C., Blackburn, H., Buzina, R., Fidanza, F., Giampaoli, S., Jansen, A., Menotti, A., Nedeljkovic, S., Pekkarinen, M., Simic, B.S., Toshima, H., Feskens, E.J.M., Hollman, P.C.H. and Katan, M.B. (1995) Flavonoid intake and long-term risk of coronary heart disease and cancer in the seven countries study. *Arch. Intern. Med.* 155: 381–6.

Hurtado, I., Caldú, P., Gonzalo, A., Ramon, J.M., Mínguez, S. and Fiol, C. (1997) Antioxidative capacity of wine on human LDL oxidation in vitro: effect of skin contact in winemaking of white wine. *J. Agricult. Food Chem.* 45: 1283–9.

Jang, M., Cai, L., Udeani, G.O., Slowing, K.V., Thomas, C.F., Beecher, C.W.W., Fong, H.H.S., Farnsworth, N.R., Kinghorn, A.D., Mehta, R.G., Moon, R.C. and Pezzuto, J.M. (1997) Cancer chemopreventive activity of resveratrol, a natural product derived from grapes. *Science* 275: 218–20.

Jayatilake, G. S., Jayasuriya, H., Lee, E-S., Koonchanok, N.M., Geahlen, R.L., Ashendel, C.L. McLaughlin and J.L., Chang, C-J. (1993) Kinase inhibitors from Polygonum culpidatum. *J. Nat. Prod.* 56: 1805.

Kanner, J., Frankel, E., Granit, R., German, B.and Kinsella, J.E. (1994) Natural antioxidants in grapes and wines. *J. Agric. Food Chem.* 42: 64–69.

Kimura, Y., Ohminami, H., Okuda, H., Baba, K., Kozawa, M. and Arichi, S. (1983) Effects of stilbene components of roots of polygonum ssp. on liver injury in peroxidized oil-fed rats. *J. Med. Plant Res.* 4: 51–54.

Kinsella, J.E., Frankel, E., German, B. and Kanner, J. (1993) Possible mechanisms for the role of antioxidants in wine and plant foods. *Food Technology* April 1993: 85–89.

Klatsky, A.L. Armstrong, M.A. and Friedman, G.D. (1990) Risk of cardiovascular mortality in alcohol drinkers, exdrinkers and nondrinkers. *Am. J. Cardiol.* 66: 1237–42.

Klatsky, A.L. and Armstrong, M.A. (1993) Alcoholic beverage choice and risk of coronary artery disease mortality: do red wine drinkers fare best? *Am. J. Card.* 71: 467.

Kondo, K., Matsumoto, A., Kurata, H., Tanahashi, H., Koda, H., Amachi, T. and Itakura, H. (1994) Inhibition of oxidation of low-density lipoprotein with red wine. *The Lancet* 344, October 22: 1152.

Lamuela-Raventós, R.M., Romero-Pérez, A.I., Waterhouse, A.L. and Torre-Boronat, M.C. (1995) Direct HPLC analysis of cis- and trans-resveratrol and piceid isomers in Spanish red Vitis vinifera wines. *J. Agric. Food Chem.* 43, 2: 281–3.

Marmot, M.G., Shipley, M.J., Rose, G. and Thomas, B.J. (1981) Alcohol and mortality: an U-shaped curve. *The Lancet* 1: 580–3.

Meade, T.W., Chakrabarti, R., Haines, A.P., North, W.R.S. and Stirling, Y. (1979) Characteristic affecting fibrinolytic activity and plasma fibrinogen concentration. *British Med. J.* 1: 153–60.

Medina, F. X. (1996) Alimentación, dieta y comportamientos alimentarios en el contexto mediterráneo. In, F. X. Medina (Ed.) *La alimentación mediterránea, historia, cultura, nutrición.* Institut Catalá de la Mediterránia dÉstudis i Cooperació, Barcelona.

Moore, R.D. and Pearson, T.A. (1986) Moderate alcohol consumption and coronary artery disease. *Medicine* (Baltimore) 65: 242–67.

Orsini, F., Pelizzoni, F., Verotta, L. and Aburjai, T. (1997) Isolation, synthesis, and antiplatelet aggregation activity of resveratrol 3-O-B-D-glucopyranoside and related compounds. *J. Nat. Prod.* 60: 1082–87.

Paquay, J.B.G., Haenen, G.R.M.M., Korthouwer, R.E.M. and Bast, A. (1997) Peroxynitrite scavenging by wines. *Journal of Agricult. Food Chemistry* 45, 9: 3357–58.

Renaud S., Beswick, A.D., Fehly, A.M., Sharp, D.S. and Elwood, P.C. (1992) Alcohol and platelet aggregation: the Caerphilly collaborative heart disease study. *Am. J. Clin. Nutr.* 55: 1012–17.

Renaud, S. and Lorgeril, M. (1992) Wine, alcohol, platelets, and the French paradox for coronary heart disease. *The Lancet* 339: 1523–26.

Rice-Evans, C., Miller, N.J. and Paganga, G.(1996) Structure-antioxidant activity relationships of flavonoids and phenolic acids. *Free radical Biol. Med.* 20: 933–56.

Rice-Evans, C., Miller, N.J. and Paganga, G. (1997) Antioxidant properties of phenolic compounds. *Trends in plant science* 2, 4, April 1997: 152–9.

Roggero, J. P. and García-Parrilla, M. C. (1995) Effects of ultraviolet irradiation on resveratrol and changes in resveratrol and various of its derivates in the skins of ripening grapes. *Sciences des Aliments* 15: 411–22.

Sato, M., Ramarathnam, N., Suzuki, Y., Ohkubo, T., Takeuchi, M. and Ochi, H. (1996) Varietal differences in the phenolic content and superoxide radical scavenging potential of wines from different sources. *J. Agricult. Food Chem.* 44: 37–41.

Schramm, D.D., Pearson, D.A. and German, J.B. (1997) Endothelial cell basal PGI2 release is stimulated by wine in witro: one mechanism that may mediate the vasoprotective effects of wine. *Nutritional Biochem.* 8: 647–51.

Siemann, E.H. and Creasy, L.L. (1992) Concentration of the phytoalexin resveratrol in wine. *Am. J. Enol. Vitic.* Vol 43, 1: 49–52.

Simonetti P., Pietta, P. and Testolin, G. (1997) Polyphenol content and total antioxidant potential of selected Italian wines. *J. Agric. Food Chem.* 45: 1152–55.

Singleton, V.L. and Essau, P. (1969) Quality and processing relationship in wine production. Phenolic substances in grapes and wines and their significance. *Ad. Food Res.* Academic Press, New York.

Soleas, G.J., Diamandis, E.P. and Goldberg, D.M. (1997) Wine as a biological fluid: History, production, and role in disease prevention. *Journal of Clinical Laboratory Analysis* 11: 287–313.

Soleas, G.J., Tomlinson, G., Diamandis, E.P. and Goldberg, D.M. (1997) Relative contributions of polyphenolic constituents to the antioxidant status of wines: development of a predictive model. *J. Agricult. Food Chem.* 45: 3995–4003.

Stockley, C. S. (1995) El vino y la enfermedad cardiovascular. *Alimentaria* Nov. 95: 131–6.

Ticca, M. (1995) Alimentazione equilibrata e salute: il ruolo del vino. *La Rivista di Scienza dell'Alimentazione* anno 24, 3: 323–42.

Teissedere, P.L., Frankel, E.N., Waterhouse, A.L., Peleg, H. and German, J.B. (1996) Inhibition of in vitro human LDL oxidation by phenolic antioxidants from grapes and wines. *J. Sci. Food Agric.* 70: 55–61.

Verhagen, J.V., Haenen, G.R.M.M. and Bast, A. (1996) Nitric oxide radical scavenging by wines. *J. Agricult. Food Chem.* 44: 373–34.

11. DRINKING
AN ALMOST SILENT LANGUAGE

Isabel González Turmo

Drinking is an act loaded with significance. It is a cultural fact on which thousands of years, millions of gestures have accumulated. The first difference appears to be between drinking and not drinking – alcohol, of course. Or, even more so, between having to drink or having to abstain from drinking, for there are few domains in which being what you are and being what you ought to be are farther apart than where drinking is concerned. In fact, even those religions which dissuade or ban the consumption of alcohol have maintained, throughout their history, more or less tolerant attitudes towards it. This is the case for Islam which has known, from Syria, Persia or India to Al-Andalus, the Muslim Andalucia during the Middle Ages, times of enormous compromise with the wine drinkers. In Al-Andalus, for example, grapevines were the second most important crop, and formulas for relieving hangovers, nearly always based on decoctions of beans and vegetables, were frequent in the prescriptions of the epoch (Rubiera Mata 1994). Occasionally, Muslims were banned expressly from making and selling wine, but not from consuming it in private. Some people consider that the cubicles or small reserved rooms found in Andalucian taverns, which allow one to drink without being seen, originated then.

It should not be forgotten that, in Mohammed's days, at Arabian fairs it was usual to drink alcohol made from palm, or beer brewed from barley or millet. Similarly, in two suras of the Koran, 67 and 219, 'the liquor of the fruit of the palm and of the vineyard' was praised, while drunkenness was condemned as the work of Satan in the ninetieth sura. As for the wine promised in the paradise of the believers, it is said that it does not inebriate and is related to pure water and milk. In fact, it was the hadiths and the Sunnite and Shiite legal schools who explicitly banned alcohol consumption and trade, and decreed punishment for the offenders.

Religious precepts apart, the capacity to produce wine is a key factor, at least until recent times, in understanding the frequency of its consumption. One's conscience might act as a restraint to its appreciation, but wherever wine was produced, it was drunk. The Mediterranean area of Europe has been producing wine for thousands of years. The production has coexisted with tolerance or intransigency, but it has not ceased. For wine, besides being a source of pleasure or of disorders, depending on the point of view, and a stimulant of sociability, is also a non-negligible source of revenue and a very important part of the diet.

Wine has been praised and insulted, consumed as basic food or enjoyed as a status symbol. It has been drunk alone, in a corner of the house, with an elbow propped on the tavern counter, or enjoyed in company, and it is this potential company, so diverse and rich in its significance, that has provided so many situations, repeated throughout generations and over the centuries. From this mosaic of countless pieces where the history of drinking has been traced, practices, attitudes and meanings have been woven into a wide and varied range of rituals, resulting in the fact that, in most areas of the planet where wine is circulating with persistent tenacity, there is hardly a gathering, a party or a rite of passage where thirst has not been quenched by the magical element. This explains the far-reaching significance of aspects such as the order in which wine is served, the tasting sequence, the mechanisms of control and solidarity established through buying rounds, of matching it to the accompanying food and the verbal pronouncement that makes it sacred during a toast.

Seen from this perspective, it does not make sense to wonder if drinking is an individual or a social act, or at least the question should be posed in another way. Drinking is always an individual act, since each drinker necessarily has to situate himself, more or less consciously, according to the change of emotions produced by the ingestion of alcohol. It is also always a social fact, even when drinking alone, since it is loaded with socially assumed meanings. It is a language that, on many occasions, needs neither words nor expressions. The case most often quoted, the alcoholic who comes into the bar, drinks alone, without exchanging a word with anybody, and goes back to his house alone, is no exception. Nor is that of the woman who drinks alone in the kitchen, while she cooks. They and those who surround them, during or after the consumption, know perfectly the meaning and the consequences of the act. All remain silent because everything has been said.

I do not believe, therefore, that it makes sense to affirm, as is done so often, that in the south of Europe drinking is a social fact and that in the centre and in the north, an individual one. Maybe in the south people drink in company and in the north it is more frequent to drink alone, but in both cases drinking is an individual and a social fact, at the same time.

Background of Drinking

Spain is the country that cultivates the largest surface of vineyards in the world. Although joining the European Union, in 1986, required a gradual decrease from 1,633,000 hectares (ha.) in 1984 to 1,198,680 ha. in 1995, Spain continues to be ahead of the other largest producers of the world, France and Italy. In 1995, France had 895,000 ha. and Italy 910,000 ha. (European Commission and Member Countries, 1995).

Also, Spain owns a great diversity of wines, due to the many varieties of vine-plants and its long history in conforming to the tastes and practices of producers and consumers. This has generated 5,500 producers and fifty-three Denominations of Origin (Ministry of Agriculture, Fishing and Food 1997). A rigorous and restrictive policy concerning the plantations has been necessary due to an important excess of production. It is well known that the surface dedicated to vineyards was one of main obstacles to Spain's being allowed to join the European Union. Today Spain sells 637,976 tons of wine annually, of which almost 80 percent goes to the countries of the European Union, while imports reach only 245,087 tons (European Commission and Member Countries 1995).

A singular case is that of Andalucia, the southernmost and largest region in Spain. In the south, it is limited by the Atlantic Ocean, the Mediterranean Sea and the Straits of Gibraltar, which separate it from Africa. To the west it has a border with Portugal and to the north limits with Extremadura and Castilla La Mancha, Spanish regions with which it shares a long history of alimentary similarities. It is a territory of about 87,000 km^2, crossed from NE to SW by the Guadalquivir River, whose wide valley provides rich and fertile lands. On both sides mountain chains run to the south, almost to the coast, as in much of the Mediterranean littoral.

The cultivated surface of vineyards in Andalucia is 41,076 ha. There are twelve Denominations of Origin and nine wine regions (Council of Agriculture and Fishing, 1997). Among the wines of Andalucia, and also of Spain, special mention should be made of the fortified wines, 'vinos generosos': *finos, manzanillas, amontillados, olorosos, Palos Cortados*, because of their singular character. Jerez, Sanlúcar de Barrameda and Montilla Moriles are their Denominations of Origin. They are nursed to maturity in wooden barrels over a minimum of three years.

As regards consumption, the national total per capita for wine is 37.37 litres annually, compared with 67.4 for beer. Eighty-two percent of the beer consumption corresponds to hostelry receipts. Andalucia is below the national average for wine consumption and above that for beer.

Besides this data, Andalucia can be considered as a privileged laboratory for the study of the cultural aspects of wine. Drinking it for centuries has resulted in a wide range of attitudes, behaviours, reactions, and meanings. It should not be forgotten that this is an area where the production and consumption of alcohol have existed for millennia and where religions and cultures have coexisted with opposing positions. All this has contributed to form a language which, through drinking, distributes roles between men and women, rich and poor, young and elders, foreigners and villagers, which is fully integrated into the life of each inhabitant. In the same way, each occasion and event has its ritual, where wine is always present.

What and how do the Andalucians drink? How have their habits changed throughout the present century? How do they behave when drinking? The investigations that I have carried out in Andalucia over the last decade point out that domestic consumption offers important contrasts depending on territory, social position, age and gender (González Turmo 1995). A few decades ago, the fact of living in a producing area implied a higher consumption of wine but this does not concern large areas only. It can also be observed in the behaviour of neighbouring districts. In towns and cities where there was no production, most of the people did not drink at home, only in taverns. A curious case is that of the territory occupied currently by the National Park of Doñana. Many kilometres of dunes, pinegroves and swamps are inhabited by very few people. Water was scarce. The fear of water-borne infectious diseases was permanent, but this area was lucky enough to be surrounded by districts of wine producers. The result was that at home and in the fields people drank more wine than water, but always prudently, to control the effects and expense. The fact is that, in spite of how much was produced, for most of the population wine was a treat, like eggs, at least at home. It was measured and reserved for special occasions. Amid such dearth, the taverns were authentic oases, reserved for the men. They were visited every evening, after dinner, by the men of the town. Wine was mostly served in individual bottles of half a litre without a label. This bulk wine was customarily from the region: must, white wine and, in the morning, *aguardiente* (spirits), served in very small glasses. A woman remembered her deceased husband, a day labourer, in the following way: 'He had dinner when he came in from the fields, and later went to the tavern to drink wine. He came back at night and, like a gentleman, sat down and took off his hat, and then he went to bed.'

Beyond this daily drinking in taverns, some categories of workers have given rise to particular consumption patterns. Fishermen and sailors from El Marco de Jerez drank wine on board, and wine only. They also used it for cooking. The fact is that the abundance of wine in the area combined with the generous attitude of the seagoers. Although they were the region's poorest people, the security of knowing that fishing was always there made them live from day to day, and also drink from day to day. If there was fishing, there was money and, therefore, one could buy wine before going aboard for two or three days. Their consumption could be higher than that of the owner of a small vineyard, who needed his production in order to sell it. The rice cultivators of the swamps also drank wine instead of water. These men, who remained far from home for weeks or even months, took a drinking bottle of must with them to the fields. They drank in small sips, measuring well how to satiate their thirst and recover enough strength to continue working, without succumbing to the drowsiness that alcohol can produce.

In early twentieth-century Andalucia, labour was very rarely paid for with wine, but with oil, vegetables or bread. However, a wise habit existed: the owners of big cellars gave their numerous workers a glass of wine before they left work, at six in the afternoon. By doing so they tried to

... In Andalucia, the gentlemen drank mainly ... manzanilla (El Rocio pilgrimage).

prevent them from drinking directly from the barrels during the working day, which would have been impossible to control in such enormous installations.

In addition to the majority of men who drank in the taverns and those groups who drank at work, a minority did so at home and in the *casinos*, as much in vineyard areas as in non-producing regions. These were the spaces of sociability reserved to the men of the elite, a sort of Spanish 'club'. In Andalucia, the gentlemen drank mainly *oloroso* or *manzanilla*. From the postwar period until the arrival of the democracy, *fino,* which is from Jerez, and also spirits were consumed.

Women, on the other hand, were condemned, at least in theory, to drink water. Their admission to taverns, bars and, of course, to casinos was unimaginable until very recently, whatever their social class. Only on special days could they go to a particular place, accompanied by their husbands, and only if his social position allowed it. If it became known that a woman drank, it was one of the worst insults that a family's good name could suffer. Sometimes it was enough for a woman to have a beer or a glass of wine in a bar for her to be considered a drunkard. The men used to like boasting that their daughters and wives hated wine, and they still do. The tranquil woman did not drink at home either. If one did have a liking for it, she had to keep it hidden, drinking in the kitchen, and rinsing her mouth with Eau de Cologne to avoid being accused. Nor did women drink during gatherings among themselves, not only not alcohol, but not tea or coffee either. Even amongst women of the upper bourgeoisie, not even water was offered. In fact, the habit of having a snack in the afternoon, which later became a custom, took a long time to be assimilated in the rural areas, even among the middle classes.

The scant permissiveness shown towards women by no means operated for the children and the young. In the wine-producing regions, babies were weaned on wine. It was also very common to give alcohol to children almost daily, be it liquor, wine or must. It was given with bread as a snack and, sometimes, diluted with water for lunch. On special occasions, such as Christmas or Holy Week, children received a glass of local wine or liquor.

There was even a time of the year when abundant consumption of alcohol and drunkenness among the young were authorised, during the *quintos* parties of the youths who were due to do their military service that year. They would go from house to house having food and wine, devoting one day and one night to nutritional and alcoholic excesses. In Andalucia it was observed mainly in the mountainous regions and among the small landowners but the quintos parties were certainly more frequent in other regions of Spain, where the community style of the peasantry favoured these practices. It was, in fact, a sort of rite of passage, through which their right to consume alcohol in public was collectively recognised.

The other ceremonials also had wine in their epicentre. On many occasions nothing, or almost nothing, was offered to eat, but wine was indispensable. In some mountain districts and also in other regions of Spain, three glasses of wine and three sweets or three candied fruits were given at christenings or when the wedding proposal was made. Always three. This way, consumption was controlled and solidarity reinforced. Only at weddings was it less common to measure the quantities. Drinking was, finally, fundamental. It also took place during wakes for the dead. The step towards death receives a very different treatment from that observed in other areas of Spain and of the Mediterranean. The passage to death involves absolute parsimony and austerity. As if, through fatalism, the negation of life was accepted. Food and drinks are not used, as in other places (Ibáñez Garcia 1990; D'Onofrio 1993), to separate the living from the dead. Nobody stops eating or drinking but nothing is served to those coming from outside, either before or after the funeral, or on its first anniversary. Life goes on and it is not necessary to mark such a difficult moment by changing one's daily habits. So as not to enhance such a hard occasion, not a bowl of soup, a glass of liquor or a cup of coffee will be served except in particular circumstances. Such occasions are decided by the most affluent who are, after all, those who can afford it.

Similarly, it is significant that, while so much wine is circulating, the habit of toasting does not exist. Until recent years it was usual for each drinker to request half a bottle of wine. In taverns, everyone had their own drink and, in the more elegant bars, people drank alone or asked for wine tasters with which to invite newcomers to a glass of fino. When they had been invited, they were served according to their age or degree of intimacy. Once the wine had been served, everyone drank without a toast, except on very rare and special occasions. Amid the conversation, each person concentrated on his glass, drinking more quickly or sipping more slowly, as everyone tried to sustain a more or less homogeneous rhythm in the number of orders. In recent years, however, some of these customs have disappeared: half bottles are no longer requested, everyone asks for a glass, which avoids having to invite other people, and toasting is more frequent than before, although not among the older generations. The toast is really a foreign habit which has been incorporated as the century has advanced, beginning in the big cities. Sometimes people offer resistance to habits that are so different from the local way of drinking. Hence, many Andalucian gentlemen exclaimed, like the hero of Visconti's film 'The Leopard', the Prince of Salinas del Gatopardo: 'One used to have the good taste not to toast. Moreover, as Calogero said, the greatest joys are silent.'

New Drinks in the Old Landscape

Today the situation is, partly, different. Market globalisation favours the consumption of imported drinks. Even so, in the producing areas local wines are still preferred. Alcohol emphasises territorial and local differences. Festive celebrations provide the best opportunities of affirming identity through wine. Among such events, the supracommunal ones, such as the El Rocío yearly pilgrimage, which assembles different villages, are those which best conciliate these manifestations of identity.

As regards differences between the classes, they have moved towards new preferences. Whisky has been incorporated as a significant drink of status, although its ingestion is much less restricted than that of fino or oloroso was in the past. In fact, it is one of those drinks that most people can afford, but which are advertised as being the prerogative of a minority. Whisky is the drink of confusion.

Neither does there exist a spatial distribution according to the social position of the clientele of the establishments where people drink, at least in rural areas. There are not zones of rich and poor, bourgeois and labourers, as happens almost without exception in towns. Of course, each class has its own bars, but this does not imply the existence of territorial class demarcations.

Behaviour is, however, very different according to social position. It is certain that people now go out in family groups more than some years ago, but the frequency of these outings varies a lot. In winter they are rare, in summer, more regular. During warm weather, bar terraces are crowded until very late and even until dawn. However, the fact that bars are full should not mislead the observer. He should not conclude that the spending power of most of the population allows them to dine out every evening. Mostly they leave home after dinner and only have a glass or two or a snack. This is in order to keep expenses under control, but this control does not involve staying at home, and even less inviting friends in for a meal. Invitations at home have always been rare in Andalucia, whatever the social class. The house is a private, family environment. One's social life takes place outside.

Women are beginning to go into bars, but limitations still exist. Access permission depends, first, on the type of establishment, i.e., cafeterias yes, taverns no. Age and civic status count too. Entrance is more difficult for older and married women unless they are accompanied by their spouse or, at least, by a group of friends. The acceptance seems to be subject to a cumulative effect: a woman alone is not welcome but a group of them is. This does not mean that they are forbidden entrance, but they tend to limit it themselves because of the looks they receive: inquiring, fixed, masculine. Eventually, the men disturb them and they leave the place precipitously. Girls, however, are not so vulnerable. They enter bars, mainly in groups. Even so there are some places, such as taverns, that continue to belong to men only.

Even inside the house, it is rare for women to drink while eating. The few who do so belong to the medium or higher strata and are less than forty years old. Here I am referring to those women who affirm that they drink because, among the older ones, it is very common for them to deny it. Often I have been able to observe that they drink beer or wine while cooking and finally they recognise it without pretence.

What happens with children and the young? Nowadays nobody gives wine to children. Among youths, however, consumption of alcohol has increased. Their preferences are one litre beer bottles and cocktails made from spirits. Another certainty is that the wines that people stopped drinking a couple of decades ago, such as manzanilla or mosto, or spirits such as aguardiente, are now resurgent. Manzanilla has replaced fino on the regional market. Such progress would not be possible with a total rejection by the younger generation. Even aguardiente, the consumption of which had almost ceased, is beginning to be appreciated among youths, at least in the producing regions – as a long drink with ice.

The youngsters, however, hardly ever drink at home. Their place is on the streets. They are that multitude that invades sites, and even neighbourhoods, changing the life of their inhabitants. This shifting of youths to their leisure centres often goes on beyond their place of origin. Each weekend they leave to have a good time in the nearby towns. Their destinations are night bars and discos. On many occasions they drink outside, next to their cars. In fact, there are companies which, with just a telephone call, provide them with drinks in a few minutes.

Their attitude towards drinking is different from that of other generations. Not because they are more compulsive. The young, through the group, are looking for the ambiguity towards which the alteration of their daily routine precipitates them for a few hours. Lights, rhythm, alcohol and speed nowadays provide the strength necessary to restore the most desired image of themselves.

Age has become one of the most distinctive means of identification and youth is, without a doubt, the golden age. Drinking thus serves in bringing together, or in separating, the generations, but there is no reason to think that the tastes and habits adopted during youth remain unchanged until maturity, and even less so in old age. Although youngsters depend on their parents, and for longer nowadays than previously, they evolve within a consumption network which is seemingly independent from the social position of the family. This is not always the case but it is more probable that the children of workers and big proprietors will meet up and drink the same drinks in fashionable bars than go to places which are frequented by their parents. These juvenile consumption networks will be dissolved as they create their own families and become professionals. Then, they have to adjust to a new spending power which allows less ambiguous and flexible possibilities than previously. Their drinking habits will also be affected by such a change.

During the fieldwork I was able to observe how youngsters undergo, between fifteen and twenty-five years approximately, a transformation in their taste concerning food and drinks. The scenario for these changes is in the street, or in bars, and no longer the home which is, as always, the place where generations confront one another.

Discos and bars are where youngsters begin to taste the food and drinks that they reject at home. The years they spend in bars play the role of a rite of passage, where each age subgroup takes its distance from the one below it. They become mature through drinking and eating in the street.

What is observed is exactly the following: age groups between fifteen and twenty-five years old are divided, in turn, in a series of subgroups, according to their tastes and habits. These subgroups appear at three- or four-year intervals which they delimit with the same clarity as that with which generations can be defined. The youngest, between fifteen and eighteen, do not patronise the same places as their immediate superiors. They prefer hamburgers, pizzas and sodas, although they already drink beer and cocktails. As they advance in age, there is a progressive acceptance of local drinks and foods. The following group, between eighteen and twenty-one or twenty-two years old approximately, drinks beer mostly and begins to abandon hamburgers and pizzas, at least as a compulsory alternative. When they are over twenty-two they already drink manzanilla, moscatel and aguardiente, besides cocktails, and, outside their homes, eat dishes which would surprise their parents if they saw them. This state of things has also been verified by market studies carried out by local producers and which register a change in the wine consumption among the young, when they turn twenty. It happens because of the desire to put aside childhood tastes and, through wine, to accept their new status as adults.

Other Uses and Habits: Cooking, Preserves and Healing Procedures

Besides being a drink, wine had, and still has, many other uses. To begin with, it is eaten, or it is used to cook with, which amounts to the same thing. The wines from Jerez have well-defined roles in the kitchen: fino and manzanilla are used for cooking fish and vegetables; amontillado for consommés, pulses and meats; old oloroso for meats, mainly roasted; and crema or cream for desserts, but most people are satisfied by just pouring on whatever wine is handy.

Once again, it is in the producing areas that wine is mainly used for cooking, while in regions where it is imported such a tradition does not exist, even though it is available in every supermarket. Only the modest, popular pastries have always required a little wine; this was their privilege. The wine used for cooking is usually cheap wine or even vinegar. For preserving, aguardiente has undoubtedly been used most frequently, with the result that preserves of this type are done almost exclusively in the producing regions. Elsewhere, food is salted, dried or preserved in fat.

Aguardiente has also been used for curative purposes more than wine. As a hypothesis, it should be mentioned that there is a certain delimitation of the healing agents, according to the ailment. Thus, water is, above all, a transmitter of external properties, a way of using other elements which cannot be ingested directly, such as bark and many plants; alcohol is, undoubtedly, tonic and reactive; oil, sedative. In emergencies and serious cases, animal foods are consumed.

Among the ailments that required the use of alcohol were those of the digestive tract: indigestion and stomach pains. The most common method was *espurreao de aguardiente*. It consisted, since it is no longer done, in laying down the patient, usually a boy, and squirting mouthfuls of aguardiente over him, hard on the stomach or the back, to produce a reaction that made him vomit. I cannot resist repeating the story an old woman told me:

The most incredible thing in the world happened to me and my daughter, Maria, with an indigestion. She was beautiful and became very ill, I was told that she had been cursed with the evil eye, and that I had to go to a woman's house who said: 'Take the child and look for three Marias (three women) and tell them to walk through different streets, praying'. Then I asked for three glasses of aguardiente and a bottle of oil, and I massaged her back with it. After, I took a mouthful of aguardiente and spat it over her and then I turned her face upwards and started again. Just two minutes later, she vomited something bad.

New Scenarios for Renewed Tastes

As habits changed, so did the establishments. It was a slow process that took almost a century, although in the latter decades it may have accelerated. Today some taverns remain, but very few. The same thing happened to the casinos and the old cafés, which have disappeared completely. However, tapas bars, cafeterias, inns, pubs, discos and restaurants have proliferated.

Taverns, the first and fundamental invention for such an important need as drinking in these latitudes, reigned on their own for centuries, frequented only by men. In comparison, bars and restaurants are recent contrivances. It suffices to remember that Seville, the capital of Andalucia, had 446 taverns in the nineteenth century and only 110,000 inhabitants, an enormous number when compared with restaurants, inns and cafés which, added together, reached thirty-six (González Turmo 1996). Today, in the same city, with 800,000 inhabitants, taverns can be counted on the fingers of one hand. There are, however, about seven thousand bars and almost eight hundred restaurants.

The tavern is in its death throes, that is certain. Consequently, it seems necessary to underline the importance it held as a space of masculine sociability. It was, after all, the locale where customers could talk together over a glass of wine, regardless of their social class, with the result that the middle class hardly ever went there. This has been the merit and the risk of the tavern, since the Roman ones where wine was consumed for the first time in a different place from where it was produced (Romero de Solís 1989).

From the early twentieth century onwards, first the breweries and then the bars began encroaching on the territory of the old taverns. In Spain beer has been drunk since Carlos V brought it in the sixteenth century from Flanders (Simón Palmer 1997). There were also breweries, mostly Dutch, English and Irish, but not until the first years of the century did places specialising in serving beer proliferate. Foreign beerhouses became fashionable among the bourgeoisie and with them arrived also the *aperitivo,* or snack. The new invention triumphed first in the capital, Madrid. In Andalucia and, in fact, in Seville it began to be served in some beerhouses at the beginning of the century, but was not generalised until the 1930s. By then there were not only taverns and breweries, but bars also became fashionable. These bars and beerhouses were the favourite meeting places of that incipient middle class that did not like the ordinary taverns and did not have the money to go to restaurants.

Appetizers were being served in the 1930s, in their local version, the *tapa*. They are small dishes of cold or warm food that accompany a glass of wine or beer at the counter or the tables of bars. In fact, they are part of that range of tidbits so frequent in the Mediterranean area (I. de Garine 1996). With time, they have become a distinctive feature of the Andalucian lifestyle. Today there are Andalucian tapas bars in New York and it seems that they have always existed.

Throughout the twentieth century, many other changes have taken place. The Civil War and the post-war period brought about a hispanicisation of the establishments. Franco's regime changed the hostelry. Names and flavours reminiscent of the Allies were rejected. Bars called Geneva, France or England had to change their names for ones from Spain or Seville. Drinks and cocktails also suffered from the process of patriotic identification.

It was in the 1960s that a middle class was consolidated, capable of filling new locales and introducing new ways. American- and British-style places appeared: cafeterias, snack-bars, pubs, whisky bars, self-service restaurants. Two decades later hamburger houses and pizza bars began to proliferate, but a local revival also took place. Regional, local cooking and Spanish wines sparkled like champagne. Clients knew about wines which, previously, were the privilege of the chosen few. Business and political lunches changed people's taste in wine. It is more a question of talking than eating. It is important not to drink too much either, especially highly alcoholised drinks. Consequently, white wine replaced red wine at lunchtime, and whisky was taken instead of brandy afterwards.

Final Considerations

Finally, the preferences about wine have changed as well as the type of places in which it is drunk, and also partly the way people drink and the drinkers' roles. Differences in relation to social position are solved nowadays, as so often in history, by changing the object of luxury. There are always better wines, liquors or sparkling wines to be used to display social status. There has not really been much change in the possibility of frequenting one place rather than another, according to one's social class. Today, as yesterday, those without money can only go to the cheapest places, while those who enjoy a better situation can choose.

As regards the distance between gender behaviour, it is obvious that it is narrowing down, although drinking still carries a masculine stamp. This is not, however, exclusive to Andalucia or to Spain. It is the norm. Moreover, in places where people have been drinking daily and with moderation for centuries, men are supposed to be self-controlled when drinking. Those who do not hold their wine well are avoided when drunk. Women, however, are not expected to be moderate drinkers nor are their sexual predispositions trusted. This results in masculine control being considered the best way of avoiding trouble.

As regards the tastes and drinking habits of the young, which often cause a lot of fuss among those who are alarmed by a possible definitive loss of competency in the taste for wine, it seems that the situation is not that desperate. The young have youthful tastes but, inevitably, they will stop being young and their tastes will change. This is reinforced by the marked current tendency to appreciate what is autochthonous and traditional.

Drinking is, today like yesterday, a powerful identification mechanism. It is also an unquestionable form of communication. What happens is that the drinks and the drinkers change, as has been the case relentlessly throughout history. The meanings of some messages also change, but the capacity to create networks and to display identities remains. Each expression, each acceptance and each rejection speaks without a voice, as has always happened, because drinking is an almost silent language.

References

Consejería de Agricultura y Pesca de la Junta de Andalucía (1995) *La calidad agroalimentaria según Andalucía.* Denominaciones de Origen y Específicas, Sevilla.

Dae, Sh. (1995) Food and Archaeology in Romano-Byzantine Palestine. In, A. Davidson (Ed.), *Food in Antiquity.* Exeter Press: 331.

D'Onofrio, S. (1993) A la mesa con los muertos. In, I. González Turmo & P. Romero de Solís (Eds.) *Antropología de la Alimentación: nuevos ensayos sobre la dieta mediterránea.* Consejería de Cultura de la Junta de Andalucía y Fundación Machado, Sevilla: 155–89.

Garine, I. de (1996) Alimentation Méditerranéenne et realité. In, I. González Turmo & P. Romero de Solís (Eds.) *Antropología de la Alimentación: nuevos ensayos sobre la dieta mediterránea.* Universidad de Sevilla y Fundación Machado, Sevilla: 83–102.

González Turmo, I. (1995) *Comida de rico, comida de pobre.* Universidad de Sevilla.

González Turmo, I. (1996) *Banquetes, tapas, cartas y menús. Sevilla, 1863–1996.* Servicio de Publicaciones del Ayuntamiento de Sevilla, 23, 38 & 174.

Ibáñez Garcia, M.C. (1990) V° Encuentro en Castilla y Léon (Alimentación y gastronomía tradicionales), Diputación de Salamanca.

Martínez García (1984) La asistencia material en los hospitales de Burgos a fines de la Edad Media. In, Menjot, D. (Ed.) *Manger et boire au Moyen Age.* Publications de la Faculté des Lettres et Sciences Humaines de Nice, 27: 349–60.

Ministerio de Agricultura, Pesca y Alimentación (1997) *Datos estadísticos de las Denominaciones de vinos y bebidas espirituosas,* Sevilla.

Ministerio de Agricultura, Pesca y Alimentación (1997) *Consumo Alimentario en España,* Madrid.

Molénat, J.P. (1984) Menus des pauvres, menus des confrères à Tolède dans la deuxième moitié du xv siècle. In, Menjot, D. (Ed.) *Manger et boire au Moyen Age.* Publications de la Faculté des Lettres et Sciences Humaines de Nice, 311–18.

Palmer Simón, C. (1997) *La Cocina de Palacio, 1561–1931.* Editorial Castalia: 64.

Romero de Solís, P. (1989) La taberna en España y América. *Terrain*: 63–71.

Rubiera Mata, Mª J. (1994) La dieta de Ibn Quzman. Notas sobre la alimentación andalusí a través de su literatura. In, M. Marín y Waines, D' (de.) *La alimentación en las culturas islámicas*. Mundo árabe e Islam, Madrid: 130.

12. GENDER AND DRINK IN ARAGON, SPAIN

Luis Cantarero Abad[1]

> Food associations are a site where gender distinctions can be enacted.
> (Gamman, L. and Makinen M. 1994: 147)

Introduction

A man and a woman, in their early thirties, enter a bar in Saragossa (Spain). It is about 8.00 p.m. She orders a mint tea and a beer. After a while the bartender (male, in his forties) serves the man with the beer and the woman with the mint tea. Another couple order a whisky and an apple liqueur. The former is served to the man, the latter to the woman. Similar situations have no doubt been experienced by many a customer. What is it, then, that makes a bartender behave in this way? Probably, as Gamman and Makinen (1994: 146) argue, it is the way sex and food (and drink, it could be added) are gendered.

In other words, culture and society establish which drinks are 'good' for men and which are for women. Although it is impossible to talk of 'women' or 'men' as homogeneous categories, each of them is characterised by a number of cultural features of gender. As Corral (1988: 227) points out, gender indicates the whole of socially marked traits, that is to say, those imposed to a greater or lesser extent, and charged with a greater or lesser degree of symbolism, indicators of one's belonging to one or the other sex. Dio Bleichmar (1996: 136) similarly argues that gender is a concept that belongs in the field of subjectivity and of symbolic order. According to Tubert (1988: 227), 'feminine' and 'masculine' do not refer to empirical entities, but are constructions that belong in the field of representation; they are the result of a symbolic operation. So, it could be argued that gender is a signifier (man/woman) that refers to signifieds (to drink beer/to drink mint tea) that are arbitrarily imposed.

In this chapter I will show quantitative and qualitative data that illustrates that preferences and aversions concerning drinks are, among other things, a gender marker. By preferring a drink, the subject is expressing her/his gender; together with the drink he or she 'swallows' those characteristics that are arbitrarily attributed to what is regarded as masculine and/or feminine. However, gender identity varies in different cultures; for this reason we will see that drink preferences are not the same in urban as in rural societies, that they change even within the same urban society, and within the same gender category. Such differences originate in individual values and motivations.

Drinks in Aragon

Aragon: Basic Data

The area of Aragon is 47,724 km^2, divided into three provinces in the following way: Saragossa 17,274,30 km^2 (36 percent of the regional area), Huesca 15,640,90 km^2 (32.8 percent) and Teruel 14,808.80 km^2 (31 percent). In the north, the Pyrenees separate it from France. In the south, there is the Iberian Range, and in the centre, the valley of the River Ebro. Aragon's area is 9 percent of that of Spain (504,750 km^2).

According to the 1991 census (Censo de población de Aragón 1991) the whole of the Aragonese population is 1,188,817, of which 586,570 are men and 602,247 are women (207,810 inhabitants in the province of Huesca, 143,680 in Teruel, 837,327 in Saragossa). The density of population is low (twenty-five inhabitants per km^2). More than half the Aragonese population and 70 percent of the province's population are concentrated in Saragossa city, the capital of Aragon, where the services sector is the main area of employment.

The working agricultural population (2nd term 1995, Gobierno de Aragón, Datos básicos de Aragón 1996) in Aragon is 11 percent of the whole of the working population. Irrigated land is a remarkable feature in the agricultural landscape (400,000 hectares of irrigated land) (ibid.). Along the River Ebro there are large stretches of cereal crops (such as wheat, barley and maize), vines, almond trees, olive trees, fruit and vegetables (such as asparagus, tomatoes, peppers, etc.). In the province of Teruel the most important agricultural areas are located in Bajo Aragon (an olive-growing region) and in the valleys of Jalón and Bajo Jiloca, and are characterised by the production of fruit (such as apples, pears, peaches, cherries, etc.), saffron, beetroots, potatoes and mushrooms. As to animal husbandry and farming, it is worth mentioning that there are more than three million sheep and pigs and around twelve million fowls.

Drink Preferences and Their Relation to Age and Gender

Table 12.1 shows the descriptive data of drink preferences in Aragon. They have been collected by handing out a questionnaire to a representative sample of the resident population over twenty years of age and 816 subjects were selected by a simple random system. The margin for error is of ± 3.5, for a population regarded as infinite and the reliability is 95.5 percent. Data has been processed with the *Statistical Package for Social Sciences* (SPSS).

As can be seen, among all the products included in the category 'drink', the population aged over twenty prefers water; 93.6 percent of the population like it, 5.9 percent are indifferent to it, 0.6 percent dislike it and everybody has tried it. Water is followed by coffee (79.2 percent like it, 12.1 are indifferent to it, 8.7 dislike it and everybody has tried it), soft drinks (76.7 percent like them,

Table 12.1   Drink preferences in Aragon (percent).

Drink	Like	Indifferent	Dislike	Has not tried	No answer
Water	93.6	5.9	0.6		
Coffee	79.2	12.1	8.7		0.1
Soft drinks	76.7	16.8	6.5		
Herbal teas	61.2	25.7	13.4		
Skimmed milk	39.6	25.4	29.6	3.7	1.9
Whole milk	72.4	16.8	10.2		0.7
Beer	57.9	20.8	21.2	0.2	0.1
Wine	60.2	22.1	17 ,	0.5	
Liqueurs	36.1	31.4	30.9	1.4	0.2
Spirits	27.8	29.2	40.6	2.3	0.1

16.8 are indifferent to them, 6.5 dislike them and everybody has tried them), whole milk (72.4 percent like it, 16.8 are indifferent to it, 10.2 dislike it and everybody has tried it), herbal teas (61.2 percent like them, 25.7 are indifferent to them, 13.4 dislike them and everybody has tried them), wine (60.2 percent like it, 22.1 are indifferent to it, 17 dislike it and 0.5 percent have not tried it), beer (57.9 percent like it, 20.8 are indifferent to it, 21.2 dislike it and 0.2 percent have not tried it).

The drinks that are less popular are: spirits (27.8 percent like them, 29.2 are indifferent to them, 40.6 dislike them and 2.3 percent have not tried them), liqueurs (36.1 percent like them, 31.4 are indifferent to them, 30.9 dislike them and 1.4 percent have not tried them) and skimmed milk (39.6 percent like it, 25.4 are indifferent to it, 29.6 dislike it and 3.7 percent have not tried it).

The inferential analysis relates drink preferences to age and gender. Statistically significant relations have been found between age and the following drinks: spirits, liqueurs, wine (see Table 12.2). Spirits are preferred by the youngest subjects of our sample, between 20–29 years of age (43.6 percent like them, 30.2 are indifferent to them, 26.2 percent dislike them) whereas they are liked less by people over 65 (4.9 percent like them, 34.1 are indifferent to them and 61 percent dislike them).

Liqueurs and soft drinks are also preferred by the youngest subjects, that is, those between 20-29, and they are liked less by people over 65. This tendency is reversed in the case of wine: it is preferred by subjects between 55–64 years of age (71.7 percent like it, 13 percent are indifferent to it and 15.2 percent dislike it), whereas it is liked less by the youngest (50.3 percent of the subjects between 20–29 years of age like it, 29.7 are indifferent to it and 20 percent dislike it). Finally, it is worth noticing that no statistically significant differences have been found in the relation between age and the following drinks: water, coffee, beer, herbal teas, milk (whole/skimmed).

Statistically significant differences have been also found in the relation

Table 12.2 Drink preferences in Aragon according to age (percent)

Drinks	Like					Indifferent					Dislike				
	20–29	30–44	45–54	55–64	>65	20–29	30–44	45–54	55–64	>65	20–29	30–44	45–54	55–64	>65
Spirits	43.6	34.9	28.6	31.1	4.9	30.2	30	27.7	28.9	34.1	26.2	35.2	43.8	40	61
Liqueurs	55.7	36.5	37.7	37	22	27.9	37.1	33.3	23.9	34.1	16.4	26.5	28.9	39.1	43.9
Wine	50.3	59.9	64	71.7	64.3	29.7	25.3	21.1	13	19	20	14.7	14.9	15.2	16.7
Soft drinks	87	77.6	77.2	78.3	65.1	9.3	17.3	15.8	19.6	23.3	3.7	5.1	7	2.2	11.6

Table 12.3   Drink preferences in Aragon according to gender (percent)

| | Like | | Indifferent | | Dislike | |
Drinks	M	F	M	F	M	F
Coffee	81.1	73.2	12	13.7	6.9	13
Herbal teas	50.6	66.4	31.8	22	17.6	11.6
Skimmed milk	32.3	48.9	30.9	26.4	36.7	24.7
Whole milk	74.3	69.4	17.7	17	8	13.6
Beer	75.9	48.2	17.7	23.5	6.4	28.3
Wine	71.1	45.6	18.9	31.2	10	23.2
Liqueurs	52.1	34.7	30.9	33.5	17	31.8
Spirits	48.6	23.2	30.6	29.2	20.8	47.6

between drink and gender. Men prefer spirits (48.6 percent of men like them as opposed to 23.2 percent of women), coffee (81.1 percent of men like it as opposed to 73.2 percent of women), beer (75.9 percent of men like it as opposed to 48.2 percent of women), liqueurs (52.1 percent of men like them as opposed to 34.7 percent of women) and wine (71.1 percent of men like it as opposed to 45.6 percent of women). Herbal teas are the only kind of drink that is more popular with women than with men: 66.4 percent of women like them as opposed to 50.6 percent of men. As to milk, the statistical differences are noticeable depending on whether it is skimmed or whole. Skimmed milk is preferred by women (48.9 percent as opposed to 32.3 percent of men). Whole milk is preferred by men (74.3 percent as opposed to 69.4 percent of women). Finally, it is worth noticing that no statistically significant differences have been found as far as the relationship between gender and water/soft drinks is concerned.

Gender and Drink

The following data on qualitative analysis supports and expands on previous results. Fieldwork has also been carried out in Aragon. More specifically in Saragossa city and in five villages of the pre-Pyrenean area of Serrablo (province of Huesca) that constitute the valley of Basa: Yebra de Basa, S.Julián de Basa, Fanlillo, Orús and Sobás.

Saragossa City

Gender, Body Image and Drink Preferences

The importance of aesthetic appearance in the selection of food was postulated by Igor de Garine as early as 1971: 'nowadays, fashion-conscious women follow frugal diets in order to acquire a silhouette which, in most traditional societies, would be regarded as a symbol of sterility, and might even lead to accusations of witchcraft' (Garine 1971: 146). This is an observation which, far from being obsolete, can still be applied to present-day society. Our body has become our visiting card. Its care (washing, clothing, tanning, adorning, etc.), aims at keeping it within the limits of what is socially valued. The high social value attached to our body motivates specific food practices, since the latter affect our image. As Camporesi points out (1995: 25), the religion of the body has innumerable hosts of followers, new ascetics and martyrs; in this Renaissance of the body there are no limits to the most challenging experiments that aim at the attainment of a life that is almost on the verge of Heaven.

Men prefer a muscular, strong and agile body and they value physical strength. To obtain their ideal body they practise a number of sports, either in the open air (tennis, soccer, etc.), or in a gym (weight-lifting, body-building, karate, etc.).

From a nutritional point of view, besides eating solid food, preferably rich in carbohydrates and proteins, people who practise some kind of sport regularly, to keep fit, believe that they must drink a sufficient amount of liquid in order to restore what they lose during the exercise (some informants say that they prepare their own drinks with the above-mentioned substances). On one hand, they prefer 'natural' drinks; large quantities of water, fruit juices with no added sugar, milk, fat-free soups and stock, to mention a few. They reject coffee, tea, and soft drinks, since they 'contain caffeine, sugar ... and they are not very healthy'. On the other hand, they value 'energy' drinks. According to the food industry, 'natural' drinks alone do not satisfy the wish to perform at one's best, whereas the publicised brands boast of not only being able to quench one's thirst, but also to immediately restore lost liquid and to better one's physical performance. In the advertisement for *Gatorade,* for example, emphasis is put on the fact that this drink is absorbed faster than water; the latter (according to the publicity) does away with the impulse to drink before the process of hydration is completed. Not only does *Gatorade* enter the blood cycle faster, it also provides one's muscles with additional energy, an advantage which, it is stressed, water cannot supply.

It is evident that this kind of publicity discredits water (apparently *Gatorade's* biggest rival), just as it does with other similar drinks that are regarded as natural, whereas the advertised product is associated with an increase in the standards of performance, and its qualities are highlighted through scientific arguments. The subjects considered, persuaded that this is how things really stand, and wishing for an increased physical performance that will satisfy their narcissism, prefer and consume industrial drinks such as *Aquarius, Gatorade,* etc.

Women wish to keep and/or obtain a slim body. The idea of slimness is related to one's individual subjective position. Some women feel fine as soon as they reach what the specialists describe as the 'right weight'. Others are over the recommended weight and do not consider themselves fat. Some women however, although their physical characteristics satisfy medical criteria, do not consider themselves slim. All of them, concerned with the quest for the social and individual ideal of slimness, reject alcoholic drinks (both drinks with a low-alcohol content like beer and wine, and stronger liquors like whisky and gin), as well as soft drinks with sugar, and fizzy drinks (soft drinks and sparkling water). Such drinks are not consumed because, according to our informants, 'they are fattening'.

For this reason, the food industry has created non-alcoholic beverages (non-alcoholic beer for example), fat-free drinks (like skimmed milk), non-fizzy drinks *(Trinaranjus, Radical, Fruitopia,*[2] etc.), and sugar-free soft drinks (according to a 33-year-old informant, one of her favourite drinks is soda water, 'because it contains saccharine'). New products include a range of drinks which are both sugar-free and still: *Nestea,* for example, (produced by Nestlé) and *Don Simón* (a Spanish brand), but the food industry goes further than that. Its latest tendency is to produce drinks which combine the absence of sugar, fat and bubbles with the addition of vitamins, fibre and the so-called 'bio' nutritional elements which are considered essential for good health. All these drinks meet the demands of women who are concerned with keeping fit and being slim. As Camporesi (1995: 31) observes, a low-caloric drink can become the embodiment of the quest for almost heavenly lightness. However, it must not be forgotten that advertising is responsible, to a great extent, for the spreading of the image of an ideal body, thus reinforcing and even shaping the characteristics of the demand. According to Gamman and Makinen (1994: 153): 'the use of gender in the marketing of food commodities, through advertising, is widespread in Western culture and bears some relation to changing ideas about diet and healthcare ... Our cultural obsession with slenderness is implicitly encoded in all food advertisements aimed at women'.

More specifically, our informants have come to consider that non-alcoholic fat-free, sugar-free and non-fizzy drinks are slimming, provided they are not combined with food. Water, for example, is associated with obesity if taken during meals. However, it is believed not to be fattening when drunk between meals. It is thought that large quantities of herbal teas (camomile, mint, etc.), are also slimming (or at least, they are not fattening).

Water and infusions are considered healthy too, since they 'help to expel liquids'. Similarly, alcoholic drinks are rejected for prophylactic reasons. Here are some examples of what our female informants think of alcohol: 'it is harmful to your liver', 'it gives you a headache', 'if I drink alcohol I think I'm going to feel very sick the next day', 'I don't usually drink alcohol ... it doesn't agree with my body, on top of it, it's fattening', etc. Coffee is another drink that has been medicalised and that is not considered to be fattening. People drink it in order to keep awake; as an informant (thirty-four, female) observes, 'I take it as medicine when I must drive'. Other people however, use it as a tranquilliser: 'coffee doesn't makes me nervous at all ... I drink it before I go to bed and I fall asleep, and it is not fattening'.

As can be seen, the concern with health and with one's body image go hand in hand. However, there is a tendency, on the part of our female informants, to justify their preference/aversion for a drink in terms of health (elimination of liquids, headache, etc.), rather than in terms of an ideal body. This strategy helps these women to deal with the social pressure exerted on them by their family, friends, etc. The latter wish them to be slim and beautiful, and yet, especially on social occasions such as invitations and festivities, urge them to reject the drinks that symbolically satisfy the ideal of a perfect body. For this reason, 'diet' drinks are preferably consumed when one is alone.

Gender, Social Status and Drink Preferences

Other informants are concerned with their social status; they want to look wealthy and refined, which motivates their food preferences. Some drinks symbolically transmit economic power. Among them, during lunch or dinner, men prefer red, vintage wine ('aged for at least five years'), of about 12–13° and of Spanish origin. As an informant (restaurateur, thirty-three, male) says: 'experts drink red wine, accept white wine if there isn't anything else ... and reject rosé because it has no complex aroma, it is acid ... it is just for helping the food through ... the *nouveaux riches,* who are no judges of wine, prefer Rioja[3] and, because they are from Aragon, wines that come from the area of Somontano'.[4] The favourite red wines for those who want to distinguish themselves socially come from the Ribera del Duero, Penedés and Rioja Alavesa. Among those of Ribera del Duero people prefer *Vega Sicilia* ('the most prestigious mark in the world'). The wines of Penedés are particularly popular due to their rich colour, high alcohol content (14° approximately) and very complex aroma. Women prefer young, fruity white wines. However, at the table, it is the eldest male subject who chooses the wine. Women accept his choice.

At the end of the meal, the favourite drinks are specific brands with high alcohol content. All of them are not only a marker of personal status, but also of gender: in this case, masculinity and economic power are closely related. Men prefer malt whisky and/or vintage brandy (8–10 years' maturation). The favourite whisky brands are *Cardhu* and *Glenfiddich.* Wealthy people ask for malt whisky such as *Macallan* and/or *Glenlivet.* They always have it with ice and avoid mixing it with soft drinks. As for brandy, the most popular is Jerez. Favourite brands are *Carlos I* and *Cardenal Mendoza.* According to the same restaurateur: 'those who want to show off, but are no experts, will ask for French cognac *Courvoisier* and/or *Remy Martin,* whereas a much-travelled wine connoisseur will ask for *Armagnac'.* Men use drinks as markers of their social position more than women do. In company, if a man orders an expensive drink or a famous brand, the others order different brands or dearer ones. In contrast, women choose the same as the first woman who orders. When women want to show off their economic position, they prefer sweet liqueurs whose flavours are considered 'traditional', such as hazelnut, apple, peach, or melon, of French or Swiss origin, regardless of the brand. They also have cocktails: gin *(Beefeater)* and tonic with a slice of lemon, and whisky with coke. The brands of whisky are popular marketing products such as *J.B., White Label* or *Cutty Sark.*

Both men and women consume the above-mentioned drinks in small quantities because large amounts of alcohol would be synonymous with lack of control and ordinariness. Furthermore, either at home or outside, alcoholic drinks are consumed in the company of other people, in contrast to what happens with diet drinks which, as already mentioned, are consumed by people when they are on their own. Thus, it can be inferred that drinks become a socialising element that favours communication because they facilitate and maintain social relationships, and, above all, because the presence of 'others' is the condition *sine qua non* to symbolically mark, through drinks, one's ascent up the social ladder or the confirmation of one's position. According to Millán (1998: 223), commensality is eminently social and cultural; to share food and drink means to form and materialise a real group and, at a symbolic level, to constitute and maintain society. Social relationships are staged round the table, in the sense that the place people occupy reproduces, in a schematic way, a structure that reveals the social hierarchy of the group and its leader.

Basa Valley: Alcohol as Gender Indicator

Basa Valley: Basic Data

The Basa Valley (province of Huesca) comprises Yebra de Basa, San Julián de Basa, Sobás, Orús and Fanlillo. According to its inhabitants, the valley is 18,000 hectares in area.

According to the 1996 census of Yebra de Basa, the total population of the valley amounts to just 103 men and 66 women. During the fieldwork I found out that two families live in San Julián de Basa and in Sobás (five people in the former and six in the latter). Two people live in Orús (the parson and a man over fifty) and a family of seven live in Fanlillo. Most of the people live in Yebra de Basa; according to its inhabitants there are about forty people who live and work there at present, of which ten are pensioners and another ten are residents but work elsewhere. Most of these places are inhabited by an ageing population. There are four very young children (between 0–6 years of age), one child between 6–14, another between 14–18 ; then four people between 19–25, three between 25–35, ten between 36–45 and the others are over fifty years of age. All of these villages have suffered from a remarkable decrease in population since the 1960s, although they have not been completely abandoned and they are inhabited by people who have been living there for a long time.

The main source of income of the inhabitants is agriculture and animal farming. On their land they grow wheat and barley to sell, and alfalfa and grass as forage for their own cattle. They also have small vegetable gardens for their own use. Sixty percent of cultivated lands are wheat crops, 20 percent barley crops and another 20 percent alfalfa crops (this data has been provided by the Town Council of Yebra de Basa). The fields are not very extensive and, according to an inhabitant of the valley (sixty–five, male), the most extensive one is about 50 hectares. Animal husbandry and farming are the principal activities; people mainly own sheep and cows. According to the 1996 animal census there are 1,053 sheep, 89 cows, 25–30 pigs approximately and, since 1996, 30–35 horses that are sold to the Basque Country and Catalonia (horse meat is not eaten in the Basa Valley). For their own consumption, people also keep hens, rabbits and pigs.

Gender and Alcoholic Drinks

The relationship between gender and alcohol is one which, as can be read in Heath (1989: 16–69), can be traced back to ancient times, and which has been highlighted by recent cross-cultural studies.

In the case of Basa Valley, gender is one of the main indicators of social difference. The patriarchal culture of this society, traditionally pastoral and agricultural, becomes evident in some of the personal traits of the men that inhabit this place: a hard and realistic view on life, uprightness, integrity, calm, stubborness, etc.[5] Men work outside the house and do not have a share in the housework; they sit at the head of the table, and are served first. Women are allotted the 'food area' (they do the shopping, the cooking, the cleaning, etc.), and also help in the fields; they are in charge of vegetable gardens as well as of farm animals and of children. Women satisfy the food needs of the men: the latter are the ones who enjoy the pleasures of food, the former enjoy the pleasure involved in pleasing the men. According to an informant (twenty-seven, male): 'women are satisfied with preparing food, and they like it when people ask for more and tell them how tasty everything is … they like to see that everybody is satisfied'.

Because of this hierarchical order, food consumption in the home is conditioned by men's preferences. A 24-year-old female inhabitant of the valley observes in this respect: 'my mother and I would eat more fish, but we don't buy it because it would be just for the two of us' (the implication being that men in the family are not keen on fish). As Arnaiz (1996: 79) points out, this phenomenon is underlied by a paternalistic ideology according to which the breadwinner is the one who 'calls the tune'. As this author goes on to say, once we understand the relationship of women with food in terms of a service they provide for the family, it can also be inferred that their preferences and tastes are subordinated to those of the beneficiaries, and that women are usually satisfied with carrying out such services, which are often disguised as *women's own* tasks.

Drinking alcohol, among other things, distinguishes men from women. In these places men have always drunk alcohol. In former times men had *cazalla* (dry aniseed) for breakfast, and/or *revuelto* (dry aniseed and muscatel) with biscuits and muffins. During the day they had *carajillos* (coffee with a dash of alcohol, mainly brandy), wine, etc. Peculiar to these places was the *sopanvino:* a slice of bread soaked in wine and sugar. It was consumed by men, women and children alike. The latter had it for breakfast or when they were back from school. As an informant (sixty-five, male) observes: 'even in the early years of our childhood, we had mellow wine with egg yolks for breakfast ... about five or six p.m. we had bread soaked in wine and sugar'.

Today, as these people themselves say, 'this tradition has been lost because of all this medical stuff, cholesterol and uric acid'. The owner of a bar in the area (sixty-five, male) says, 'now people drink more coffee, juices, cider and must (unfermented grape juice)'. The decrease in alcohol consumption has been caused not only by medical checkups, but also by inspections of the blood-level of alcohol carried out by the Guardia Civil.[6] However, shepherds still take a leather gourd of red wine with them every time they take the sheep to the pastures.

Among other alcoholic drinks, wine, which is very traditional in this place, functions as a gender marker. It is essential to men: it is a source of strength and nourishment and it cheers one up. Sitting at the table without wine is out of the question. As a seventy-year-old man observes, 'if they give me food without wine, to hell with it!' It is drunk with the traditional mid-morning snack, at lunch time, with the afternoon snack and at dinner time. People are never short of wine in the mountains. As a local saying paraphrases, 'when the bottle goes to the mountain it is full, when it comes back home it is empty'. Some people still remember the time when there were vines in this area and how they had to root them out because the climatic conditions were not favourable. Today wine is purchased in Sabiñanigo[7] and, they say, it comes from Cariñena. In contrast with the general tendency to drink light wines, the inhabitants of this area still prefer those with higher alcohol content. After they have bought the wine, they put it into barrels or big casks (most of the houses have a wine cellar) so that it matures, because, they say, 'in this way you get a much better wine'. This sweet-tasting wine is consumed together with sausage and ham for the mid-morning or the afternoon snack, and with cakes after lunch. This last combination, offered to foreign guests, is a local cultural marker.

On occasions such as festivities and invitations there is always a glass of cognac and/or home-made *pacharán* (liqueur made of sloes), a drink that appeared only recently. A seventy-year-old man observes, 'when the parson comes, we have some cognac *Soberano* or *Veterano*'.[8] This brandy, in the popular imagery, is synonymous with strength, masculinity and national identity. In order to consolidate these values, the image chosen to publicise it is that of a black bull and its advertising slogan reads more or less 'just for men'. Guests are also offered beer, soft drinks (orange, lemon and coke) and/or mellow wine with biscuits or muffins. As with other alcoholic drinks, beer is mainly consumed by men. It is associated with rest, it symbolises the end of hard labour and it is drunk at home as well as in bars.

Women prefer water, they reject wine and, of course, alcoholic drinks, since, they say, 'it makes you dizzy'. This indisposition, far from having a physical origin is, in fact, sociocultural. Women, since their early childhood, are warned against drinking and about alcohol's harmful effects. In other words, it is the social control exerted by men on women that causes the dizziness. In fact, men do not like the idea of women drinking alcohol, going to bars, smoking, etc. As a 66-year-old man says, 'it's not nice to see a woman drinking a glass of brandy'. In her work on Andalucia, González Turmo (1997: 119–20) similarly observes that: 'if a woman drank hard liquor and especially if she did so in excess and in public, it was considered as one of the ugliest and most dishonourable acts for her family. The women preferred, or "should prefer" less alcoholic drinks, like beer, and sweeter drinks.' It can be inferred that, in other parts of Spain, men can get drunk, whereas women cannot. A sixty-year-old man from the Basa Valley says, 'women get drunk very fast. If they drink a couple of glasses or three it's okay, but if they go on we must tell them to stop.' Such 'properly' small quantities of alcohol are always consumed by women on festive occasions like Christmas, Easter, birthdays, etc. In this case they prefer, as a fifty-year-old woman says, 'tiny glasses of sweet liqueurs'.

Throughout the year, there are also a number of occasions on which the women of the Basa Valley gather for communal meals from which the male members of the community are excluded. This allows them to consume alcohol. On St Agueda's day (29th January), for example, women eat together to celebrate 'women's day' and to claim a more active role for women within society. On this day, the women of Yebra de Basa have lunch together in one of the two local bars and there, as the men say, they take advantage of the situation and have a few drinks.

Another chance for women to be together and drink is the so-called 'gym lunches'. Lately some of them have taken up, as a hobby, long after-lunch walks in the surrounding areas; others do some exercise in the gym. Afterwards, they usually have a drink together in the local bar. This shows that, for these women, these physical activities are not only a way of keeping fit, but also an excuse for going on excursions and having lunch together. According to a 65-year-old man, 'they go over the top, they have apple and peach liqueurs or home-made pacharán'. Yet, both the celebration of St Agueda's day and gym lunches, which are apparently the assertion of women's freedom, become the means by which men contextualise and control women's consumption of alcohol.

In the Basa Valley, other drinks are not gender specific. Coffee, for example, is a favourite drink for men as well as for women. It is consumed in large quantities; as a seventy-year-old woman observes, 'we have coffee at any time from dawn 'til sunset'. In their opinion coffee does not keep one awake, that is why they also drink it after dinner. Infusions, tea and camomile are mainly associated with illnesses. For this reason they are rejected. As the same woman asserts, 'I drink infusions when I have a stomachache, the very smell of them makes my stomach turn'. Some families, for health reasons such as high cholesterol rates, consume skimmed milk, although they prefer milking their own cows.

Conclusion

Drinking is a practice whose function is not only that of satisfying one's thirst. Gender is a socially constructed category that carries specific meanings and triggers the drinking practice itself and the drink preferences and aversions. However, gender is not a homogeneous category. Values and individual beliefs produce intra-gender differences that influence drink preferences as well as the very action of drinking.

Notes

1. Translated by Monica Stacconi.
2. *Trinaranjus* (Schweppes), *Radical* (Pepsi) and *Fruitopía* (Coca Cola), are three brands of still, sugar-free drinks. Trinaranjus can be found in a number of flavours (lemon, apple, orange, tea etc.). Radical and Fruitopía, besides the 'traditional' flavours (orange, lemon, etc.) combine fruits that are regarded as 'exotic' or 'wild'. The last two drinks are presented in brightly-coloured bottles (blue, green, pink, etc.). Further information on food and colour can be found in Barusi, Medina and Colesanti, 1998.
3. Rioja: mark of origin, 10–12° proof, red, white, rosé made in the homonymous region divided into Rioja Alta, the most humid area, Rioja Alavesa, similar to the former but with steeper slopes, and Rioja Baja, characterised by a warmer and drier climate. The main varieties of grape used are *tempranillo* and *garnacha* (sweet, red grape) for red wines, and *viura* and *malvasia* for white wines (Delgado 1988).
4. Mark of origin of wines in Huesca, at the foot of the Pyrenees. It was acknowledged in 1980. In Aragon there are other three marks of origin: Calatayud, Campo de Borja and Cariñena.
5. On the identity of the Aragonese and of pastoral societies, see Ortiz-Oses 1992.
6. Guardia Civil: security corps whose main duty is to keep the public order in rural areas and to watch sea and land frontiers, as well as roads and railways *(Diccionario de la lengua española)*.
7. A village near to Basa Valley.
8. *Soberano* and *Veterano* are brands of Brandy of Jerez, produced in Jerez de la Frontera, Puerto de Santa María, and Sanlúcar de Barrameda, in the province of Cádiz (Andalucía, Spain). Its maturation, in oak barrels, lasts from six months up to more than three years. The alcoholic degree ranges from 36° to 45° *(MAPA, 1995)*.

References

Barusi, A.F., Medina, F.X. y Colesanti, G. (Eds.) (1998) *El color en la alimentación mediterránea. Elementos sensoriales y culturales de la nutrición.* Icaria, Barcelona.

Camporesi, P. (1995) *Il governo del corpo.* Garzanti, Italy.

Corral, N.(1996) *El cortejo del mal. Ética feminista y psicoanálisis.* Talasa, Madrid.

Delgado, C.(1988) *Diccionario de gastronomía.* Alianza, Madrid.

Dio Bleichmar, E. (1996) Feminidad/masculinidad. Resistencias en el psicoanálisis al concepto de género. In, Burin, M. y Dio Bleichmar, E. (comp.) *Género, psicoanálisis, subjetividad.* Paidós, Barcelona.

Gamman, L. y Makinen, M. (1994) *Female Fetishism. A New Look.* Lawrence & Wishart, London.

Garine, I. de (1971) The Socio-Cultural Aspects of Nutrition, *Ecology of Food and Nutrition* Vol. 1: 143–63.

Gobierno de Aragón, (1991) *Censo de población de Aragón Pirámides de población.* Zaragoza. Diputación General de Aragón. Departamento de Economía y Hacienda. Instituto Aragonés de Estadística.

González Turmo, I. (1997) The Pathways of Taste. The West Andalucian Case. In, H. Macbeth (Ed.) *Food Preferences and Taste. Continuity and Change.* Berghahn Books, Oxford: 115–26.

Gracia Arnaiz, M. (1996) *Paradojas de la alimentación contemporánea.* Institut Català d'Antropologia, Icaria, Barcelona.

Heath, D. (1989) A Decade of Development in the Anthropological Study of Alcohol Use: 1970–1980. In, M. Douglas (Ed.) *Constructive Drinking. Perspectives on Drink from Anthropology.* Cambridge University Press, Cambridge: 16–69.

Millán, A. (1998) Alrededor de la mesa: aspectos normativos, rituales y simbólicos de la comensalía. In, F. Checa y P. Molina (Eds.) *La función simbólica de los ritos. Rituales y simbolismo en el Mediterráneo.* Icaria, Barcelona.

MAPA – Ministerio de Agricultura, Pesca y Alimentación y Mercasa (1995) *Alimentos de España. Denominaciones de origen y de calidad,* Madrid.

Ortiz-Oses, A. (1992) *La identidad cultural aragonesa.* Alcañiz. Centro de Estudios Bajoaragoneses.

Real Academia Española (1992) *Diccionario de la lengua española.*Vigésima primera edición, Espasa, Madrid.

Tubert, S. (1988) *La sexualidad femenina y su construcción imaginaria.* Ediciones el Arguero, Madrid.

13. TAPEO
AN IDENTITY MODEL OF PUBLIC DRINK AND FOOD CONSUMPTION IN SPAIN

....

Amado Millan[1]

The Tapa

In the *Diccionario del uso del español* (Moliner 1971) one can read: '*Tapa* (Andalucia) Slice of ham, bacon or sausage served in taverns on top of *cañas* and *chatos* [glasses] of wine. Any variety of appetizer (olives, pickles, cold cuts, sausage, squid and other types of fried fish, shellfish, salads or any kind of light and appetising food) served in bars and similar establishments as an accompaniment to a drink'. Originally, the *tapa* (from *tapadera* – lid), was served on top of the glass as a protection against flies, etc.

A tapa is, then, a portion of food: *pincho* or *banderilla* (food served on a cocktail stick), *montado* (served on a small slice of bread), plate or portion, *tabla* (choice of cheese, ham or sausage presented on a wooden board), chosen among a variety of food combinations that are placed on some kind of edible base and can be found in certain bars of the Hispano–European area. All the various tapas are displayed, or accessible to customers for self-service; when they are not immediately visible or available, the bartender reels off the list of tapas, which is known by heart. They can be found in bars at specific times of the day and are accompanied by some kind of drink, preferably fermented (beer or wine). *Tapeo* is the action of eating tapas.

Inter-Regional Differences

Tapeo has spread throughout Spain and has also affected certain bars of the *Spanish milieu* in other countries, e.g., New York, Paris, Cape Town. Some regions are famous for their sophisticated *pinchos*. Others, such as Andalucia, are popular for their wide variety of food portions combined with their particular wines *(mosto, fino, manzanilla, amontillado)*. In the Basque country, for example, we find as a common practice the so-called *chiquiteo*, small quantities of wine or beer successively drunk by a group of friends in a number of different bars (Ramirez Goicoechea 1991).

Historical References and Changes

Capel and Barbacil place the origin of tapeo[2] in Andalucia. It might also have originated in the grape and wine growing area of La Mancha, producer of strong-tasting seasoned cheese. Whenever the tavern owners of other regions came to La Mancha to buy wine, they were given a taste of it together with some cheese – due to the strong flavour of the cheese, the bad quality of the wine was concealed.[3]

To return to Capel's account (1995: 13), tapas probably spread from Andalucian taverns to other regions, especially during the first third of the twentieth century. Originally, local specialities (sausage, cured ham, cheese, vegetables) were used for their elaboration, but later on other products were introduced through the trade, such as pickles and tinned preserves (cockles or tuna fish), consumed mainly with local wine.

Pre-war period

Tapas made their appearance in Saragossa in the 1930s with the boom of beer-shops and modern bars and the decline of cafeterias. In the area called Tubo, next to the Plaza de España, the symbolic core of the city, one can still see some of the bars that, in the period preceding the Spanish Civil War, served slices of melon, sherbet, almonds and olives. Later on these bars served *banderillas* of pickled tuna and *salmueras* (salted anchovies) (Repollés y Romero 1996: 9). It was here that, in 1944, the squid sandwiches peculiar to tapeo were first prepared.

Post-war Period

During the post-war period, although many of the taverns and inns in Spain did not provide meals (Romero de Solís 1989), customers could consume their own food provided they bought the drinks from the inn.

1960s–Present Day

The increase in income made the spreading of tapeo possible and facilitated women's entry into bars and taverns, which had always been the area of masculine interaction. This change was due to the fact that taverns now provided food as well as drinks. From 1980 onwards, and even before, tapeo increasingly spread and the structure of consumption changed. If at the beginning tapeo was considered an activity preceding the main midday and evening meals (which were eaten privately or in a restaurant), today they very often replace dinner (45 percent of the interviewees substitute their lunch or dinner with tapeo).

Eating tapas shows the shift from cooking in times of scarcity (when the palatal characteristics of food and drinks were secondary to satiety) to cooking in times of abundance and of gastronomic knowledge (the *Nouvelle Cuisine* influenced the elaboration of tapas). Along with this shift, there has been a transformation of local wines that were formerly considered too strong, with an excessive alcohol content. Tapeo transformed and displaced a private activity, that of eating in a home whose walls concealed the scarcity experienced during the post-war period, when visits during mealtimes were not proper (Fournier 1990), into a public activity that would foster the ostentation of economic wealth. Furthermore, since tapas are eaten in the company of other people, everyone, in turn, can play the part of the host and buy a round of tapas.

Structure

The ingredients can be of animal or vegetable origin (meat, fish, shellfish, cheese, vegetables, mushrooms, etc.) They all belong in the food cultural selection. Tapas are small-sized (20–30 g) and, in general, there is no need to cut them into pieces in order to eat them. Portions and *tablas* (a choice of food on a wooden board) are bigger in size.

As to the rules concerning the combination of ingredients (composition, combination, substitution), tastes (salted, seldom sweet, sour, etc.), texture (crunchy, soft, etc.), they are an extension of the rules that govern the food culture itself. Food portions, as we will see, are combined with certain kinds of drinks.

Such portions are already made and displayed on the counter or are very quick to prepare. They are usually prepared in the presence of the customer, sometimes in the kitchen. There are various ways of elaborating food (I have listed at least nineteen varieties) including marinating and smoking (fish, cheese, etc.), frying (prawns, squid, rolls of fried pig intestines), steaming (fresh cockles, etc.), pickling (olives, gherkins, egg plants, spring onions, etc.), sousing (bonito, mussels, mackerel, etc.), dressing in various ways (shellfish, vegetables, etc.), preserving in oil or brine (cockles, leeks, peppers, etc.), roasting and baking (potatoes, lamb's heads, etc.), stewing (bull meat, lamb's legs, pig's trotters, etc.) salting (anchovies, etc.), grilling, boiling, curing (ham, sausage, salted tuna, etc.), frying in batter (prawns, eggs, egg plants, zucchini, etc.).

Barbacil's guide for Saragossa covers 173 kinds of tapas and 73 selected bars. Some of these tapas can be found in more than one establishment, others in only one bar. Recurrence might help define the 'typical tapa'. The most common tapas, classified according to their main ingredient, are: peppers, codfish, squids, anchovies, ham, potatoes, omelette, traditional potato omelette, etc. (Barbacil 1996).[4] These ingredients are consumed at room temperature or hot.

Drinks

Tapas are usually accompanied by small quantities (10 cl minimum) of fermented drinks such as wine or beer (occasionally mixed with soda water) whose alcohol content may range from 1–4.5 percent in the case of beer and from 9–12 percent for wine. Cider and vermouth are also consumed, but less often. Other common drinks are alcohol-free ones such as bottled water, grape juice, bitters and non-alcoholic beer. Soft drinks (cola and fruit beverages) are not considered proper for tapeo although some people do drink them, but never milk, distilled liqueurs or *sangría* (drink made of wine and fruit juice, first consumed by the young generation of the 1960s, which the initial tourist boom turned into emblematic, typical and topical of the country).

In 1995 the average consumption of wine was 30.53 litres per person per year; 57 percent of it was consumed in establishments (MERCASA 1998: 225). Wine consumption is higher in the north, north-east and north-west of the country than in Andalucia and the Canary Islands; it is higher in rural areas than in urban ones; in the lower socio-economic classes than in the upper classes, and in smaller family units with older members (MAPA 1996: 303). In 1987 (MAPA 1988: 473), families consumed 58 percent of the 47 litres of wine per person per year, and consumption in winter was higher than in summer (ibid: 474); similarly, the north-east, north and north-west showed a higher wine consumption than Levante, the south or the Canary Islands.

In 1996 beer consumption was 64.7 litres per person per year, less than the European average (83 litres); 79 percent was consumed in catering establishments (MERCASA 1988: 218). Beer consumption was higher in Andalucia and Levante, in urban areas, in lower socio-economic classes, in younger family units of two or three members (MAPA, 1996: 303). In 1987 it was static, although higher in summer. Beer was consumed, as it is today, out of the home (69 percent in bars and cafeterias), and its consumption was higher in Andalucia and Levante, which exceeded (and still does) the national average (MAPA 1988: 519–21). Family beer consumption was not recorded by MAPA until 1987 (ibid: 519).

Beer consumption has increased at a higher rate than wine. The consumption outside the home and during the tapeo is characterised by the availability of greater quantities which, in turn, favour a longer halt in the bar at a minimum expense (Fournier 1992: 92–93). Although the quality of beer is similar to that of wine, the unit is more expensive.

In 1995 the average cider consumption was 1.53 litres per person per year; 53.78 percent was consumed in establishments (MERCASA 1998: 240). In 1995 the consumption of soft drinks and soda water was 64.76 litres per person per year, of which 47.64 percent was consumed in the catering sector (ibid.). In 1995 the consumption of bottled water was 57.69 litres per person per year, of which 36.10 percent was consumed in the catering sector (ibid: 215). In 1995 the consumption of spirituous drinks was 5.54 litres per person per year, of which 79.96 percent was consumed in the catering sector (ibid: 235).

Gender

The consumption of alcoholic drinks is higher for men, aged from forty-five on. Higher consumption of alcohol corresponds to a greater degree of education of the subject; the same is true for women (De Miguel 94–95: 372).

Women's appropriation of symbolic elements that in the 1960s were almost the sole prerogative of masculinity (except for upper classes and urban areas), such as the use of bars or tobacco, dissolves – or at least reduces – gender discrimination of behaviour and space differentiation.Tapeo has facilitated this transformation.[5]

Men are more concerned with the proximity and price of bars than women, who are concerned with quality, taste (hedonism) and variety. Furthermore, women are more prone than men to trying new bars and elaborations that are recommended to them.

Complexity

Tapas show great variety and increasing complexity, stimulated by contests and prizes.[6] As to drinks, although they are apparently simple and less varied (mainly wine and beer), they become increasingly complex due to the deployment of new technologies, globalisation of economy, etc. A large amount of information concerning the organoleptic characteristics of wines, marks of origin, vintage years, commercial brands, etc., has become accessible to consumers, creating a discourse of 'gastronomic knowledge' that bestows prestige on those who display it.

Uniformity/Variety

Eating and drinking rounds are an essential aspect of tapeo. Each round takes place in a different bar, in search of, on one hand, food variety, and on the other, drink uniformity. In the case of wine it is more difficult to find the same mark of origin or brand whereas beer is considered to have a more homogeneous taste. This perceptive characteristic has favoured the increase in beer consumption.

Functions

Sociability seems to be the prime function of tapeo: drink consumption is also usually carried out in the company of other people (De Miguel 1996: 221). Tapeo is a way of commensal interaction where verbal (and non-verbal) exchange plays an essential role: 'good-humoured chats are the protagonists of tapeo. Serious matters are wound up or else they are wrapped in irony and very often people make fun of one another' (s.n.a., 2ª Muestra Gastronómica de la Tapa en Zaragoza 1998: 7). Jokes, criticism (political and sports), comments on news and gossip, service offers, and business are frequent subjects of conversation in Andalucian taverns and bars (Fournier 1992: 98).

The needs of present-day consumers, such as the demand for healthy food, speed, body aesthetics, sobriety, tasting hedonism, etc., are met through this way of drinking and eating. Small quantities of food and drink help maintain the predominant ideal of body image (no more than 10 percent of the customers are overweight,[7] according to our observations).

The combination of food and drink, both consumed in small quantities, ensures the customers' sobriety: 'Sobriety and calm are essential to this kind of consumption, while people stand side by side and chatter friendlily around the best local wines and gastronomic dainties that each bar offers' (2ª Muestra 1998: 7). The quest for gastronomical pleasure can be satisfied by the wide assortment of tapas in each bar and by the frequent moving from one bar to another.

Exteriority

Eating tapas, Capel points out (1995: 12) 'is neither comfortable nor cheap, although it is amusing and pleasurable'. Yet, tapas bars are easily affordable due to the wide variety of prices, and the customer, in turn, is only requested to be well-mannered and respectful of the privacy of a public place.

If we exclude sleeping hours, the average time spent at home by 32 percent of the Spanish population, except for housewives, is four hours or less on working days. It is 5–6 hours for 30 percent of the population, from 7–9 hours for 20 percent of the population and 10 or more hours for the remaining 16 percent (De Miguel 1994: 420). Men of any age spend less time at home than women, and young women less than older ones. The average time, in minutes (CIRES 1991: 331), that is devoted to bars and cafeterias daily is 15.6 on weekdays, 37 on Saturdays and 38.4 on Sundays. The average time, in relation to gender, devoted to activities out of the home (such as having a drink in a bar), is 65 percent for men and 37 percent for women (De Miguel 1994: 433). Thus, the spatial dichotomy outside-public-masculine/inside-private-feminine, which is not so patent at a young age, still persists, temporal data that corroborates the external quality of Hispano–European culture (outside social life, public places, etc.)

Consumption Times

Opening times of bars that specialise in the elaboration of tapas are usually from 11–11.30 a.m. to 3–4 p.m., and from 6–7 p.m. to 11–12 p.m. Such a timetable places tapeo well beyond breakfast time, and makes it coincide with the mid-morning snack (or immediately after), and with the time preceding lunch (or with lunchtime). Similarly, in the afternoon, tapeo is made to coincide with the time following the mid-afternoon snack and preceding dinner (or with dinner time, and even after dinner time).

Our informants[8] do not have tapas for breakfast, only two eat them for the mid-morning snack, twenty-one eat tapas before lunch, only two at lunch-time, no one eats tapas for the mid-afternoon snack, seventeen do so before dinner, most of them (25) replace dinner with tapas and some of them eat tapas for supper *(recena)* .

The importance of sociability in this kind of food and drink consumption demands an amount of leisure time which the customer can only enjoy at the end of the day and on festive occasions, weekends and holidays. Tapeo, just like other identity markers, even though it is a daily activity, is still associated with festive commensality. Within the weekly cycle, tapeo concentrates on Saturdays (24 informants), followed by Sundays (18), Fridays (17) and working days (8).

Tapeo is not only affected by the weekly cycle, but also by climate, season, and even televised sport events since they condition people's outings and attendance in bars. The time spent in the same bar, standing next to the counter or sitting on the stools, never goes beyond 30 minutes.

Tapeo, from the 1930s until almost the 1980s, was placed in the phase preceding the ritual of commensality, before the main midday meal, especially on Sundays and holy days: 'we had an appetizer after the church service, together with family and friends' (S.G.L. – Santiago Gómez Laguna).

When people were paid weekly and in cash on Saturdays, after work they had a drink and an appetizer. It was a popular activity, cheaper than it is nowadays, which has now spread to the middle and upper-middle classes. Together with tapas, people had wine, (in the south of the country *finos, manzanillas,* etc.), as well as alcoholic bitters, which have now been replaced by alcohol-free bitters. People also had vermouth, a wine spiced with cinnamon and cloves, now replaced by grape juice (S.G.L.). Vermouth consumption in the last five years has decreased by 10 percent (MERCASA: 238). Another change was the introduction of cola and lemon soft drinks that took place about ten or fifteen years ago. Alcohol consumption, the glass of brandy drunk together with coffee after lunch, has also been discontinued (S.G.L).

Customers

The attendance of bars and cafeterias is very high; such places become essential to the social functions carried out in them, whereas nourishment becomes secondary. Tapas and drinks are mostly consumed at the counter, standing or sitting on stools, less frequently at tables – indeed some bars have none.

Although there are no precise statistics on tapeo, we can note that 65 percent of men and 37 percent of women who were questioned nationwide had been to a bar the day preceding the interview; 61 percent belonged to the working population, 66 percent were youths, 30 percent were housewives and 27 percent were elderly (De Miguel 93–94: 433). As to the relationship between class and tapeo, Fournier (1992: 96) points out that tapeo is common in the middle and middle-upper classes: 'low-class people eat, they do not nibble'.

Youths (male) are the most assiduous customers of tapas bars; they tend to be left-wing and smokers. Drinking and smoking seem to be the way of expressing extroversion and sociability (De Miguel 1993–94; 443).

Social class influences women when it comes to going to bars (De Miguel, 1994: 443). However, we can assume that tapeo has contributed to facilitating women's access to areas that were only masculine and solely associated with the consumption of alcohol. Tapeo is also an alternative to *chiquiteo, ir de vinos,* etc., activities that only involve drinking. People usually go to tapas bars with their partner (especially women), with a group of friends (both women and men), with schoolmates or colleagues, and with their family (especially women) (Repollés y Romero 1996).

Capel points out that tapeo 'is inseparable from hubbub and narrowness' (1995: 12). Fournier also points out that the place is saturated with noise (1992:91). Multiple voices reiterate a conversation that we might call polyphonic, or, as Pitt-Rivers observes on Spaniards (1990: 42), 'everybody is speaking and nobody is listening', yet people seem to understand one another.

Stock, which in former times people had together with wine (when the consumption of tapas was not so high), was drunk out of a glass and counteracted intoxication. We find here further evidence of the fact that alcohol becomes secondary with respect to sociability; people do not drink in order to reach a state of unconsciousness, but to stimulate social integration. Everybody gets their portions out of a common recipient (earthenware pot, plate, wooden board), whereas drinks are consumed in individual recipients and vary from one commensal to the other. The individual *pincho* can also be shared with a person with whom one is on very close terms, such as a partner or intimate friend. Other commensals' behaviour can be easily observed, and when somebody does not follow the rules of equality (by eating the biggest share) and reciprocity (cadging, eating without ever paying) he or she can even be excluded from the group.

When, after having eaten all the portions on the plate there is only one left, this is called the 'shameful portion'. People, in turn, refuse to eat it up and, very often, that last bite is left on the plate. We could assume that there is a taboo associated with survival, according to which the leftovers must stay available and nobody dares appropriate them. The consumption of the last portion would break the egalitarianism among the commensals, since one person would be attributed a status that the other members of the group reject.

The bill is not paid on being served, but after the consumption and before leaving the bar; this shows the manager's trust in the customer, and avoids the repetition of bills in case there are further orders. In some bars (Repollés y Romero: 14) the cocktail sticks of *pinchos* are kept in order to count them at

the end and sum up the bill. The bartender often asks customers what they
have had in order to establish how much he has to charge.

Conclusion

Tapeo is not only about particular kinds of food and drink, but also about elaborations, quantities, space, time and ways of consumption related to identity.
Thus, sociability (verbal interaction, reciprocity, community, conviviality),
outward appearance and externality, the game of appearances and the subsequent ostentation, the hedonistic enjoyment of ingestion joined with the utili-
tarian availability of fast food (yet eaten slowly), etc., are ways of asserting
one's identity.

   This kind of consumption, combining drink and food, maintains the nutritional balance, and it also promotes people's 'good manners', and the ability
to 'stay sober while drinking'. It prevents scandals, drunkenness and, in the
long run, it does not produce cirrhosis, as happens with other forms of alcohol
consumption (Fournier 1992: 97–98). This ritual favours sobriety in spite of the
ingestion of alcohol.

   Commensals value the interaction produced by tapeo more than eating and
drinking. At the counter (a common table), symbolic, physical, interpersonal
and inter-group distances are minimised. Verbal and bodily contacts take place
and last, or not, depending on the other person's reaction.

   As to ostentation, what is displayed is the economic power (capacity to
consume, to treat others to the most expensive bar or tapa) as well as one's
knowledge of drinks or ingredients, of their origin, qualities, methods of elaboration etc., all things that are thought to confer prestige. Although personal
preferences are stratified (Cantarero 1999), people do not usually boast of the
higher prestige of a preference with respect to others, since *de gustibus non
disputandum.*

   A few bars sometimes display the record of tapas and drink consumed in a
day, although only the initials of the winner appear, e.g., Taberna Andaluza 41
on 20.12.97, IEA-JAS. Sometimes, but less than before, people bet on the
quantity of tapas and drink that someone can ingest.

   In Aragon (INE 1996) the average expenditure per person was 606,449
pesetas; the average spent on food, drinks and tobacco was 176,368 pts.; on
clothing and shoes it was 82,195 pts. (it is worth mentioning here that 4,849 pts
was spent on personal care, 7,075 pts. on toiletry articles, 1,757 pts. on jewellery, watches, fashion jewellery, etc., all things relative to the construction of
a personal image); the expenditure on medical services and medicine was
16,195 pts. and, finally, the expenditure on restaurants and cafeterias was
54,882 pts.

   National expenditure on restaurants, cafeterias and hotels is three times the
medical expenditure (the investment on sociability is proportionally inverse to
medical services), it is twice the expenditure on personal transportation, and

the same on housing; they are 'significant markers of Spanish social life' (CECS 1994: 93).

The different gastronomic cultures of the country are homologated in the social use, the manner, technique or art of convivial interaction that constitutes tapeo. This relation between food, drink and commensality is confined to the country and nostalgically longed for by emigrants. Tapeo is a model of sociability specific to Spanish identity: '... that amusing way ... and absolutely Spanish art of eating as you are standing' (Barbacil 1996: 8).

Except for the bottled water (62.84 percent) or coffeee and infusions (57.91 percent) consumed in the home (MERCASA 1998), the consumption of drinks, alcoholic as well as soft, takes place in outside places such as bars and cafeterias, reinforcing the interpretation of externalisation as a differential cultural characteristic embodied by tapeo.

The group, community, sociability, outward appearance, visibility, supposed conformity, social control, hedonism in taste, moderation, tradition ... all constitute the model of Spanish social life in which one can participate through the consumption of drinks and exquisite food portions in the company of friends.

Acknowledgements

I wish to thank Dimás Repollés, Pablo Romero, Luis Cantarero, Santiago Gómez Laguna, former students of my courses of Anthropology of Food, Alicia Dóiz, Joaquina Fuertes, Monica Stacconi, Carmen Montesinos, Chepo, Gabriel Crespo, Joaquín Martínez, Luis Roche, Manolo Vaca, Miguel Sánchez, Pilar, Rosa, Luis and many others whose collaboration has made this work possible.

Notes

1. Translated by Monica Stacconi.
2. The tavern, already present in Classical Rome, can be considered the ancestor of the *tapas* bar. Written references to it, in Spanish, date from 1228 (Romero de Solís 1989: 65). It can be inferred that food was served in taverns even though, as Romero de Solís observes, various laws prohibited the elaboration and consumption of game, fish (1585) and food in general (1613) in these places. Only from 1795 onwards would the elaboration of fried food be authorised, although the prohibition on boiled foodstuff was maintained (ibid: 68).
3. Hence apparently the popular expression 'to give something with cheese', i.e., 'to cheat somebody'.
4. The list might well go beyond the 173 varieties included in the guide.
5. Laws of the end of the 18th century still prohibited women to frequent taverns (Romero de Solís 1989: 67).
6. For example, the tapas competition 'San Jorge Prize' awards the originality of

elaboration and also the use of Aragonese or regionally traditional products, i.e., originality and identity consciousness are encouraged.

7. Nineteen percent of the Spanish population are overweight, nine percent of which are between 18 and 29 years old (8 percent men and 9 percent women), and 29 percent are over 65 (De Miguel 1997).

8. A sample of 78 customers, male and female, from 18–65 years of age, all urban residents belonging to the middle and upper-middle class. Another five interviews were held with proprietors and staff working in the catering sector.

References

Barbacil, J. (1996) *De tapas por Zaragoza*. Madrid, El País-Aguilar.

Cantarero Abad, L., (1999*) Preferencias y rechazos alimentarios: factores psicológicos y socioculturales. Un estudio en la población aragonesa*. Tesis doctoral (Universitat de Barcelona).

Capel, J.C. (1995) *De tapas por Madrid*. El País-Aguilar, Madrid.

CECS (Centro de Estudios del Cambio Social) (1994) El consumo como indicador de las preferencias de la sociedad. In, *España 1993, una interpretación de su realidad social*. Fundación Ramón Areces e Iberdrola y dirigido por la Fundación Encuentro, CECS, Madrid: 88–96.

CIRES (Centro de Investigaciones sobre la Realidad social, Madrid).

De Miguel, A. (dir) (1994) *La sociedad española 1993–94*. Complutense, Madrid.

De Miguel, A. (dir) (1995) *La sociedad española 1994–95*. Complutense, Madrid.

De Miguel, A. (dir) (1996) *La sociedad española 1995–96*. Complutense, Madrid.

De Miguel, A. (dir) (1997) *La sociedad española 1996–97*. Complutense, Madrid.

Fournier, D. (1990) Toros: Vídeo y Tabernas. *Taurología*, (3): 31–36.

Fournier, D. (1992) Del mosto al cuba libre. *El Folk-lore Andaluz*. Fundación Machado, Sevilla, 9: 81–103.

Fournier, D. et D'Onofrio, S. (Eds.) (1991) *Le ferment divin*. Maison des Sciences de l'Homme, Paris.

INE: Instituto Nacional de Estadistica (1991) *Encuesta de Presupuestos Familiares 1990–91*, Madrid.

MAPA: Ministerio de Agricultura, Pesca y Alimentación (1996) *La Alimentación en España 1995*. Secretaria General de Alimentación, Madrid.

MAPA: Ministerio de Agricultura, Pesca y Alimentación (1998) *El consumo alimentario en España 1987*. Dirección General de Política Alimentaria, Madrid.

MERCASA (1998) *Alimentación en España. Producción, industria, distribución y consumo*, Ministerio de Agricultura, Pesca y Alimentación (MAPA), Madrid.

Moliner, M. (1971) *Diccionario del uso español*. Gredos, Madrid.

Pitt-Rivers, J. (1990) España vista por los antropologos. In, Catedra, M. (Ed.) *Los españoles vistos por los antropólogos*. Júcar, Madrid.

Ramirez Goicoechea, E. (1991) La cuadrilla: modelo tradicional de grupalidad. In, *De jóvenes y sus identidades. Socioantropología de la etnicidad en Euskadi*. Siglo XXI, Madrid: 286–331.

Repolles, D. y Romero, P. (1996) Documento de trabajo, Universidad de Zaragoza.

Romero de Solís, P. (1989) La taberna en Espagne et en Amérique. *Terrain*, MPE (Mission du Patrimoine Ethnologique, Ministère de la Culture de de la Commuication), Paris, (9): 63–71.

S.n.a. (sin nombre de autor) *2ª Muestra Gastronómica de la Tapa en Zaragoza*. 5-7 de junio 1998.

14. CANTINAS AND DRINKERS IN MEXICO

Ricardo Avila Palafox

Introduction

For more than a century, *cantinas* in Mexico have been a social space of tolerance and letting off steam where social norms can be transgressed momentarily. In the beginning they were established and accepted as assembly places for men, who could thus release tensions, feelings, and passions, although only in a theoretical and fleeting way. Alcoholic drinks, this essential lubricant, a true balm for social tensions, are acquired in cantinas.[1] Popular belief holds that alcohol removes evils from the soul, and since evils appear to be eternal, it seems necessary to maintain oneself drinking a good part of the day. However, when the levels of alcohol pass certain limits, occasionally or over a long period, the initial release and joy offered by moderate drinking can lead to suffering and destruction.

Mexican cantinas are frequented by a plethora of clients with specific tastes, customs, ideas, and fantasies. These, for social or cultural examination purposes, can be grouped in different ways. There are two types of drinkers: those who enjoy and those who suffer. Suffering in this case refers to the physical ravages, the product of hangovers and long-range after-effects, as well as the moral afflictions, be they of an individual or collective nature.

In this text, based on informal interviews and participant observation,[2] I give a brief account and some general reflections about Mexican cantinas (especially considering those in the city of Guadalajara), describing their spaces and patrons. I will briefly point out how the practice of consuming alcoholic drinks has developed in Mexico. Finally, a reflection will be made about alcoholism in Mexico in terms of its inhabitants' cultural character.

Cantinas and Patrons

It is difficult and useless to assign an exact date when cantinas appeared in Mexico. Still, everything seems to indicate that it was during the second half of the nineteenth century, after decades of war and political instability. Of course, before cantinas were established, Mexico had places were liquor could be drunk, like stores selling wine and spirits, roadside inns and hostelries. These places were not only devoted to the sale of alcoholic drinks, they served

food and one could rest or spend the night there, and they offered other services for travellers, merchants, or muleteers. This did not prevent many of the
clients from taking libations with delight and ending up drunk, as numerous
travellers from the period tell (Erskine 1959: 239; Eisenstein 1989: 210).

In contrast to inns and hostelries, which were essentially rural places, the
cantina is a typically urban phenomenon. It is a public establishment, created
to offer its clients a space for enjoyment, communication, and for savouring
different types of alcoholic drinks. Although the concept of cantina was
imported to a certain extent, in Mexico its precursor was the store selling
spirits, *pulque*, or wines which controlled the trade of fortified wines (*vinos
generosos*) and fine liquors imported from overseas. These places responded
to the social demand for alcohol.

The well-stocked and even luxurious cantinas began to proliferate towards
the 1870s in cities such as Mexico City, Veracruz (the port of entry for almost
everything that arrived from Europe), Puebla and Guadalajara. A large
variety of imported alcohols were offered in them, rubbing shoulders with local
drinks such as rum and tequila. The latter was first marketed in the area of
Guadalajara, its place of origin, and subsequently made available throughout
Mexico. With time, and circumstances, tequila, obtained from a cactus *(Agave
tequilana weber)* was elevated to the status of national emblem, but that is
another story.

Until about twenty years ago, women, save those of ill repute, were not
allowed to enter cantinas, which reveals something of the recent moral habits
of Mexican society. It was said – and some of the righteous still maintain – that
cantinas were places for men, where women were 'spoken' about. Even today,
only a minority of women frequent cantinas.

For drinkers, waiters, and owners of cantinas, these places are the proper
environment to drink in a relaxed, happy fashion. Further, the drinks are considerably cheaper than in restaurants or other types of more elegant establishment, such as ostentatious bars. The cantina is considered a neutral zone,
where, in principle, differences and disputes stay outside, although if a certain
dose of alcohol intake is exceeded, both can enter the premises and take over
the drinkers.

The cantina is the public space of tolerance par excellence, where social heterogeneity meets to give vent to happiness, sadness, passions, etc. In cantinas
there is a permissive atmosphere where, in principle, people speak with
freedom. Today, various types of drinkers can be distinguished, ranging from
regulars, who go every day to have a drink, to the well-to-do young who have
adopted the fashion of going to these establishments, believing that they will
find a good time there, synonymous in this case with informal, popular, decadent, and even slummy. Of course, this crowd adopts snobbish postures that
appear cyclically in societies, such as when the young Spanish nobles and
aristocrats of the late eighteenth century frequented the poor neighbourhood
taverns (Fuentes 1992: 235–6; Ginzburg 1991: 185).

In addition to these two groups, situated at the extremes, there are occasional drinkers who, when they drink, do it seriously. Also, there are cyclical drinkers, who drink on weekends or paydays. There are sporadic drunks, who drink on few occasions, but when they indulge, they almost always achieve their aim: to benumb themselves. There are also professed alcoholics who drink daily 'to forget' say the waiters. Likewise, prostitutes are on hand, tolerated only in certain cantinas. And some cantinas are frequented more or less often by businessmen, reporters, professionals, officers, and myriad others.

In some way, all these individuals find in cantinas a festive and pleasant ambience, proper for preliminary sex play and nonsense; to relieve the tensions, where alcohol functions as a social lubricant. Further, since women have been admitted and as alcohol relaxes people, in some cantinas flirting has become institutionalised, to the satisfaction of those who seek to drink and flirt at the same time. Thus, one drinker stated that people go to cantinas 'to take off their clothes', metaphorically speaking.

Alcoholic Consumption in Mexico

Before the Europeans' arrival, consumption of alcoholic drinks was limited and strictly controlled. The most widely consumed drink was *pulque*, the fermented product of agave, known as maguey *(Agave atrovirens)*. Its consumption was restricted to ceremonial uses and on special occasions old people were given permission to drink it. Young people who became drunk were severely punished, so severely that they sometimes died as a result (Davies 1988: 223).

Evidently, once the social order of pre-Columbian Mexico had broken down, the control over pulque and other intoxicating drinks was lost, and consumption increased. In addition, the Europeans offered the native Americans, specifically the Mexicans, a poisoned gift: sugar cane. By cultivating and multiplying its production, they made cane spirit, cane alcohol and rum (called *chinguirito* in Mexico) appear (Braudel 1994: 39). Widespread production of this drink caused enormous ravages in New Spain's economy and society, because the attempt made to control it had little result. Only towards the end of the eighteenth century could an *entente* be reached between rulers, producers and consumers, through which its production was accepted under another name and certain rules were agreed upon for its production and consumption (Enciclopedia de Mexico 1993: 2159). In the end, consumers and producers won the battle, obviously.

The other drink whose consumption increased, above all on Mexico's high central plain, was pulque. In New Spain, taxes on pulque brought to the state half of what taxes on silver mines provided, especially throughout much of the seventeenth century (Braudel 1994: 39). Like chinguirito, the excessive consumption of pulque caused serious problems in public health and order in colonial Mexico, and even during the nineteenth century, as numerous accounts from the epoch attest (Corcuera 1990:75, 123). However, its low percentage of alcohol (between two and seven percent) lessened its social impact compared to the brew distilled from sugar cane.

During the second half of the nineteenth century and throughout most of the twentieth century, until twenty or thirty years ago, pulque was drunk in establishments called *pulquerias*, very rudimentary places frequented by consumers of mostly rural origin and character. The majority of pulquerias had suggestive names, such as La Encantadora (The Enchantress), La Dominadora (The Dominating Female), or El Recuerdo del Porvenir (Memory of the Future) (Chadourne 1989: 225), and most of them had a small section for women, where they could imbibe at ease. Chinguirito and other drinks with a high alcoholic content could also be found and consumed in the wine shops, offshoots of the little alcohol shops from the colonial epoch, which became mostly urban establishments. Although dirty, grim, and even dangerous, every type of alcohol was sold there retail or wholesale (Novo, 1967: 227).

Towards 1870, when the civil war ended and social order was restored, the economy grew, benefitting more social strata, who began drinking alcoholic drinks in this novel establishment of purely Spanish pedigree, called the cantina in Mexico. In these establishments characteristic of the city, one could consume quality alcohols – rare and expensive – that before were found only occasionally in wine shops. Also, fortified wines and other grape derivatives started being imported from Europe, above all from Spain, as well as rums and local spirits. In addition, towards the end of the nineteenth century, beer began to be consumed in cantinas, since it was during this time that the first breweries were established in Mexico. Ice-cold beer, in a generally warm country, soon became Mexicans' favourite drink with relative ease, to such a degree that beer now accounts for 80 percent of alcoholic beverage sales in the country (Publico 8/25/1998: 8).

The country's public life was losing its ostentatious and heavy sacredness, the product of a pristine religiosity, and habits became more secular. Tolerance for spaces devoted to the sale and consumption of alcoholic beverages grew, above all as the new social elite accepted eating and drinking fashions imported from abroad, especially from Spain and France. In this context the first cantinas appeared and flourished, where society men met to savour imported drinks, eat appetizers that were really abundant meals, and tackle all kinds of social and political questions. Many of those cantinas survived for decades, maintaining their style and service, but the majority adapted themselves to local tastes. Thus, beside ham, cold cuts, and all kinds of fish and canned seafood – so-called imported foods – appeared drinks like rum and tequila, and traditional Mexican dishes such as *tacos* with chile, *quesadillas*, and many others that accompany the cantina clients' libations.

Cantinas not only adapted to local tastes, they adjusted to the country's social and economic conditions. Most of them limited themselves to certain neighbourhoods and responded to the taste and generosity of the habitués' pocket books, which, more often than not, were strapped by the ups and downs of the Mexican economy. Only a few cantinas, those with more cachet, sustained themselves as they were conceived. At present, for those who represent reality as a state of order and cleanliness, the greater part of cantinas are informal places, run-down, a little decadent, and even dirty, but for the assiduous clients, they are one of the few places where they can enjoy good moments.

The opening of cantinas in Mexico gave the population a way and style of drinking that had consolidated some time ago in Spain: to imbibe an age-old drink, wine in different forms, accompanied by snacks. However, wine was and still is practically unknown among most of the Mexican population, so that in Mexico the cantina had to adapt to local tastes, to cane alcohols, beer, tequila, spicy snacks, and later, grape spirits of mediocre quality. Likewise, the cantina adjusted to the Mexicans' style of drinking, with its endemic and excessive alcohol consumption and public drunkenness.

The Drinkers

The conviviality experienced in cantinas is very interesting and attractive, as anyone who has been in a good Spanish tavern can verify: one or two drinks accompanied by snacks clearly foster social relations. Moderate drinking encourages good conversations and identifies and brings people together, but only personal balance and education, the type of family and social education that corresponds to a drinking style imposed by society itself, permit temperate drinking.

In some European societies, such as that of Spain, for example, collective procedures have been established for controlling antisocial behaviours that arise when overindulging. These rules, unwritten, but more or less observed by all, would explain the limited tendency in Spain for violence and disturbances. Obviously, this does not imply that there is no-one in this country who drinks to excess, nor that there is a certain structural alcoholism in Spanish society, but it is uncommon to find drinkers who cause disturbances and, above all, become violent.

On the contrary, Mexico has no social control procedures for drunkenness, disturbances, or violence. Of a withdrawn and suspicious character (which could be explained by delving into history), the Mexican begins to drink in a discreet and circumspect manner, but once alcohol has performed its uninhibiting effect, he will throw himself into chatting, partying, euphoria, and complete drunkenness. If these circumstances do not lead to disturbances or violence, the Mexican returns to his doubting state, sinking into deep and solitary introspection, with the bonus of a terrible hangover as a result of his excess.

Further, although it is true that in Mexico there are temperate drinkers, or those who control their confirmed alcoholism, the Mexicans' way of drinking is generally cyclical. Every weekend, as a release from workdays that are alienating and full of tensions, a large number of Mexicans devote themselves to drinking, many of them to excess. The party begins with the famous 'social Friday' (if not Friday, it is Saturday, depending on when the working week ends), when the first drinks of non-workdays are consumed, and so it continues with greater or lesser excess until Sunday or Monday, which is a social institution in Mexico: the renowned 'San Lunes' (Corcuera 1990: 66), a day of repose that a large number of workers use to rest and alleviate the hangover from the weekend.

During these cycles, countless persons participate in true collective drunken binges; many of them lead to violence, and others end in tragedy. A glance at the newspapers suffices to realise how alcohol is consumed with little temperance in Mexico. Take these crime-page headlines: 'In drunkards' quarrel, construction worker beaten to death' (El Informador 05/06/1996); 'One dead and four wounded in highway crash. Empty beer cans found in auto' (El Informador 05/09/1996); 'Labourer found stabbed to death in a well; body identified by his son who said he was an alcoholic' (El Informador 05/13/1996); 'One dead and two wounded in drunk driving accident' (El Informador 05/19/1996); 'Murderer sentenced to fourteen years in prison. In the heat of drinks, he argued, took out a pistol and killed the person who tried to intervene and the victim's daughter was wounded' (El Informador 05/20/1996).

These news items give a good idea of the social violence linked to alcohol. However, this panorama does not take into account the family and social violence that is known to exist and is considerable, even if no inkling of it reaches the police's jurisdiction or the newspapers. Although in appearance the percentage of crimes related to alcohol on the crime page is not high, in the context of robberies, traffic accidents, or injuries due to various causes, the quantity of events is really significant. At present, however, the number of cases of violence related to drug consumption is outstripping those caused by alcohol consumption (El Occidental 05/1998-09/1998).

Beyond the weekly cycle of alcoholic consumption in Mexico, whose peaks are outlined in the newspaper crime pages, there is the group of veteran alcoholics who go to bars, breweries, cantinas, or who drink in their homes and even in the street, where drinks of terrible quality are consumed – many of them adulterated, even 96 percent alcohol mixed with flavoured soft drinks. Those who usually consume these drinks, take drugs, some of them strong.

The greater part of everyday drinkers who go to cantinas, that is the group with which we could talk the most, does not recognise its addiction to alcohol. Save some exceptions, the majority of them consider that they do not depend on alcoholic drinks, and they argue that they could give them up whenever they want. In fact, it was quite difficult to talk to drinkers about this topic, which is a taboo. Of course, it is easier to ignore it than to recognise it. One of them, however, talked without reticence about his fondness for alcohol:

– How many cantinas are you familiar with?
– Eighteen or twenty.
– Which do you like most?
– I like cabarets the best.

– Do you suffer when you drink?

– No! I enjoy.

– Are there people who suffer when they drink?

– Yes, but the majority don't drink to suffer, but to enjoy.

– Suffering is the hangover?

– Yes, but it is physical, not moral suffering. One knows who has a problem when he drinks, because it suddenly comes out.

– And alcohol helps to bring it out …

– Of course! It brings out suffering.

– But with so many problems people have, you have to be drinking all the time to 'bring out' the problems …

– That's how life is! Look: once I drank alcohol and took pills (barbiturates), and I was happy for two days.

– But, afterwards, how did you feel?

– A little bushed, but nothing happened.

– How do you cure a hangover?

– With some pancakes and lots of syrup or jelly.

Various lines of reflection can be taken from this conversation, but this will be material for another text.

Waiters and cantina owners have another vision of their clients' drinking. In principle they recognise that the majority of people who go to cantinas do have a certain dependence on alcohol, but it is different for each person. That is, there are those who need to consume alcohol daily; others consume it with regularity, according to the cycles of group sociability, and they do not show an insurmountable dependence; and there are those who only do it sporadically. The waiters of cantinas and the proprietors establish a typology of drinkers, who they identify by their manner of drinking, their dress, and their behaviour.

Drinking Mexico

When they begin to drink, from the first sips, those who drink begin to enjoy. Of course, it is necessary that the palate be trained and accustomed to the rather acrid taste of intoxicating drinks. Beyond the second drink, and depending on the type of drink that is consumed and the custom acquired, the drinker passes to a state of excitation or ecstasy that lasts a certain time and whose outcome, in fact, can only take two paths: the return to sobriety or unconsciousness and potential madness, although these are only temporary.

In both cases, there are physical ravages, some are perceptible, but most of them are not; some are temporary, others leave after-effects. Both bartenders and some self-critical drinkers agree that the joy in the act of drinking ends when physical after-effects appear, that is, a hangover. Practically no-one refers to, or is aware of, the long-range effects left by daily and/or excessive drinking, and there is even less awareness of possible afflictions of a moral order.

Recently, the Ministry of Health in Mexico published a report through which it informed the public that the level of alcoholic consumption in the country was not high, but rather low. The document's arguments revolve around some data that shows, according to its authors, that 80 percent of men in Mexico drink some type of alcohol, while only 45 percent of the women do so. Further, consumption per capita of absolute alcohol in the country is six litres annually, without mentioning the type of alcohol, although I imagine this total includes beer. Also, it says that the greatest alcoholic consumption takes place in homes. However, the most remarkable thing about this document is that 10 percent of males drink 50 percent of all alcoholic drinks consumed in Mexico (Publico 05/16/1998). That is, if we estimate that Mexico's population is currently ninety-five million people and that consumption per capita is six litres, it turns out that 9.5 million people each consume annually 30 litres of drinks containing at least 40 percent of alcohol.

Now then, independently of whether this data strictly corresponds to reality (since official statistics in Mexico are not completely reliable) the fact that a significant number of Mexican men consume, each of them, thirty litres of drinks that contain alcohol annually is not a flattering statistic, the less so since it deals with the economically active population. This without considering the other population sectors who are barely dealt with in the study and who, in some way, are affected by consumption, such as women drinkers who every day become more numerous. Nor do these figures take into account the drinkers of 'alcoholic drinks' produced by the extensive and efficient network of bootleggers which, according to the Mexican Chamber of the Alcoholic Drink Industry (a distillers' association), is beginning to match its members' production, that is, some 180 million litres annually.

This leaves the impression that Mexico's health authorities do not recognise as a public health problem the significant alcoholism that their own figures reflect. Facing this attitude, the question that remains is: what figures are necessary to consider alcoholic consumption a public-health problem?

Beyond the data from official – always debatable – statistics, the question of alcoholism in Mexico would have to be examined through another conceptual recourse, a cultural ethos. Through this, it is possible to come up with some explanations about the behaviour and lifestyles of members of a society, of a nation. Although it is not always tangible and often ungraspable, cultural character makes more sense than cold numbers, above all when something as complex and intimate as the people's 'soul' is explained.

Almost fifty years ago, Octavio Paz, the noted poet and intellectual, achieved 'taking an X-ray' of the Mexican soul. This X-ray is still valid and constitutes a reference *de rigueur* to explain many phases of the Mexican's social and cultural character. In his noteworthy essay, suggestively and provocatively entitled 'The Labyrinth of Solitude', Paz (1993) digs for explanations in the remote past about the Mexican's character.

He begins with the supposition that Mexicans are a people hurt by the conquest, a fact which implies – idyllically – that, before the conquest, Mexico's ancient society was better. The Mexicans are, then, according to this author's idea, bastards, because when conquered by their symbolic father, they did not find affection and support, but disdain and rudeness. Their only source of relief and protection was a resigned indigenous mother, whose essential object in life, after the conquest, was to preserve the race. Thus, Mexicans resulted as incomplete beings, unbalanced and hesitant, whose best and only refuge was solitude, the solitude of their social being.

But solitude is a heavy burden, so that from time to time it should be abandoned to achieve a little relief, although only momentarily. Thus, when the solitary Mexican – who deep down loves parties – has the opportunity to organise and participate in them, he does it in an effusive and crazy manner: 'Thanks to parties, the Mexican opens up, participates, communes with his fellow beings and with the values that give meaning to his existence ... Parties liberate us, however fleetingly, from these impulses to escape and from all these inflammable materials stored in our interior' (Paz 1993: 51).

To escape their solitude and sadness, Mexicans not only use the party, but also the vehicle of alcohol, that allows them to be – in a growing scale that, fortunately, does not always reach its extreme consequences – friendly, agreeable, talkative, funny, loquacious, aggressive, and sometimes extremely violent. This would explain why party nights can also be nights of mourning, due to the fact that in the paroxysm of releasing solitude, mixed with alcohol, they can easily meet death.

Indeed, one of the attitudes of Mexicans that foreigners note is their stance towards parties and their rough relationship with alcohol. One of these foreigners, an acute observer in possession of a brilliant mind, visiting Mexico in the first years of the nineteenth century, left numerous examples of these talkative and volatile parties in her correspondence, and the torpid relationship of Mexicans with intoxicating drinks. The illustrious visitor tells that on numerous occasions she observed how happy parties, with music and dancing, and an excess of chinguirito, became quarrels, some extremely violent. She also noted how different women, under the effects of alcohol, maintained relationships with men, between permissive and surly, whom today we would call sadomasochists, and some of them, in fits of drunken jealousy and madness, murdered their mates, ending up in asylums (Erskine 1959: 89, 335, 353). Fortunately, not all the Mexicans' parties and drunkenness end in violence and death, or they would exterminate themselves, but the foregoing delineates an image of a complex social and individual relationship with alcohol.

Before crossing the threshold of violence and death, extremes of this sort of centrifugal – and therefore antisocial – force that is excessive drinking, there are prior levels of transgression for Mexicans: the insult (to another person) and the very act of drinking without moderation, considered morally unacceptable and, in more than one case, sinful.

When the party or drunken binge that the Mexican has enjoyed ends, there appears, along with the physical discomfort of the hangover, suffering provoked by violations that infringed on an unwritten but implacable code of ethics: joy becomes suffering, above all moral suffering, that generally is the most lacerating. The Mexican then returns to his solitude, to his doubtful retreat, to his metaphorical insularity, from which (especially if he is obsessive) he will part a moment to drink again and forget the ignominious reality that has transformed into a vicious cycle.

To Conclude

Thanks to their spontaneous development, fermented drinks were known practically from the time of the agricultural revolution in all the corners of the planet. It was distillation, however, well adopted by the European peoples, which revolutionised the consumption of alcohol in the Occident and in the world in general. While the fermentation scarcely reached an average 10 percent alcoholic content, with distillation more than 50 percent was obtained. This allowed ordinary people to maintain a certain state of well-being, since the stimulus of consuming alcoholic drinks, above all distilled, provides certain energy if it is consumed every day, and even makes it possible to fool the stomach when there is not enough to eat. Further, distillation of drinks in Europe, added to the fermentation of liquids, already known, gave states an important and inexhaustible source of revenue. However, the increase in alcoholic drinks, above all those that are distilled, and their limited control, brought the terrible plague of alcoholism to the West.

The high consumption of alcoholic drinks and alcoholism itself is a typical phenomenon of modern times, of the expansion of the West, although their concrete expressions are typical of each country and place. In Mexico, specifically, the paths of high consumption of alcoholic beverages and of alcoholism can be traced, from its strict regulation and control in pre-Columbian Mexico up to the present. For practical and immediate effects, it must be pointed out that the consumption of alcohol – and of drugs, which is not necessarily a horse of another colour – has frankly increased. The devastating effects can be easily observed.

Why do people drink? Why in particular do Mexicans drink? It must be said, in the first place, that there is a social context that encourages it. As in many other countries, young people in Mexico begin to drink mainly in imitation and due to the stimuli displayed in the media. Also, social controls in relation to alcoholic consumption are very lax, and there is a context of corruption that makes it possible to infringe without much difficulty the elemental controls established.

Furthermore, the threshold for drinking with temperance and pleasure is constantly transgressed by drinking in excess and suffering the consequences, to the degree that there are no effective social mechanisms to control the excessive consumption of alcoholic drinks and, above all, their violent and destructive tendencies.

Inveterate and radical drinkers have multiple explanations and justifications about their way of drinking. However, one of them, strangely lucid, when explaining why he drank so much – realising his own affliction – responded: 'We, the fucked over (poor) drink because the rich fuck us over (exploit us).' Then he was asked why the rich drink, to which he replied: 'Because they are also fucked. This stinking world doesn't work.'

This drinker's reflections explain, in some way, why the problem of drinking is so acute in Mexico and the Occident in general, and why it does not stop, but keeps rising. On the one hand, there is immoderate social exploitation and excessive and grotesque inequality. On the other hand, and this is the most serious aspect, drinking, taking drugs, or alienating oneself in any way, is perhaps the least violent method of surviving in a society plunged in a sickness of paradigms, in a deep crisis of its own logos which poorly supports the whole of the social structure.

Thus, to achieve moderate consumption of alcoholic drinks in Mexico and in other regions, is perhaps a circumstance more related to a deep and global social change than with the proselytizing intentions of the 'clean consciences', who have never stopped pointing out the way to hell, although they have not realised that we perhaps live in it.[3]

Notes

1. The forerunner of the cantina and its closest model is the Spanish tavern.
2. More than thirty 'open' interviews with different drinkers conducted in twelve cantinas in Guadalajara, Mexico.
3. This essay is part of a broader investigation about cantinas in Guadalajara, Mexico. I thank Maria Teresa Ruiz and Cristina Ramirez for obtaining some of the data presented here.

References

Braudel, F. (1994) *Bebidas y excitantes*. Alianza Editorial, Madrid.

Corcuera de M., S. (1990) *Entre gula y templanza*. Fondo de Cultura Economica (FCE), Mèxico.

Chadourne, M. (1989) Anahuac o el indio sin plumas. In, J. lturriaga de la Fuente (comp.) *Anecdotario de viajeros en Mèxico – siglos XVI–XX*. Fondo de Cultura Economica (FCE), t. II, Mèxico.

Davies, N. (1988) *Los antiguos reinos de Mèxico*. Fondo de Cultura Economica (FCE), Mèxico.

Eisenstein, Sergei, M. (1989) Memorias inmorales. Autobiografla. In, J. lturriaga de la Fuente (comp.) *Anecdotario de viajeros en Mèxico – siglos XVI–XX*. Fondo de Cultura Economica (FCE), t. II, Mèxico.

El Informador, perïodico de la ciudad de Guadalajara.

El Occidental, periodico de la ciudad de Guadalajara.

Enciclopedia de Mèxico (1993) Mèxico, Edicion de la Encyclopaedia Britannica.

Erskine, Frances, I., Marquesa Calderon de la Barca (1959) *La vida en Mèxico durante una residencia de dos anos en ese paìs*. Editorial Porrua, Mèxico.

Fuentes, C. (1992) *El espejo enterrado*. Fondo de Cultura Economica (FCE), Mèxico.

Ginzburg, C. (1991) *El queso y los gusanos.* Muchnik Editores, Barcelona.

Novo, S. ([1967] 1997) *Cocina mexicana o historia gastronomica de la ciudad de Mèxico.* Editorial Porrua, Mèxico.

Paz, O. ([1950] 1993) *El laberinto de la soledad.* Fondo de Cultura Economica (FCE), Mèxico.

Publico, periodico de la ciudad de Guadalajara.

Vallée, B.L. (1998) Alcohol in Western World. *Scientific American,* June: 62–67.

15. TAMADOBA
DRINKING SOCIAL COHESION AT THE GEORGIAN TABLE

Mary Ellen Chatwin

Occasions to drink wine and stronger alcohol are both frequent and ceremonial in Georgia, and their distinctiveness lies in drinking behaviour with its close intermingling of social, ritual, sacred and recreational meanings. Preeminent at these moments is the *tamada* and his (the great majority are men, reasons for which we examine) role in controlling the direction these occasions will take. The term *tamadoba* designates that role, or the institutional fulfillment of heading the table and controlling all drinking through a long series of *sadhregrdzelo* (a short speech with a drink which can be seen as situated somewhere between a toast and a blessing) during significant food moments. Usually events are those of the *supra* (literally tablecloth) which signifies a special food occasion, solemn or festive. The term supra is derived from the Arabic *sufratun,* the cloth spread on the floor for eating. The meaning has been enlarged in Georgia to include the formal and festive meals themselves. In most regions of the Caucasus hospitality and feasting have gone hand in hand for many centuries. In Georgia, traditions linked to the supra or festive food occasion have gained a reputation for opulence, extravagance and ostentatious behaviour. It should be noted, however, that uncontrolled drunkenness is extremely rare. We will look at the reasons for this control, as well as deeper meanings which are being conveyed at the supra.

It is not within the scope of this paper to discuss various notions of hospitality – yet we should bear in mind anthropological approaches to the study of hospitality, and especially within Mediterranean society, such as notions of 'honour-and-shame', and – perhaps a more salient notion – that of 'englobing'. Englobing is a term originally coined by E. Ardener (1975: 25) designating the process or condition of dominance whereby 'one structure blocks the power of actualisation of the other'. In the case of Georgian hospitality, especially when food and drink are material representations of exchange, the strict coding is so absolute as to prevent social expression of another kind, or even the introduction of another mood at the table. This is a first indication of the control of consumption, but simultaneously and more importantly, we can see how identity is forged and transmitted within the group.

In the context of meals and occasions where observable displays of hospitality call for subsequent recognition and acknowledgement of the host family's honour, then 'letting oneself be englobed' (in Ardener's sense of the term) is as important as 'positioning' oneself to play host. 'Playing hosted' and paying tribute to the host family's honour, are the basis of strict table rules, especially the structured drinking process. This system, or tamadoba at the supra, is recognised in all the Caucasus, and specific expressions can be seen in neighbouring countries; yet Georgians have a particular reputation in the Caucasus and the former Soviet Union as well, for the distinctiveness of their conviviality at table. Within Georgia itself the tamadoba process has regional variations that are familiar to most Georgians. We cannot go into the details of these variations here, but I will mention the types of differences in my description of a typical supra.

For the outsider, for example European travellers for whom the meanings are hidden, I often observed confusion and even attempted refusal to enter into the system. The following example illustrates the quandary for the outsider. Odette Keun (1924), a traveller through the Caucasus early in the twentieth century, wrote:

> My disgusted orderly officer presented me as a European without endurance and without manners. Social conventions are a perfect tyranny among the Georgians … Again and again I have arrived half dead at a village, tortured by a bad saddle … asking only to be allowed to eat a bite of bread and drink some tea, so that I might wash and lie down immediately, and I have been made to wait … for hours … while they prepared a feast. I laugh now when I recall all the tears of exasperation that these attentions cost me, but at the time I did not feel at all hilarious. When I had dismounted, it is true they would offer me maize cakes and tea; but when I spoke of going to bed, I would learn, to my unspeakable horror, that they had gone to kill a sheep.

Today as well, in Tbilisi, it is common that a supra brings foreigners and Georgians into the context of what – to the outsider – looks at first like a long drinking spree at a heavily laden table, with many consecutive toasts. It is a common complaint of businessmen or officials who have come to Georgia to 'get a job done' in a short time, that they spend most of their time at the table, and that meetings are terminated early so that a supra can begin. Foreigners who remain in Georgia for longer than a few days or weeks, however, begin to perceive that something else is happening.

Very intricate social processes are woven into the evident, sometimes even boisterous, declarations and observations voiced by the participants at the event. Under the leadership of the 'toast-master' or tamada, guests at the table become cohesively linked into a process of identification – of their ancestors, their families, their friends and those present.

This process has also been studied by economists Mars and Altmann (1983), who showed how economic and financial ties are subtly created and reinforced through the process of conviviality during the supra. Whatever the phenomena that take place, the procedure is carefully and skillfully managed by the toast-master and adhered to by all at the table. It allows for the re-identification of self and close others, as well as a reconfirmation of worldviews of the group.

Aspects of tamadoba which have been most studied are the ritual and social, while there is still room for research to examine links between the sacred and the profane in this context. Abundance, aesthetics, complexity and difficulty of preparation enter into the definition of the prestige linked to hospitality, manifest at such food events. Drink is the most important mediator of food's prestige. Wine – many times produced by the host family – imposes a sense of temporality, both during the meal and over the seasons, closely linked to the vineyard in many rural areas of Georgia. Such occasions help to readjust the space and distance between members of the family when one member has disappeared, or when another joins the group. They project the participants' hopes and attention towards the future, while underlining what has been acquired – sometimes attained through personal sacrifice, sometimes through time, or through force.

Drink at the Georgian table is heavy with meaning and is not taken lightly by those who participate in the repasts it structures. Food, though usually abundant, aesthetically prepared and varied, often takes second place to drink. Symbolically we can say that regional family identity as well as hospitality is represented by food, while values and personal identity – including honour – by drink.

During the Soviet period, such occasions were what the anthropologist Thorstein Veblen (1899), a century ago, called 'conspicuous consumption', as food under the socialist regime was plentiful and very cheap, and infrastructures to organise ever-larger feasts were accessible even to the working classes. During that period, however, exaggerated expressions of the supra were forbidden by the authorities. Mars and Altman (1991: 276) studied the phenomenon during the 1970s and stated that:

It is understanding this role of the feast and the latency inherent in the links it encourages, that we can appreciate why the feast is so important in Soviet Georgia and perhaps too why it should be officially discouraged by the Soviet authorities. This is because it is in the manipulation of such ego-focused networks that Georgians can and do influence and manipulate the organisations of the State.

Ostensibly proscribed for economic and political reasons, such feasts created in fact still another point of social resistance, as large repasts with wasteful consumption not only reeked of capitalism, but provided a constant reminder of who owed social debts to whom, links which were to prove stronger within a second, shadow, economy than the Soviet State itself.

Such socio-economic aspects of the supra are indeed essential for understanding the importance of the tamada's role, which is closely linked with his personality. Usually someone from the host family, with a certain gift for speaking, this head of a family – still considered first masculine in Georgia – must provide the guests with group identity. He should possess psychological characteristics that create empathy between him and each guest, and must know how to exclude all forms of animosity and quarrelling at table. It is unusual indeed at the Georgian table to hear any unpleasant statement. (We can perhaps include this feature in the process of controlled drinking from a psychophysical point of view, as alcohol intake from such occasions rarely – if ever – results in conflictual interaction, even after hours of drinking.)

Without going into more detail about the traits of a good tamada, it appears that inherent personality traits, refined and encouraged within the family context, contribute to making a boy become a successful tamada as an adult. We can also mention that skills are acquired through experience, through imitation and within a specific social context, through many years and situations. This balance of personal traits and experience make an effective tamada who can create innovations at each feast, upon a background of a deeper theme, which all those present have already heard many times, at many other occasions, and voiced by other tamadas.

One man who is often asked to be tamada told me he felt he was a jazz-player, innovating on an on-going theme that everyone knows.

It is up to the tamada to 'open' the feast with a first raised glass, joined by all at the table, and to continue this process with successive statements at frequent intervals during the whole meal. An average supra lasts several hours, and wine consumption varies from 2–6 litres of wine per person during that time. There is no drinking of wine unless the tamada calls for a *sadhregrdzelo* (though non-alcoholic beverages are also on the table for drinking anytime during the meal). Here again, we discern a means to control of alcohol consumption, as a good tamada keeps his eye on each person's mood and behaviour, and takes into account quantities consumed and mood within the tamadoba process.

We must differentiate between this and the idea of 'toasting' in the Anglo-Saxon or European mode. The anglophone meaning of 'toast' is very unsatisfactory for the present context, as European and American drinking frameworks are very different from the Georgian one. In this presentation, the word 'toast' will signify the Georgian 'sadhregrdzelo' which is a phrase spoken as a glass of wine is raised and then drunk. However the resemblance of the Georgian type of toast is strikingly like a 'blessing' *(dalotsva)*, and sacredness is an important part of the underlying meanings at a supra. However jovial and light the mood may be, there is a strict underlying understanding that the drink – especially wine – is sacred. If it is spilled there are specific words that are uttered, and it is praised as an entity. In Edward Shevardnadze's book 'The Future Belongs to Freedom' (Shevardnadze, 1991: 3–4) he stated that Georgian society is 'dominated by the vineyard, to which much of Georgian culture can be traced … the Georgian's feeling (is) that his vineyard is like his own child ... From childhood I had been taught to respect the vineyard'. If a glass is knocked over accidentally, a special toast is said for the dead. If this happened to have been the last toast, another will be offered, as toasts to the dead cannot close a feast.

While the anglophone toast conjures up individual brilliance of speech, and especially that of personally produced ideas which lead the process of the repast's mood in as many different directions as there are 'salutes' and 'social debts' to pay at the table, the Georgian toasting system is a ritual process, familiar to all participants, and one which will not deviate according to personal whim. Though individual variations may intervene in the recognition of context and participants, changing the process is impossible.

Sadhregrdzelo includes the idea of 'salute' in the anglophone sense of the term 'toast', yet honouring and paying tribute to a person present is but a small part of the salutation. Celebrating ideals, pledging love and fidelity to family – living and dead – to country and to social ties are essential components of the 'blessing' of the wine by the tamada, and subsequently by the others present. The participants around a table consume the wine after each toast only in the right order, and from left to right, acknowledging and underlining the principal utterance of the tamada, then drinking themselves. At times it is essential to empty the glass to emphasise the seriousness of one's words. One does not propose a toast if one is not tamada (except under certain conditions and with permission of the tamada). One does not change the theme of the toast proposed (an important difference from anglophone toasting behaviour), and one does not drink wine without the tamada's sadhregrdzelo uttered first.

The number of toasts at a supra ranges from five to twenty and more. For an evening repast of from three to five hours, the festivities can mean individual consumption of from one-half to at least two litres of wine for a woman and from two to six litres per man.

The process which I describe below proceeds through the most structured social identity (for example with those who are dead, one's parents or other) to the least structured. I believe it is pertinent to remember theories of status, such as Ralph Linton's published in 1936, which describes 'achieved' and 'ascribed' types of status and identity. Ascribed status is that which is inherited, in a certain sense, or relatively 'inescapable' in the given society, such as sex, age, race, and ethnicity. It is crucial to defining the basic patterns of one's life. Achieved, or acquired, status, in contrast, is due to personal effort, to chance, or to educational and occupational attainment.

In Georgia, as in many traditional societies, status is a position in a social structure and involves rights, duties and reciprocal expectations of behaviour, none of which depends on the personal characteristics of the individual. Yet in Georgia too, as a modern society, status involves the personal gestures and decisions, achievements and attainments that only the individual can bring about. Within the tamadoba process, drinking at the supra, the toasts begin with ascribed and continue with achieved status themes. An essential point of this presentation is that the Georgian supra illustrates and perpetuates strong traditional status and identity through its show of respect and enforcement of ascribed status, while it integrates social transformation and new cultural aspects through recognition of achieved status. I believe this has been one of the secrets of Georgia's particular style of adaptation to the sometimes-violent social transformation after the breakdown of the former system and a key to its success for future means of addressing social change.

We will illustrate this process by the following example taken from a supra situation in Georgia during my fieldwork. This *keipi* (a word derived from an ancient Persian word for joy), or festive meal, celebrated the occasion of a friend's birthday in 1995. The word *Gaumardjos* means, literally, 'Victory' in Georgian.

Ascribed Status

1. *'Gaumardjos,*[1] *chvens tamadas!'* – Gaumardjos for our tamada!
   To the newly announced tamada. If the master of the house has asked someone else to accept the role of tamada, he will make this first toast himself, to thank the tamada for accepting. When someone other than the family head has been invited to act as tamada, this is an exception to the usual toasts in the first series which concern an acquired status.

2. *'Iubilars gaumardjos!'* – Gaumardjos to the person whose celebration it is!
   To the person for whom the keipi is organised, for example in the case of a birthday. This toast is omitted if there is a collective instead of an individual reason for the keipi.

3A. *'Odjakhs gaumardjos!'* – Gaumardjos to the family (in whose home we are)!
   To the immediate family of the person for whom the keipi is organised, or the family in whose home the keipi is taking place. This toast may alternatively include 'the head of the household and his (…) spouse'. It may also be to the parents of the person for whom the keipi is organised, and through them to parents in general, so that those present also feel the need to recognise their own parents through the parents of the other.

3B. *'Salotsalevs da odjakhis upros gaumardjos!'* – Gaumardjos to the sacred family site and to the family elders!
   This toast, proffered by mountain dwellers and all those who consider their origins to be a specific mountain area, salutes the origins of the family *(odjakhi)*, the sacred 'salotsavi' site, where the family saint is buried or where the saint's relics are found; the term *uprosi*, or elder, carries the signification of 'authority', 'superior' in other contexts, thus the table's structure builds upon the absolute unchallengeable authority of the past. For mountain dwellers and their relatives on the plains, countless toasts for hundreds of years for the same ancestors provide a solid certainty of social belonging. City dwellers with roots in the urban tradition were never observed making this toast.

If elderly persons are present, they are then toasted. As 'transition' into another generation, a toast is then proposed to the adult generation as per their relationship to the elders:

4. *'Dedmamisshvilebs gaumardjos!'* – Gaumardjos to mother and father's children (brothers and sisters). Literally, 'mother's-father's children, victory!', one's brothers and sisters are toasted through their relationship to common parents.

The elderly may have been toasted already, and the family's ancestors, living or dead are saluted:

5. *'Odjakhis tsinaprebs gaumardjos!'* – Gaumardjos to the family's ancestors
6. *'Khsovna gardatsvlilebis!'* – Gaumardjos to those who have died (whom we knew). 'In memory of the deceased'.

For those who have passed on, perhaps with the names of recently deceased evoked by the tamada, each person remembering loved ones by pouring wine onto (or dipping) bread. Especially emotional remembrances are uttered concerning those who have died early or before members of the family of the preceding generation. The bread is eaten or not, according to personal habit. One informant said she leaves this bread on the table. According to informants who live in the mountains and from my own observations there, wine is poured on the ground upon this toast; these informants stated that because of a lack of 'ground' in urban areas, pouring wine onto bread instead has become a symbolic substitute for this salute to the deceased. Urban Christian believers argue, however, that it is the combination of the body and blood of Christ. The borders of urban and rural belief systems are thus drawn through a common cultural practice. Often, certain participants in this ritual feel they are directly sharing wine with the person, and bread is the material form of the deceased person.

Most important, as wine is poured from each glass onto bread, the deceased participate in the keipi. Often this toast is celebrated with men standing (women always remain seated during Georgian toasts).[3]

7. *'Gaumardjos patarebs!'* – 'Small ones, victory!'

To the children; a sense of renewal is now toasted, and the youngest of all present, the *tamadobit*[4] is especially honoured by these words, brought to the attention of all participants. Through children, hope for the future is toasted and mentioned in the words of each respondent.

8. *'Samshoblos gaumardjos!'* – ' To the parentland'.[5]

Though some observers have seen this toast as the first one marking a passage into less specific and more general considerations ('After this point, the tamada begins to propose general toasts' Holisky, 1985: 16), it still smoothly follows the process of identity. One guest responded to this toast, 'Armenians have a saying that the most beautiful country in the world is the one in which you belong'. If foreign guests are present, the toast may begin with special welcoming words to them, as representatives of their country, then come around to saluting Georgia, and all places where one has a feeling of belonging. This could include Georgians from other regions. Social 'belonging' is primordial for this toast, and if the guest is American, for example, she or he will be toasted as belonging to that country, with *'amerikas gaumardjos!'* This is often in the urban, cosmopolitan context, however. In rural areas, a more simple social 'belonging' to one's own territory is considered enough for Georgians present.

9. *'Chvens kalebs gaumardjos!'* or *'kartvel dedas gaumardjos!'* – 'Victory to our women!' or 'Georgian mothers, victory!'
   To women and the specific roles they embody (women come from the kitchen if they are not seated, to drink and acknowledge this toast).[6]
   The role of mother is especially honoured during this toast, and the tamada tries to point out how many children each woman present has. If she has none, she will not only wish she had, but she will be wished by others to have many in the future.

Acquired (Achieved) Status Toasts

After the above toasts denoting ascribed social and cultural 'belonging', follow 'circumstantial' toasts which englobe through another mechanism than automatic or ascribed status, that of more or less voluntary identity, or acquired status, often in networks which the participants have consciously created.

During interviews, informants who explained the 'déroulement' of the toasting process could remember clearly the general order of the first part, but no longer seemed to remember which toasts should be proffered after those, even though a keipi is at best only halfway finished at this point. Drinking is, of course, still dictated by the tamada, but gradually related to more contingent ideals and/or issues, for example:

10. *'Damtsuravs gaumardjos!'* – Gaumardjos to 'the one who made (pressed) this wine!'
11. *'Chvens shvilis gaumardjos!'* – Gaumardjos to 'our son', meaning a local hero.
    To 'our son', who may be anyone from Joseph Stalin in the Gori region, to Beria or Shevardnadze in Guria, and Zviad Gamsakurdia in Mingrelia. We witnessed this toast in the Caspi region to the Kartlian King Vakhtang Gorgasali, and to a priest from the nearby Ertadsminda who was said to have led invaders in the wrong direction to save the village, and was martyred himself. Queen Tamara is often the object of this toast in mountain regions.
    A primordial aspect of Georgian acquired identity manifest through the drinking process is that of honouring regional heroes. At this point there will certainly be an expression of admiration or regret for local and

regional heroes, often with song or poetry recited emotionally. The men frequently stand. This toast was especially common in villages or at repasts in urban areas where a large part of the participants were from one region.

12. *'Megobrebs gaumardjos!'* – Gaumardjos to friends.
To friends, victory! Many services and favours have been performed by the participants for others at the table, or not present. This toast idealises friendship as an almost-ascribed notion, pointing out that some friends are more like brothers, fathers, mothers, etc. Mars and Altman (1991: 277) mention 'ego-focused networks' which are strengthened by the keipi feast: 'participants in the feast become concrete representatives, – "embodiments" – of more abstract entities...they become archetypes of their wider affiliations'. From the authors' economic point of view these affiliations produce a very tangible economic support system. The obvious englobing aspect of this and future toasts is quite consciously performed by the tamada for psychological reasons as much as, if not more than, material ones.

13–20. *'Rezos gaumardjos!'* – Gaumardjos to Rezo (and to other people in turn).
'Rezo', 'Zura' or 'Levan' will be toasted personally, as the series of toasts to specific participants, if they have not been recognised by other toasts. This is a variation on no. 12. As the above authors mention, each person becomes the embodiment of values, accomplishments and ideals. Very reserved or timid participants who have remained in the shadows are saluted personally, made to feel part of the group, and valued – this is part of the tamada's skill. These personalised toasts intersperse all following ones, so that each participant has been honoured and included.[7]

21. *'Am chers gaumardjos!'*
To the place, in this case 'to the ceiling' of the house where the keipi is taking place. Among my fieldwork situations, for example a keipi by the river, this toast was 'to the river and its goodness'.

22. *'Tamadas gaumardjos!'*
To the tamada (understood, too, is the good execution of his role). This toast is usually omitted if the tamada is the host himself, and terminates the occasion.

In conclusion, I hope that this short overview of an important aspect of Georgian culture has been enough to transmit the essence of the central role of drinking for all the society. The wider implications of these foodways into Georgian life and the professional and economic realm, the religious, gender and family spheres or other socio-cultural domains, are potential areas of further study. Other prospects for research include the control of alcohol consumption and comparative studies in the prevention of alcoholism. Finally, there are interesting studies to be made of interethnic studies and even conflict mediation in the Caucasus region through such processes as the tamadoba.

Notes

1. *Gaumardjos* literally means 'victory' and is used as the toast's pivotal expression. Even if no other words are spoken, 'gaumardjos' is uttered before raising a glass of alcohol or wine to drink. An alternative expression is *itsotskhle*, or 'life to you'.
2. My informants (male and female) could only evoke the reason for a difference in physical position during toasts (men standing, women seated) as 'not wanting to bother the women who may feel tired'. Indeed, if the participants have not been socialised into the rigorous, physically trying, experience of a long keipi through much experience, they may well feel tired. This impression has been evoked even by male foreigners, such as Mars and Altman (1991: 274): 'Such gargantuan reveling can be appreciated as doubly competitive when it is realized that men are not only expected to drink, but are not expected to relieve themselves during the evening and that they are indeed required to stay in the room ...'
3. The tamadobit represents the person favoured or accentuated by the tamada for a certain toast. In this case the youngest child received the accent by the tamada; in another case it could be an adult whose friends are far away, while the toast is to friends in general. The tamada would then accentuate that person as being 'tamadobit' for that toast, as if a special blessing is made for an individual as embodiment of the toast's highest intentions.
4. The 'parentland' in Georgian has no gender-related connotation as do terms in other languages, such as 'fatherland' or 'motherland'.
5. There is no specific toast to men, which marks the specificity of women's roles and personae, which must be englobed by a toast, instead of being considered totally as the englobers themselves. We distinguish the power structure of roles through repasts, by noting that those who literally 'dictate identity' are men, and those who undergo it are women, though they participate in their own englobing.
6. We are reminded here of Y. Preiswerk's description of the convivial meal (1986: 204):

   ... more than that (preventing division and dispersion – author's note) it offers each the occasion to take the same amount of food, and the same time to speak. In principle, one can suppose a sort of equality – quantitative, objective and measurable – of elementary justice. In conferring on each at least a minimal status of equality, the meal reminds us that those who are sitting around the table have an equal right to social esteem.

References

Ardener, E. (1975) The 'Problem' Revisited. In, Shirley Ardener (Ed.) *Defining Females: the nature of women in society.* John Wiley, London (2nd edition, Oxford, 1993): 19–27.

Chatwin, M.E. (1997) *Foodways and Socio-cultural transformation in the Republic of Georgia, 1989–1994.* Metsniereba Press, Tbilisi, Georgia.

Goldstein, D. (1993) *A Georgian Feast.* Harper Collins, New York.

Keun, Odette (1924) In the Land of the Golden Fleece, quoted in Goldstein 1993.

Linton, R. (1936) *The Study of Man.* Appleton-Century Publ., New York, 204 p.

Mars, G. and Altman, Y. (1983) The Cultural Bases of Soviet Georgia's Second Economy, in *Soviet Studies* vol. 35, (October): 546–60.

Preiswerk, Yvonne (1986) Signification et sens du manger: Quelle table pour quels échanges? *Les cahiers médico-sociaux,* Geneva, no.3-4: 203–210.

Shevardnadze, E. (1991) *The Future Belongs to Freedom.* Sinclair-Stevenson Ltd, London.

Veblen, Thorstein (1899) *The Theory of the Leisure Class.* Macmillan, New York.

16. AN ETHNOGRAPHIC ACCOUNT OF THE MANY ROLES OF MILLET BEER IN THE CULTURE OF THE DUUPA AGRICULTURALISTS, (POLI MOUNTAINS) NORTHERN CAMEROON

Eric Garine

Over the last thirty years a few books, collections and articles have shown what a promising subject drinking could be for study in the field of social sciences (Mandelbaum 1965; Everett et al. 1976; Heath, 1987; I. de Garine, this volume). It is clear today that drinking is a multi-dimensional phenomenon which Marcel Mauss might have well have called a *phénomène social total*. Depending on the various cultures in which it has been investigated, and on the interests of fieldworkers and scholars, different aspects have been studied: the physiological aspects related to liquid ingestion or to alcohol consumption; the psychological and behavioural aspects of inebriation; the symbolic meaning of drinks and their role in ritual systems; the economic dimension of the production of beverages and their exchange value; and the role of drinking in the expression of social ties or in the making of them. These topics have been documented in various parts of the world, and there are quite a few references to drinking in the social science literature devoted to Africa (Curto 1989). It seems that ethnologists not only thought that it was a relevant subject to study, but that, at least for a few societies, it might become *the* major topic as drinking appears to be at the core of social life.

Studies of alcohol consumption in African cultures have focused on very different cultural situations, the so-called 'traditional' agrarian communities (such as the one I will describe later on), and colonial and postcolonial, mostly urban, societies. Colson and Scudder (1988) and, more recently, Akyeampong (1996) have described in detail the historical evolution of the ways of drinking in two distant locations (rural Zambia and urban Ghana). It is striking that in such contrasting social and political conditions, the importance of drinking as a major social fact remains central to the understanding of these cultures. These scholars have demonstrated convincingly that there is a strong relationship between drink and power. It seems that whatever the nature of the beverage (traditional beer, distilled alcohol or manufactured liquor) and the political organisation (colonial or ancient states, lineage-based systems or acephalous societies), this relationship could be investigated and serve as a guideline for the social scientist. Drinking is classically viewed as expressing the social system, and in Africa it seems to be creating it.

For the small-scale rural societies described in the ethnographic literature, home-made beverages such as millet beer were seen as a 'locus of value' for the Kofyar of Nigeria (Netting 1964); Ivan Karp (1987) wrote about the 'pervasiveness of beer' in Iteso social life; and Walter Van Beek (1978) entitled his doctoral dissertation about the Kapsiki of Northern Cameroon 'Beer brewers in the mountains'.[1] All these statements could well be applied to the ethnographic example presented in this paper, an ethnic group from Northern Cameroon called the Duupa. Another common feature of these groups is that the basis of their subsistence is farming, and that part of the work devoted to agricultural activities is performed during collective work parties when beverages are distributed to the workers. I shall attempt to explore the link between agricultural work and drinking in the shaping of that society.

The Ethnographic Setting

The Duupa number approximately six to eight thousand people and live in a mountainous area near the small town of Poli. Their neighbouring, and closely related, ethnic group, the Dowayo, are quite famous in the anthropological

Figure 16.1   Seasonal distribution of productive activities

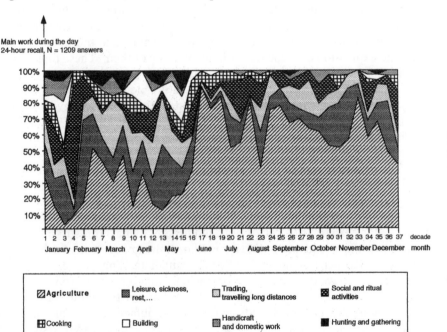

Main work during the day
24-hour recall, N = 1209 answers

100% 90% 80% 70% 60% 50% 40% 30% 20% 10%

1 2 3 4 5 6 7 8 9 10 11 12 13 14 15 16 17 18 19 20 21 22 23 24 25 26 27 28 29 30 31 32 33 34 35 36 37   decade

January February March April May June July August September October November December   month

| ▨ Agriculture | ▨ Leisure, sickness, rest,... | ▨ Trading, travelling long distances | ▨ Social and ritual activities |
| ⊞ Cooking | ☐ Building | ▨ Handicraft and domestic work | ■ Hunting and gathering |

literature since Nigel Barley spent some time with them and wrote accounts of his stays (1983a, b). At the southern fringe of Duupaland, the Dìì group, also closely related to them, have been studied extensively by Jean-Claude Muller (1996, 1999).

An Agrarian Society

The Duupa are an acephalous group with regard to their social, political and religious organisation. Their main feature is that they constitute an agrarian society as farming is, by far, the most commonly performed activity. The agrosystem involves many different species, including various yams *(Dioscorea spp.)*, but the most important plants are cereals: sorghum *(Sorghum bicolor)*, pearl millet *(Pennisetum typhoides)* and finger millet *(Eleusine coracana)*.

Apart from its importance in the material life, agriculture is also the most valued activity from both the symbolic and the social point of view. It could be said that to be a proper Duupa, one needs to be a good cultivator.

Bumma Beer in the Food System

The major role of agricultural products is clearly seen in the food system, where nearly one hundred percent of the food is produced locally by the agri-culturalists themselves. Until recently, salt was the only food purchased from outside the area. It should be mentioned here that wild species of animals or plants are rarely eaten.

The Duupa take few proper meals, which constitute just 26 percent of their intake. According to Koppert et al. (1996: 240) it seems that, over one day, only a third of the people actually eat a structured meal. Hence, snacking is the most frequent way of feeding among the Duupa. Snacks include fruits, tubers and some pulses ... and a large amount of millet beer *(bumma)*, which represents 43 percent of the intake. It is the most frequently consumed food item, and one of the most important as regards both quantity and nutritional value (Matze and Stappers 1989). It is difficult to measure snacking in general, and drinking in particular, but even if the data is not completely accurate, we think the average consumption of beer is close to half a kilogramme per capita per day, thus making millet beer by far the most important item in the Duupa's diet (Koppert et al. 1996: 253).

Apart from millet beer, the Duupa drink water. It has an important sym-bolic value and is used during various rituals, but, as far as I know, water drink-ing is not governed by explicit social rules. Tea and milk are occasionally drunk during social or commercial interactions with Fulani pastoralists, but these beverages are not really enjoyed. The Duupa know the manufactured beer that can be found everywhere in Cameroon since the colonial period, but they cannot afford it on a regular basis and it is not very much appreciated. In all

Figure 16.2 Intake frequency of different foods (24-hour recall year long, N = 819 answers)

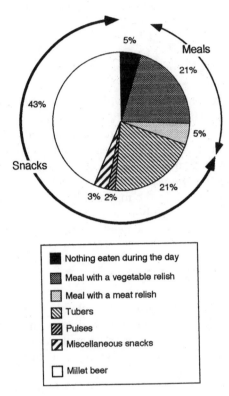

my fieldwork periods[2] I never saw a bottle in the remote villages, nor did I ever see or hear about the distilled alcohol made from sorghum that exists in other areas of Northern Cameroon (I. de Garine, this volume).

Bumma Beer

Apart from being the main food item in their diet, for the Duupa millet beer is also the most important drink. In every compound there is a hut where big jars are half-buried, and this place is devoted to the preparation of bumma beer. This used to be exclusively a man's job but it is no longer the case. However, when women prepare beer, it is for themselves and not for their husbands. Among the Duupa, the preparation of bumma is the main cooking job undertaken by the men.

The bumma is made from cereal flour, which can be sorghum but is more often pearl millet. The beer that is brewed from finger millet is known to be the strongest and it is appreciated during the rainy season when this cereal is

Figure 16.3   The recipe of *bumma* beer.

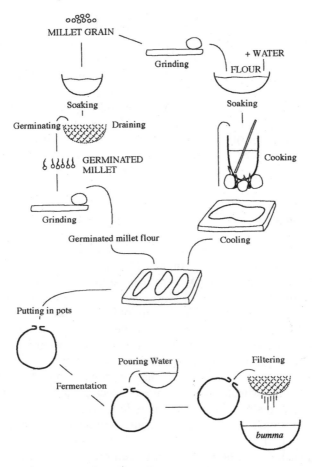

the only one available. The fermentation is initiated with some germinated millet flour that is added to the paste made from the cooked cereal. The fermentation takes from four to fifteen days, normally about seven.

The date of a festival or a work party can be deduced if one knows what operation of the brewing process is currently being done by the organiser. If someone is cooking his bumma, everybody knows the ritual will take place eight days later. The enumeration of the different stages of beer making as a way of computing time is known for other societies of Northern Cameroon (Vincent 1991: 334).

The fermented paste remains in round clay beer pots, which are left in the brewery until the day of consumption, and then brought to the drinking area. There, water is poured into the pots and the mixture is filtered in front of all the consumers just before it is drunk. The beer is then shared in calabashes and distributed to the people. The final beverage is quite thick. It is difficult to assess its alcoholic level because it depends very much on the dilution during the final operation. The few analyses we were able to carry out indicate that it can reach a little more than 4°, (between 4° and 6° according to the laboratory of the Garoua SABC *(Société Anonyme des Bières du Cameroun)*), which is comparable to other traditional beers in Africa (Chevassus-Agnès et al. 1975). As a matter of fact, the ethnographer can confirm that it is quite enough to produce intoxication ...[3]

Drinking is not an epiphenomenon of the nutrition of the Duupa. This is true from the etic and the biological point of view, but it is also the case from the Duupa emic point of view. In the classification of foods, bumma occupies the highest rank of the 'real' foods, alongside the staple millet porridge which is the basis of the main meals (E. Garine 1996).

Drinking Bumma

Who drinks bumma? Everyone except small children; even dogs are fed with the residue. As in other African contexts (Netting 1964; Jolly 1995), moderate inebriation is appreciated, but violent behaviour is avoided and the general atmosphere of drinking episodes is characterised by mutual gentleness between the drinkers. A particular feature of beer drinking among the Duupa is the habit they have of sharing a calabash between two friends, each with an arm around the other's shoulder – the contents are drunk in one gulp.

The most important point is that you never drink alone among the Duupa. It is possible to drink quite often but this does not mean that you can drink at any time, only in particular social contexts. Occasionally you can see a small group of people, mainly close kins or people from a single domestic group or neighbourhood, quietly talking and sharing a couple of calabashes of *bumma* at the end of the day. This would be an informal recreational drinking occasion but, in such cases, the beer has not been brewed specifically for such an event but comes from another source, for example, a ritual festival or a work party.

Bumma Beer on Ritual Occasions

The two main themes of the Duupa's religious life are the ancestors' cult and the initiation of the boys; millet beer is necessary for performing both of these rituals. The role played by drinking in religion is common to many cultures around the world (Fournier and D'Onofrio 1991) and it is no surprise that *bumma* is the sacrificial food *par excellence* offered to the spirits of the dead throughout the year. Spirit ancestors are given sacrifices quite often, at least once a year during the threshing of the crop, but also on various other occasions, notably when someone in the compound feels ill. The diviner will be asked to determine the cause of the illness, and most of the time it is an ancestor craving for *bumma*, just like a living human being. Sacrifices to the spirits are, then, quite common in everyday life but this flux between the living and the dead is not more important than the one between living people. However, regarding the quantity, if you need just a few drops of bumma to content the spirits of a great-grandfather, you will need a lot more to satisfy your brother-in-law or your sister's sons!

Apart from sacrifices and the purely ritual aspects, the big festivals (for celebrating the dead or initiating the boys) are also the occasion for honouring affines, neighbours and allieds by offering food and, especially, large amounts of beer. This social aspect is so important that the Duupa do not have a precise ritual schedule or a calendar. For instance, to organise the boys' initiation ceremony, the people of a village will wait for a year that has yielded a good crop so that they will have enough millet to brew sufficient bumma. This is as important as the ritual dimension because one also gains prestige by organising these feasts and distributing beer as lavishly as possible. In the Duupa ideology, it is doubtful that the symbolic value of bumma is more important than its social one – the reverse could just as well be true.

Feasting with Bumma

Beer drinking itself may be the main reason that takes people to feasts (Eguchi 1975), and, in a way, it could be said that ritual festivals are 'beer festivals'. The offering and the consumption of food and beverages is a matter of prestige and power in most past and present societies (Wiessner and Schiefenhövel 1996), and the role of feasting in the political system can be viewed as a general phenomenon (Hayden 1996). There is another feature which is common to many agrarian civilisations in Africa: the symbolic capital gained through the offering of beer. Among the Mambila of Western Cameroon, beer festivals, organised every year by a different person, could be seen as a competition during which the organiser displays as much beer as possible, gaining prestige and fame by doing so (Rehfisch 1987). For the Koma, a group living close to the Duupa, the life cursus of a man is marked by the different rituals that he must organise, each involving the preparation of large quantities of beer, to gain his rank in the age grade system and acquire prestige and the valued status of elder (I. de Garine 1996).

The Duupa share many cultural and economical traits with the Dìì, their closest neighbours, except for their political system which is organised around the power of a village chief who has important prerogatives in the ritual and the economic life of the community. In the Dìì ideology, clearly expressed in myths and rituals, the chief is viewed as a rich, generous man who, on ritual occasions, offers to his population some of his cattle and the largest amount of millet beer he can manage (Muller 1999).

This codified ritual display among the Dìì, or the prescribed ritual life history of the Koma, does not exist as such in the Duupa culture, even though agonistic dimension is also part of the ideological basis of the Duupa beer 'system'. While the prescription is not fixed so clearly, any Duupa man will have to prepare large amounts of beer on various occasions during his lifetime. This is at least the case when he organises the circumcision of his sons, and even on other occasions, such as funerals, generosity is always appreciated. It is expected from someone who has gained the bigman-like status of some elders. However, this competitive attitude is never seen by the Duupa as the dominant feature of their way of drinking, it is compensated by the reciprocity involved in offering beer.

Drinking Bumma Beer in the Work Parties

The largest amounts of bumma are consumed during rituals but the most frequent occasions for drinking are during the profane, common work parties. Foods, and notably drinks, are a way to recruit labour in a large number of civilisations (Moore 1975; Dietler 1990), including in Africa where various forms of 'work parties' are widely distributed in agrarian and peasant societies (Richards 1939; Watson 1958; Meillasoux 1964; Netting 1968; Pontié 1973; Saul 1983; Kuckertz 1985; Pottier 1985; Colson and Scudder 1988).

Among the Duupa, throughout the year the ethnographer can see a few people, from five to twenty, not necessarily belonging to the same domestic group, performing a task. It is certain that some millet beer will be consumed by these people. The Duupa call such occasions *kôm bumma*, which means literally /work beer/. A person, whom we shall call 'the owner', needs some work to be done for him: house-building, roofing, threshing the cereal crop (an important social occasion), or even hunting or carrying things from one village to another, but most often it is an agricultural task. He prepares some bumma and asks a few people to come to his place or his field on a particular day to do the work. When the day comes, the owner, members of his household and the people he has personally invited, come to the field and start to work all through the morning. A little before noon, a few other people will join the group, people just passing by – neighbours, friends, and a few thirsty people who found out where beer was to be drunk. By noon, the workers will stop and some bumma will be offered to everyone, both the people who started to work in the morning and the latecomers. After this midday break, everybody goes back to work until the evening. Another distribution of beer will take place at the end of the afternoon, when the work is done. Before the beer is shared between all the workers, some will be given to those people who were directly called upon and who had worked since the morning. This beer is called *bum tikka* /beer bottle gourd/ because it is poured into each person's gourd and he or she will carry it back home to share with family members. Very often it is this beer that is drunk in the recreational way I mentioned above. After the 'beer for the gourd' has been given to all who deserve it, there is always some left over for everyone else, and people drink until the end of the day.

Table 16.1 Proportion of domestic and collective work among the Duupa.

	Household		Work Party		Total
	N days	*% of days devoted to the task*	*N days*	*% of days devoted to the task*	
Swiddening cereal fields	16	50.0%	16	50.0%	32
Swiddening, preparing and sowing secondary fields and orchards	31	47.7%	34	52.3%	65
Sowing cereals	6	85.7%	1	14.3%	7
Weeding cereal fields	139	66.2%	71	33.8%	210
Weeding and maintenance of secondary crops	111	98.2%	2	1.8%	113
Harvesting cereals	5	20.0%	20	80.0%	25
Harvesting secondary crops	47	94.0%	3	6.0%	50
Threshing cereals	3	6.3%	45	93.8%	48
Miscellaneous agricultural tasks	18	94.7%	1	5.3%	19
Total for agricultural work	376	66.1%	193	33.9%	569
Non-agricultural work and activities	613	95.8%	27	4.2%	640
Total	989	81.8%	220	18.2%	1209

24-hour recall for 34 people, year long, N=1209 days

The work party system of the Duupa has two important features:

1. Work parties are very frequent and anybody can organise them, they are not reserved for a special category of people (elders, chiefs ...).
2. They are organised on a reciprocal basis.

They cannot be considered in commercial terms and I do not think that a Duupa would equate the exchange of work for beer as a 'payment' since, at the end of the day, the act is not over. This is very similar to the Mambwe organisation described in ex-Rhodesia by Watson some years ago (1958: 107–108):

Beer is not considered repayment for the work done, but rather as an essential refreshment for work done. The basis of Mambwe cooperative work is reciprocity... Beer is not pay: it is the work which is reciprocated... A man cannot get his gardens dug simply by providing beer for others to come to work for him; if he does not work in turn, no one will accept again his invitation.

The Duupa owner of a field is in a similar situation. Having benefitted from other people's work, he is now committed to them, and especially to those he invited personally. One day he will have to give some of his time and energy to someone else's field. The date is never specified but he will not have to wait very long before doing so since work parties are so frequent, especially during the rainy season, when all the agricultural work must be done. Work parties are not a secondary way of working, but the most important one: nearly 20 percent of the days are spent in working parties. Anyone who was not willing to 'give back' some work would quickly be dropped out of the system as no one would come to his beer parties any more, even if the beer is good and there is plenty of it. So everyone is playing the game and it is an important one. More than one third of the work input for weeding is achieved through beer parties, each 'owner' will organise at least one party just for weeding during the year. It is the key agricultural task in the African savannah: it is also a major occasion for drinking. The vital importance of weeding the fields should not be overlooked; a family who cannot complete this work might lose the whole crop and would be in danger of starving the following year. It must also be stressed that this weeding has to be carried out during the annual hungry season. By the end of July and August, there is little grain left in the granary and the next crop is yet to be harvested. In some cases, the small amount of millet available is used to brew bumma because it is a food as well as a means of production and a social medium.

Conclusion

It seems to me that the Duupa offer an interesting example of a small-scale agricultural society that is 'driven by drink'. Bumma beer is a major element to: the nutritional well-being, the social and ritual life, and the economic process. It is not a secondary aspect of the way of life, what we would call a 'social dimension' of the economic system, but it is its very basis.

The Duupa ethnographic example illustrates the generality of the significance of drink in what Dietler (1996) might call the 'commensal politics' of African societies. The role of beverages as a prestigious marker of social 'distinction' (Bourdieu 1979) seems common to many precolonial complex or stratified societies and to the class struggle in modern Africa since the colonial period. It is also an important element in the conspicuous consumption process for the accumulation of prestige gained through the display of food and drinks in many simple small-scale egalitarian societies. This aspect could be viewed as essential in the Duupa organisation, but in their case the quest for status is not a clear notion and the role of beer is ambiguous. 'On the one hand, beer may symbolise an egalitarian ethos; on the other hand, it may mark hierarchy and status differentiation' wrote Pottier (1985: 110) about the Mambwe of Zambia, and this statement can well be applied to the Duupa. Beer simultaneously creates hierarchy and differential status in some contexts (feasts and ritual festivals), and egality and reciprocity in others (work parties); it always represents the fundamental ambiguous dynamics of social life. As Karp (1983: 83) put it for the Iteso, 'beer drinking is [Duupa] social theory', and this 'pervasiveness of beer' is a common feature to many African 'traditional' societies.

This is at least true for agrarian populations; little has been said about drinking among hunter-gatherers and pastoralists. Even if alcoholic beverages are well known to them, it does not seem to be a 'locus of value' as it is for agriculturalists. This is especially true for cereal cultivators in the savannah belt, or at least more so than for tuber growers in the humid zone. A detailed review of the literature is still to be carried out, but the brewing of beer, and its use in the network of the work parties system does not seem to be widespread in the forest zone, at least in Central and Western Africa. Palm wine is the most valued drink there; it has an important ritual role and is used as a sacrificial substance, and it is also an important economic and social item, used in the bridewealth payments (see, for instance, Linares 1993; Haxaire 1996). The social and ritual dimensions of beverages are clearly present in the value accorded to palm wine. However, palm wine appears to lack the 'productive' value cereal beers seem to have when they play a part in the work party system. In his detailed relation of palm wine drinking among the Lele, Ngokwey (1987: 115) states that 'agriculture, hunting, weaving, house-building, and productive work in general exclude palm wine drinking ... Palm wine drinking thus marks the transition from the working period to the relaxed atmosphere of the evening'. This is contrary to the Duupa appreciation of bumma, but parallel to what Gusfield (1987) wrote about alcohol drinking in contemporary American society, where drinking is associated with leisure time. The relation between drinking and productive work has not been looked at closely when it is not associated with competitive feasting. It is puzzling to the occidental evaluation of drinking, but I would like to suggest that this might be an interesting feature to look at in African agrarian societies. Many classical views about the social dimension of drinking apply to the Duupa. Beer is pleasurable, it is a sign of sociability and relaxation, a mark of social boundaries towards other groups that do not drink millet beer or drink it in a different way. It is a feature of celebration and transcendence and a way of signalling or creating status, but, over and above all that, bumma beer is work, work to produce the grain, to make the beer, and beer itself is directly convertible into work, to the same agricultural work required to produce the millet. This is a techno-economical situation proper to agrarian societies that are brewing beer with the same grain they use to prepare solid foods. The appreciation of beer might be especially important in this case (Jolly 1995).

Thus, the 'productive' dimension of drinking is not limited to competitive feasting, or to the recruitment of labour for the profit of those who have a high status in the society, but this kind of 'constructive drinking' (Douglas 1987) appears also in a context where reciprocity and an egalitarian social ideology prevail. The Duupa offer an interesting example of a small-scale agricultural society that is 'driven by drink' (Dietler 1990), because, when you are a Duupa, you must have some millet beer to drink in order to cultivate the millet you need ... to brew some more beer. Among its many values, bumma can be turned into work, but not any kind of work – joyful, socially prized work – and this may well make a big difference ...

Notes

1. A title of which I am very envious because I could well have used it for my own thesis entitled 'Le mil et la bière' (1995), which is far from being as elegant.
2. Thirty-five months between 1988 and 1993.
3. Fieldwork observations, and feelings, obtained through the well-known method of participatory observation.

References

Akyeampong, E.K. (1996) *Drink, power and cultural change: A social history of alcohol in Ghana, c.1800 to recent times*. Heineman/Currey, Portsmouth, New Hampshire.

Barley, N. (1983a) *Symbolic structures. An exploration of the culture of the Dowayos*. Cambridge University Press/Maison des Sciences de l'Homme, Cambridge/Paris.

Barley, N. (1983b) *The innocent anthropologist: Notes from a mud hut*. British Museum Publications, London.

Bourdieu P. (1979) *La distinction – critique sociale du jugement*. Editions de Minuit, Paris.

Chevassus-Agnès, S., Favier, J.C. et Joseph, A., (1975) *Technologie traditionnelle et valeur nutritive des bières de sorgho du Cameroun*. ONAREST/IPM/ORSTOM, Yaoundé.

Colson, E. and Scudder, T. (1988) *For prayer and profit. The ritual, economic, and social importance of beer in Gwembe district, Zambia 1950–1982*. Stanford University Press, Stanford.

Curto, José C. (1989) Alcohol in Africa: A preliminary compilation of the post-1875 literature. *Current bibliography on African affairs*. (Washington) 21, 1: 3–31.

Dietler, M. (1990) Driven by drink: the role of drinking in the political economy and the case of early iron age France. *Journal of anthropological archaeology*, vol. 9: 352–406.

Dietler, M. (1996) Feasts and Commensal Politics in the Political Economy: Food, Power and Status in Prehistoric Europe. In, P.Wiessner and W. Schiefenhövel (Eds.) *Food and the Status Quest: An Interdisciplinary Perspective*. Berghahn Books, Providence, Oxford: 87–125.

Douglas, M. (Ed.) (1987) *Constructive Drinking. Perspectives on Drink from Anthropology*. Cambrige University Press, Cambridge.

Eguchi, P. K. (1975) Beer drinking and festivals among the Hide. *Kyoto University African studies*, vol. IX: 69–90.

Everett, M.W., Waddel, J.O. and Heath, D.B. (Eds.) (1976) *Cross Cultural Approaches to the Study of Alcohol. An Interdisciplinary Perspective*. Mouton Publishers, The Hague/Paris.

Fournier, D. et D'Onofrio, S. (Eds.) (1991) *Le ferment divin*. Maison des Sciences de l'Homme, Paris.

Garine, Eric (1995) Le mil et la bière. Le système agraire des Duupa du massif de Poli (Nord-Cameroun). Université de Paris-X, Nanterre, Thèse de doctorat, multigr.

Garine, Eric (1996) Une bonne sauce de mauvaises herbes. Note sur les repas des Duupa du massif de Poli (Nord-Cameroun). In, F. Cousin et M.C. Bataille (Eds.) *Cuisines, reflets des sociétés*. Editions Sépia /Musée de l'Homme, Paris: 77–96.

Garine, I. de (1996) Food and the Status Quest in Five African Cultures. In, P. Wiessner and W. Schiefenhövel (Eds) (1996) *Food and the Status Quest: An Interdisciplinary Perspective.* Berghahn Books, Providence, Oxford: 193–218.

Gusfield, J. (1987) Passage to play: rituals of drinking time in American society. In, M. Douglas (Ed.) *Constructive drinking. Perspectives on drink from anthropology.* Cambrige University Press, Cambridge: 3–90.

Haxaire, C. (1996) Le vin de palme et la noix de Kola: nourritures aradoxales, médiateurs de la communication avec les dieux. In, C.M. Hladik, A. Hladik, H. Pagezy, O.F Linares, G.J.A. Koppert et A. Froment (Eds.) *L'alimentation en forêt tropicale. Interactions bioculturelles et perspectives de développement.* Editions UNESCO MAB, Paris: 923–938.

Hayden, B. (1996) Feasting in prehistoric and traditional societies. In, P.Wiessner and W. Schiefenhövel (Eds.) *Food and the Status Quest: An Interdisciplinary Perspective.* Berghahn Books, Providence, Oxford: 127–47.

Heath, D.B. (1987) A decade of development in the anthropology of alcohol use: 1970–1980. In, M. Douglas (Ed.) *Constructive drinking. Perspectives on drink from anthropology.* Cambridge University Press, Cambridge: 16–69.

Jolly, E. (1995) La bière de mil dans la société Dogon. Université de Paris-X, Nanterre, Thèse de doctorat, 2 tomes multigr.

Karp, I. (1987) Beer drinking and social experience in an African society. An essay in formal sociology. In, I. Karp and C.S. Bird (Eds.) *Explorations in African systems of thought.* Smithsonian Institution Press, Washington D.C./London: 83–119.

Koppert, G.J.A, Rikong Adie, H., Gwangwa'a, S., Sajo, E., Matze, M., Pasquet, P. et Froment, A. (1996) La consommation alimentaire dans différentes zones écologiques et économiques du Cameroun. In, A. Froment, I. de Garine, Ch. Binam Bikoi et J.F. Loung (Eds.)*Bien manger et bien vivre. Anthropologie alimentaire et développement en Afrique tropicale: du biologique au social. Actes du colloque tenu à Yaoundé du 27 au 30 avril 1993.* ORSTOM/L'Harmattan, Paris: 237–254.

Kuckertz, H. (1985) Organizing labour forces in Mpondoland: a new perspective on work-parties. *Africa* vol. 55 n° 2: 115–32.

Linares, O.F. (1993) Palm oil versus palm wine: symbolic and economic dimensions. In, C.M. Hladik, A. Hladik, O.F Linares, H. Pagezy, A. Semple and M. Hadley (Eds.) *Tropical forests, people and food. Biocultural interactions and applications to development.* UNESCO/Partenon, Paris/Lancs/New York, Man and the Biosphere Series n° 13: 595–606. Mandelbaum, D.G. (1965) Alcohol and culture.*Current Anthropology* vol. 6 n° 3: 281–93.

Matze, M. et Stappers, H. (1989) Alimentation et mode de vie des Duupa de la montagne de Poli (Nord-Cameroun). Yaoundé/Wageningen. ORSTOM-ISH-CN-CNRS Projet Anthropologie Alimentaire des Populations Camerounaises, multigr. 52–XIX pages.

Meillassoux, C. (1964) *Anthropologie économique des Gouro de Côte d'Ivoire. De l'économie de subsistance à l'agriculture commerciale.* Mouton & Co, Paris/La Haye

Moore, M.P. (1975) Co-operative labour in peasant agriculture. *The Journal of Peasant Studies* vol. 2 n° 3: 270–91.

Muller, J-C. (1996) Ideology and dynamics in Dìì chiefdoms. A study of territorial movement and population fluctuation (Adamawa Province, Cameroon). In, H.J.M Claessen and J. Oosten (Eds.) *Ideology and the formation of the early states.* E.J. Brill, Leiden: 99–115.

Muller, J-C. (1999) Du don et du rite comme fondateurs des chefferies. Marcel Mauss chez les Dìì du Nord-Cameroun. *Cahiers d'Etudes Africaines*154 XXXIX–2: 387–408.

Netting, R. McC. (1964) Beer as a locus of value among the west African Kofyar. *American Anthropologist* vol. 66: 375–84.

Netting, R. McC. (1968) *Hill farmers of Nigeria: Cultural ecology of the Kofyar of the Jos Plateau.* University of Washington Press, Seattle/London.

Ngokwey, N. (1987) Varieties of palm wine among the Lele of the Kasai. In, M. Douglas (Ed.) *Constructive drinking. Perspectives on drink from anthropology.* Cambridge University Press, Cambridge: 113–21.

Pontié, G. (1973) *Les Guiziga du Cameroun septentrional. L'organisation traditionnelle et sa mise en contestation.* ORSTOM, Paris.

Pottier, J.P. (1985) Reciprocity and the beer pot: the changing pattern of Mambwe food production. In, J.P. Pottier (Ed.) *Food systems in Central and Southern Africa.* School of Oriental and African Studies, London: 101–137.

Rehfisch, F. (1987) Competitive beer drinking. In, M. Douglas (Ed.) *Constructive Drinking. Perspectives on Drink from Anthropology.* Cambrige University Press, Cambridge.

Richards, A. (1969) *Land, Labour and Diet in Northern Rhodesia. An Economic Study of the Bemba Tribe.* Oxford University Press, Oxford (1° ed 1939).

Saul, M. (1983) Work parties, wages, and accumulation in a Voltaic village. *American Ethnologist* vol. 10 n° 1: 77–96.

Van Beek, W.E.A. (1978) *Bierbrouwers in de bergern. De Kapsiki en Higi van Noord-Kameroen en Nord-oost Nigeria,* ICAU Medeling, Utrecht, n° 12 Instituut voor Culturele Anthropologie.

Vincent, J-F., (1991) *Princes montagnards du Nord Cameroun. Les Mofu Diamaré et le pouvoir politique.* 2 tomes, L'Harmattan, Paris.

Watson, W. (1958) *Tribal cohesion in a money economy. A study of the Mambwe people of Northern Rhodesia.* Manchester University Press, Manchester, 246 pages.

Wiessner, P. and Schiefenhövel, W. (Eds) (1996) *Food and the Status Quest: An Interdisciplinary Perspective.* Berghahn Books, Providence, Oxford.

17. SOCIO-ECONOMIC AND CULTURAL IMPLICATIONS OF ALCOHOLIC BEVERAGES AMONG THE ABAGUSII OF WESTERN KENYA

Wilfred K. Subbo

Introduction

All societies have their own form of alcohol (Douglas 1987). Gefou-Madianou (1992) observes that the uses of alcohol and the meanings attached to it vary widely, while the act of drinking is present in every society. Alcohol has been used for changing one's mood and as a socialising agent, especially during ceremonial occasions.

Alcohol drinking has been part and parcel of the Abagusii culture since time immemorial. In Ekegusii, the language spoken by the Abagusii, a Bantu community in Western Kenya, Nyanza Province, their traditional beer is called *busaa*. It is made from fermented sorghum grains that are ground to produce flour which is mixed with fermented maize flour. The mixture is then smoked, and dried for one to two days in the sun. Its alcoholic content is estimated to be between three to five percent (Silberschmidt 1991: 63).

Changaa is a much more purified form of busaa. It is mixed with balls of sugar and then heated, its moisture is passed through traditional filters (still) before it comes out as a colourless liquid. This liquor has a much higher alcoholic content than busaa, estimated at between 60 and 70 percent pure alcohol (Silberschmidt 1991: 63).

Traditionally, i.e., during the precolonial period, the consumption of alcohol was reserved for the elderly and the respectable members of the society. Other people were only allowed to participate in drinking alcohol during special occasions such as weddings, circumcision ceremonies and funerals.

However, in the recent past alcohol drinking has been transformed into an economic and social activity. Beer brewing and selling have become a booming business, out of which many parents have acquired money for the education of their children. In spite of this positive aspect, the beer business carries with it a number of negative aspects emanating from the processing and selling procedures observed by the people who participate in it. The brewers of the local beer are usually women, who brew it in their households and sell it from there. In a number of cases the women convert their homes into private bars. It would rightfully be said that this practice greatly compromises the privacy of the members of their families and encourages a proliferation of family conflicts. The majority of customers who come to buy beer are men. Some of them end up causing disturbances within the homestead once they become drunk, sometimes even fighting with family members.

In addition, it raises suspicion and accusations of immorality between the spouses. A number of men frequently accuse their wives of engaging in immoral practices with some of their male customers, resulting in divorce cases being common among families that sell beer. In brief, selling traditional beer from the home creates an environment conducive to family conflicts.

A number of key respondents I interviewed during my research, such as religious leaders, community development officers, and health officers, condemned the beer brewing and selling business as being a major cause of low moral standards and the spread of sexually-transmitted diseases in the populace. One education officer had the following to say concerning the beer selling business: 'It is responsible for the low educational standards in this district because once children get exposed to alcohol consumption while they are in school, this interferes with their academic progress. This often makes them drop out of school because of their low academic achievements.'

A health officer I interviewed said that the business is a great hindrance to the improvement of health standards in the area. In particular he condemned *changaa* which, because of its very high alcohol content, makes people too drunk and generally damages their health. Children whose mothers devote all their working time to beer brewing and selling are usually malnourished. Some have even been admitted into Family Life Training Programmes (FLTP), which are centres where malnourished children, together with their parents, are admitted for a period of twenty-one days for rehabilitation purposes.

Economic Implications of Alcoholic Beverages

A number of people in the Abagusii community derive their livelihood from selling busaa and changaa. Respondents reported that the minimum wage for a casual labourer was 1,500 Kenyan shillings, approximately $ 20.3 (U.S.), whereas a beer brewer can earn a minimum of Ksh 5,000, approximately $67.6 per month. This is why they prefer selling beer in spite of the risks involved because most of them do not have the permits for conducting the business, which explains why it is usually sold from their households.

Social Implications of Alcoholic Consumption

While drinking alcohol used to be reserved for the elderly, mainly on ceremonial occasions, in the recent past drastic changes have occurred in the etiquette of alcohol consumption, resulting in young married men and women engaging in heavy drinking. Papagaroufali (1992: 48) observes that, in many civilisations, women are excluded from taking strong alcohol and prohibited from experiencing the pleasures that accompany relative tipsiness. Similarly, Friedl (1967) points out that hot pungent substances were usually drunk by men while women were expected to like drinking womanly drinks such as fruit juices. These examples, drawn from developed societies, show that restrictions concerning women and alcoholic drinks are not confined to the Abagusii community per se but could be a cultural universal.

Traditionally women were not allowed to drink busaa and changaa, the main reason being that they could ruin their family's honour. It was anticipated that once the women got drunk, they might become easy-going, hence making it possible for drunken men to take sexual advantage of them. Women were thus strictly prohibited from engaging in beer drinking although they were the main brewers of the drink. It is perhaps for this reason that beer brewing is associated with illicit sex, especially nowadays that women seem free to drink beer in the company of men other than their husbands.

In the past, women's drinks were normally milk, porridge and warm water. Milk was particularly recommended for women and children, and a married man who did not have a milking cow was automatically considered to be a poor man, *Omonto Omotaka*. Currently, the usual drinks for women and children among the Abagusii are tea and coffee, taken with milk.

Times for Drinking Busaa and Changaa

In the precolonial period, busaa and changaa were usually taken during the afternoon hours, when people had completed their tasks for the day. Thus they were drinks that marked the transition from work to leisure or from normal time to special time. Based on the belief of male dominance, it was considered a sign of maturity for a man to be able to drink large quantities of alcohol without losing self-control. Furthermore, drinking alcohol helped to enhance social solidarity among the men by bringing friends and relatives together. It fostered friendship and masculinity. It was a kind of ritual for friends to meet in each other's homes and engage in drinking beer that their wives had brewed for them. This enhanced social harmony.

According to Pitt-Rivers (1977: 10): 'Food and drink always have a ritual value, for the ingestion together of a common substance creates a bond'. Furthermore, he emphasises that drinking not only creates a bond but also serves to reinforce existing bonds and express the cultural substance of social relationships.

Alcohol Consumption and Domestic Violence

Nowadays, however, among the Abagusii, beer drinking has become increasingly associated with domestic violence. A number of women said that their husbands usually quarrelled or even beat them when they came home drunk after having spent most of their resources in buying traditional beer in the homesteads of other women. Domestic violence against women is a common-place feature among the Abagusii although we cannot affirm that this is one of the hallmarks of their culture. Some of the people I interviewed considered that nowadays cases of domestic violence have become more common because of the increasing number of womenfolk who have taken to the habit of drink-ing alcohol.

It should be mentioned that in almost all countries and cultures women are frequently victims of abuse both by their intimates (Davidson 1977) and by strangers. They are often battered, sexually abused and psychologically injured by persons with whom they should share the closest trust in places considered the safest, e.g., their homes. Many more live constantly with the threat of domestic violence, whether from beating, rape or emotional abuse. This is a worldwide problem that affects all women irrespective of their age, socio-econ-omic status, colour, creed or place of residence. It should be noted here that in the traditional African society, wife-beating was acknowledged but not seen as a serious problem (Brieness and Gordon 1983) because women were never considered equal to men.

Studies by Davidson (1977) indicate that there is a close relationship between alcohol, the abuse of women and other forms of domestic violence, and that it is often used as an excuse for such acts as beatings and rape. Mention has been made of women who are beaten only when their husbands are drunk (Gayford 1975), which would indicate that there exists a close association between the con-sumption of alcohol and domestic violence.

Busaa: An Illegal Alcoholic Beverage

The Kenyan Parliament recently made recommendations for the legalisation of traditional alcoholic beverages that are brewed under hygienic conditions and which meet the required standard for such drinks. Previously, the illegal-isation of busaa brewing and selling caused a lot of problems for those involved. In their efforts to escape being noticed by the law enforcement agents, such as chiefs and administrative policemen, they brewed their beer in far-away places, for instance, in the banana plantations under very unhygienic conditions.

Furthermore, the illegalisation of the traditional beer business caused dis-advantages to those who engaged in it. Sometimes clients who had taken the beer on credit refused to pay their debts, knowing that the beer sellers could not report them to the police for fear of being arrested and charged for engag-ing in illegal business.

As well as the domestic violence due to the consumption of alcohol, many road accidents occur through drunken drivers. Many of the local policemen I talked to said that road accidents in Kisii are mainly caused by drivers who have consumed busaa and changaa. As with all other forms of alcohol, their consumption results in fatigue, weight loss, irritability, insomnia and gastritis. It should be mentioned here that Kenya has one of the highest records of road accidents emanating from people driving vehicles while under the influence of alcohol.

Competition Between Modern Beer and Traditional Beer

One might imagine that, since factory-produced beer has a well-controlled alcoholic content and is brewed and packaged in very hygienic conditions, beer drinkers would automatically prefer it to the traditional beers. However, contrary to this expectation and in spite of the competition it faces from modern industrial beers, busaa is still a very popular beverage among the Abagusii. This is true more especially in the rural and urban slum areas, where the majority of the poor Abagusii live. One of the people I interviewed gave the following reasons for preferring the traditional drink to the modern brands of beer, such as Tusker, Guinness and White Cup.

First and foremost, he said that busaa is affordable because it is very cheap. While a half-litre bottle of factory beer costs no less than forty-five Kenyan shillings (depending on where you get it from), busaa costs only ten shillings for the same volume. Note that some high-class restaurants charge up to one hundred shillings for the half-litre bottle.

Secondly, most beer drinkers claim that busaa tastes much better than factory-made beer, which they find to be too diluted. Thirdly, traditional beer enables people to identify themselves as members of the Abagusii community. They say that busaa is the drink of their ancestors; it should, therefore, be drunk when the people are giving sacrifices to their ancestors. It should be mentioned that, in spite of the spread of Christianity among the Abagusii, which prohibits ancestral worship, there are still a significant number of people who believe in their traditional religion.

Etiquette for Busaa and Changaa Drinking

In the traditional Abagusii community, beer drinking was a social norm practised by almost all adult males. It was associated with being sociable and masculine. A person who abstained from engaging in beer drinking with his colleagues without good reasons for doing so was viewed with suspicion, and was accused of being antisocial. The community had various sanctions that it used to force such a person to conform to the social norm, such as gossip, or the reluctance of friends and relatives to help him with heavy tasks like clearing his fields in preparation for the planting of crops.

However, intoxication was looked down upon. A real man was one who drank and yet maintained self-control. Therefore a man who easily became drunk lost face among his colleagues. It is important to observe that drunkenness was not tolerated among the men, even during ceremonial times.

Recent Changes Concerning the Consumption of Alcoholic Beverages

It has been established from key informants that there have been notable changes in the consumption of busaa and changaa. While in the traditional period only the elders of the community were allowed to drink alcohol, nowadays the youth have joined them in the consumption of the traditional alcoholic beverages.Various reasons are given for this change in behaviour. It is suggested that, as the youth now get married at a considerably earlier age, they feel that they are mature enough to drink alcohol. In the past men married when they were thirty years and over, whereas today young men of twenty get married. Another reason that was given is that there are many young men idling around without gainful employment due to the lack of opportunities in the rural areas. Most of them find consolation in the consumption of alcoholic drinks.

Some of the elders attributed this change in the behaviour of the youth to the influence of Western culture which has greatly contributed to the erosion of traditional cultural values, emphasising that the youth nowadays have no respect for the elders at all. Others attributed this change in behaviour to women's liberation movements, saying that this has resulted in the women joining men in the drinking of alcohol as a way of undermining the dominance hitherto enjoyed by their male counterparts. In brief, it was established that there have been significant changes in the system of consuming alcoholic drinks.

Conclusion

Busaa is a traditional alcoholic drink that is still popular with a significant number of the Abagusii people. However, a number of problems are posed with regard to processing and selling it. The government of Kenya has taken decisive moves in streamlining this business by legalising it, thus ensuring that people prepare and drink it in a harmonious environment. This is a welcome move as the role of the traditional brew as an entertaining, relaxing and economic activity should be recognised and appreciated.

As well as legalising the busaa business, I recommend that the government should fix an age limit for the purchase and consumption of traditional beer. Twenty-two years should be the right age for people to be allowed to drink busaa.

Furthermore, the women who sell it should not do so in their private homes but in market places so as not to interfere with the privacy of their families. Finally, the people should be exposed to more advanced methods of brewing so that the alcoholic content of the drink can be determined accurately.

References

Brienes, W. and Gordon, L. (1983) The new scholarship of family violence signs. *Journal of Women in Culture and society* n° 8.

Davidson, T. (1977) Wife beating, a Recurring Problem throughout History. In, M. Roy (Ed.) *Battered women: A Psychological Study of domestic violence*. Van Nestrand Reinhold, London.

Douglas, M. (Ed.) (1987) *Constructive Drinking: Perspectives on Drink from Anthropology*. Cambridge University Press, Cambridge.

Freeman, M.D.A. (1990) Violence against women, does the legal system provide solutions or itself constitute a problem? *British Journal of Law and Society* n° 7, Oxford.

Friedl, E. (1967) The position of women: appearance and reality. *Anthropological Quarterly* 40, 3: 97–108.

Gayford, J.J. (1975) Wife battering: A preliminary survey of 100 cases. *British Medical Journal* n° 1.

Gefou-Madianou, D. (1992) *Alcohol, Gender and Culture*. Routledge, London and New York.

Papagaroufali, E. (1990) Greek women in politics: Gender ideology and practice in neighbourhood groups and the family. Ph.D. dissertation, Columbia University.

Pitt-Rivers, J.J. (1977) *The Fate of Shechem or the Politics of Sex. Essays in the Anthropology of the Mediterranean*. Cambridge University Press, Cambridge.

Silberschmidt, M. (1991) *Rethinking Men and Gender Relations. An Investigation of Men, their Changing Roles within the Household and the Implications of Gender Relations in Kisii District, Kenya*. Centre for Development Research, Copenhagen.

18. ALCOHOL, SLAVERY, AND AFRICAN CULTURAL CONTINUITY IN THE BRITISH CARIBBEAN

Frederick H. Smith

Alcohol played an important role in the daily lives of British Caribbean slaves, yet little is known about slave drinking practices and the symbolic meanings slaves attached to alcohol. An examination of the rich historical, ethnographic, and archaeological records indicates that alcohol drinking may have fostered slave spirituality and promoted group identity. These symbolic uses of alcohol suggest African drinking practices, particularly those associated with the Akan and Igbo of West Africa. The persistence of African drinking behaviours helped support resistance ideologies that challenged European efforts to suppress African cultural beliefs. Further, British Caribbean slaves may have used their unique drinking practices to distinguish themselves from poorer classes of whites. Alcohol was familiar to newly arrived Africans in the British Caribbean and the symbolic meanings slaves attached to drinking appear to have transferred from Africa to the Americas. Understanding slave alcohol use provides important insights into the cultural development of the African diaspora in the British Caribbean and furnishes a prism through which to view underlying principles that helped shape slave life.

Historical-ethnographies of Caribbean slave life commonly stress the strength of African cultural traits and the survival of these traits in the Americas. Beginning with the pioneering work of Melville Herskovits, historically minded anthropologists have sought to connect West Indian slave traditions to Africa. Although Herskovits used broad 'culture area' concepts of West Africa to reconstruct African survivals in the Americas, his research often illustrated the specific origins of particular cultural influences (Herskovits 1941). For example, he made links between Haitian *voodu* and the religion of Fõn-speaking peoples of Dahomey and identified the Yoruba roots of Shango cults in Trinidad (Herskovits 1937; Herskovits and Herskovits 1947). Sidney Mintz and Richard Price (1992) revised the Herskovitsian model in an attempt to explain commonalities across the African diaspora despite the cultural heterogeneity of slave societies. They believed that the survival of West and Central African cultural beliefs in the Americas represented a dialectic between the shared mental constructs of West and Central Africans and the colonial social contexts in which slave societies developed. For example, Mintz and Price argued that shared beliefs about the active role of ancestral spirits led to syncretic religious adaptations that transcended cultural differences on the plantation. Thus,

Jamaican *Obeah* and Haitian *voodu* combine underlying principles of West and Central African belief systems. The 'additive' nature of West and Central African religions encouraged the syncretism in slave religions (Mintz and Price 1992: 44–46). A comparative examination of historically documented drinking behaviours in West Africa and the British Caribbean may contribute new insights about the ideological forces that helped shape slave life. Further, ethnographic studies concerning contemporary British Caribbean peoples may also provide invaluable evidence about the persistence of African social customs in the Americas.

The 2.5 million slaves transported to the British Caribbean in the seventeenth and eighteenth centuries came from diverse West and Central African cultural backgrounds. Yet, historical evidence from travellers' accounts, mission reports, and trade records indicates that alcohol figured prominently in precolonial West and Central Africa and that many slaves came from cultures with traditions of alcohol use. In fact, only in the Muslim-controlled areas north of the region was alcohol use of little significance. Many West and Central Africans shared common beliefs about the connection between alcohol and spirituality. It is likely, therefore, that the drinking behaviours of slaves in the British Caribbean reflect a braiding of West and Central African drinking practices. However, it is important to note that the Igbo from the Bight of Biafra and Akan peoples from the Gold Coast had a significantly greater cultural influence in the British Caribbean than other African groups. According to Douglas Chambers (1997: 77), between 1700–1809, the Igbo represented as much as a third of all slave arrivals in the British Caribbean, a higher percentage than any other Africans in this period. The Akan also greatly influenced slave life in the British Caribbean due to their seventeenth-century presence in the region. This early presence meant that Akan slaves would have had a significant socialising impact on later slave arrivals from other West and Central African backgrounds (Herskovits 1966: 96–98; Mintz and Price 1992: 42–51). Thus, the drinking practices of Igbo and Akan slaves would have significantly shaped drinking behaviours in the British Caribbean and understanding traditional alcohol use among the Igbo and Akan should reveal important insights into the symbolic meanings of slave drinking.

Alcohol use in Igbo and Akan societies predated the rise of the British transatlantic slave trade in the seventeenth century. For example, Al-Bakri of Cordoba, as early as the eleventh century, referred to 'intoxicating drinks' served at the burial of the king of the ancient kingdom of Ghana (cited in Pan 1975: 20–21). Precolonial West Africans produced alcohol from a variety of indigenous materials. Honey, plantains, and various species of millets provided numerous opportunities to ferment alcohol. Palm wine, produced from the raphia variety of palm, appears to have been one of the most common indigenously produced drinks. Although its origin is unclear, oral traditions collected in the late nineteenth century intimate a long history of palm wine use in the Gold Coast dating back to the Asanti's initial migration into the region in the early sixteenth century (Akyeampong 1997: 27). Palm wine was also common in Igbo lands prior to the seventeenth century. For example, in 1589, James Welsh wrote that in the Bight of Biafra 'there are a great store of palme trees, out of which they gather great store of wine' (cited in Isichei 1978: 9). In the mid-seventeenth century, Dutch traders named the main village just inside the mouth of the New Calabar river 'Wyndorp' due to the large amounts of palm wine produced there (cited in Jones 1995: 26).

The slave trade was another important source of alcohol in West and Central Africa. The Portuguese established the alcohol-for-slaves model as early as the sixteenth century (Vogt 1979: 71; Curto 1996). Rum became an important slave trade item with the rise of the Brazilian, British and French West Indian, and North American rum industries in the seventeenth and eighteenth centuries. British Caribbean and North American rum producers developed direct trade along the West African coast by the beginning of the eighteenth century. For example, between 1700 and 1727 rum sloops from the British Caribbean exported 690,183 litres of rum directly to African traders (Sheridan 1974: 344). In the 1770s North American rum exports to Africa averaged over 1,135,500 litres (McCusker 1989: 481–2). According to Raymond Dumett (1974: 81–81), slave trade liquors, such as rum, entered a pre-existing social structure that embraced alcohol use and replaced the traditional palm wine as early as the seventeenth century. Thus, evidence indicates that foreign and locally pro-duced alcohol was common in West Africa and its use predates the rise of the British transatlantic slave trade. Akan and Igbo peoples transported to the British Caribbean as slaves, therefore, came from societies with long traditions of alcohol use and were familiar with alcohol upon their arrival in the British Caribbean.

But why was alcohol important in Akan and Igbo societies? The physical and spiritual worlds were closely linked in traditional Akan and Igbo religions and a study of their interactions with spiritual worlds reveals the central importance of alcohol. For example, Emmanuel Akyeampong's (1997) social history of Gold Coast drinking practices provided important insights into the spiritual significance of alcohol. Akyeampong argued that alcohol was con-sidered a sacred fluid among the Akan and was necessary for opening lines of communication between the living and ancestral worlds. Akyeampong (1997: 30) stated 'Rites of passage illustrated the conception of life as a progression from the spirit world, through the living world, and back into the spiritual world. Naming, puberty, marriage, and funeral ceremonies represented differ-ent epochal stages in life's journey'. Alcohol, therefore, helped link the physi-cal and spiritual worlds ensuring the progression of life for the individual and community.

The practice of pouring libations reveals how alcohol opened interactions between the living and spiritual worlds. Libation is best described as prayer accompanied and punctuated by the pouring of alcohol (Akyeampong 1997: 24). Individuals, families, and clans poured libations in order to seek favour from ancestral spirits and deities. Libations protected the community from evil, propitiated angry spirits, accelerated an individual's recovery from illness, and, thus, created a path to the spiritual world that helped secure community needs. For example, in 1602, Pieter de Marees (1602: 42–43) described an Akan drinking ritual in which the first portion of palm wine was thrown on the ground in reverence for their ancestors and, if they had 'fetishes' tied to their arms and feet, they would spit the first mouthful of palm wine on them. Otherwise they believed that they would not be allowed to drink wine together in peace. One of the most powerful spiritual symbols among the Akan is the ancestral stool: a sacred representation of a deceased relative. Several times a year the Akan bring out their ancestral stools and place food and offerings on them followed by the pouring of alcohol libations. Libations showed reverence to the ancestors and, in return, the living received ancestral blessings (Akyeampong 1997: 40). The Igbo also poured alcohol libations and made sacrificial offerings of alcohol to their ancestors and deities in public and private ceremonies. For example, the Igbo *ofo-stick*, like the Akan ancestral stool, represents an ancestral spirit. According to Geoffrey Parrinder (1961: 124), the Igbo periodically pour alcohol libations over the ofo-stick in the hope of appeasing ancestral spirits and receiving ancestral blessings in worldly endeavours. In the early twentieth century, George Basden (1966: 220–1) recorded that the Igbo set a place apart in their households for their *alusi* (gods) which commemorate departed relatives. These do not become sacred representations of ancestral spirits until libations of gin or palm wine are poured.

In precolonial Akan and Igbo societies, birth represented a return to earth from the spirit world. The successful transition required the assistance of a powerful and sacred fluid. For example, a newborn was often given rum to wet his or her parched throat after the long journey from the spirit world. 'The gesture [of giving rum] was an expression of welcome, an entreaty to the newborn baby to stay with its earthly family' (cited in Akyeampong 1997: 31). According to Akyeampong, an Akan child was believed to have two mothers: an earth mother and a spirit mother. Fear that the spirit mother would reclaim her child produced the nine-day moratorium on naming during which time rum was offered to appease the spirit mother (ibid: 32). A.B. Ellis (1887, cited in Akyeampong 1997: 32) stated:

The child is then brought out and handed to the father, who returns thanks to the tutelary deity, and then gives it its second name (its personal name and not the day name given at birth) squirting at the same time a little rum from his mouth into the child's face ... After the second name was given rum was poured as a libation to the ancestors and the day ended with festivities.

Akyeampong pointed out that this ceremony does not occur when the child is named for a living person, confirming the link between ancestors and alcohol. The Igbo also link newborn children and the ancestral world. In fact, a newborn represented the reincarnated spirit of a deceased relative and they performed special ceremonies to determine the particular ancestral spirit (Ilogu 1974: 45–46). As a greeting to the reincarnated spirits, gifts of palm wine were given to newborn Igbo children. The naming ceremony soon followed and, according to Basden (1966: 60), it 'is a time of great rejoicing and feasting and large quantities of palm wine are consumed in celebrating the occasion'.

Marriage cemented bonds between families, clans, and lineages. The act, therefore, required spiritual approval and ancestral guidance which alcohol helped attain. Slave traders Jean Barbot (1732: 502), Pieter de Marees (1602: 19–21) and William Bosman (1705: 198–9) all noted the important role of alcohol in Akan weddings. The ceremony itself took the Akan word for alcohol, *nsa*, and was simply 'the exchange of drinks in the presence of witnesses and the pouring of libations to the gods and ancestors' (Akyeampong 1997: 36). The importance of alcohol in marriage ceremonies continued into the nineteenth century when the increasing role of women in the market economy of the Gold Coast put a premium on brides and led to the institutionalisation of brideprice known as 'head-rum' (ibid: 37). Among the Igbo, once a man selected the woman he wished to marry, he proceeded to her family's home and offered a small gift of a bottle of gin or a pot of palm wine to begin negotiations (Basden, 1966: 69). Brideprice often included quantities of alcohol and wedding ceremonies involved copious amounts of drink (ibid: 71; Parrinder 1961:106).

Death marked the end of physical life and a return to the spirit world and alcohol was central in this transformation. Proper Akan and Igbo funerals included alcohol which helped ensure the successful transition of the deceased to the spirit world. It also guaranteed the future help of the deceased and, thus, prosperity for the family and community left behind. For example, according to de Marees (1602: 184) the Akan put food and drink on the grave of the deceased believing that the dead 'live on it, and [thus] pots of water and palm-wine are constantly renewed'. In 1732, John Barbot noted that in the Gold Coast 'As soon as the corps is let down into the grave, the persons who attended the funeral drink palm wine, or rum plentifully ... and what they cannot drink off at a draught, they spill on the grave of their deceased friend, that he may have his share of the liquor' (Barbot 1732 :591; Parrinder 1961: 107). The Igbo also made tremendous use of alcohol at funerals. According to Basden (1966: 112–26), gin was sprinkled on the deceased prior to burial. During the important second burial feast, 'cases of gin and an unlimited supply of palm wine is consumed'. Francis Arinze (1970: 87–88) also noted that the Igbo made offerings of wine to their ancestors at funeral ceremonies so that the ancestral spirits would welcome the newly departed soul.

The use of alcohol in many of these ceremonies, particularly at funerals, may reflect the need to bring the community through an anxious period of spiritual liminality. These transitions can be seen as times of stress in a community when living and spiritual worlds were closely, but precariously aligned. The pacifying effect of alcohol on spirits and deities may have produced a perception of order and control that helped stabilise the community during uncertain times.

The presence of alcohol at Akan and Igbo ceremonies suggests that it helped establish the strength and cohesiveness of the community. These social gatherings required the participation and economic assistance of the family, clan, and lineage. For example, de Marees (1602: 23) stated when an Akan woman has given birth 'all the people – men, women, boys and girls – come to her ... They give the child a name upon which they have agreed, and swear upon it with the Fetissos and other sorcery ... on which occasion they make a big feast, with merry-making, food, and drink, which they love'. Such festivities required the participation and organisation of the community which helped magnify the group's shared identity, highlight its community ties, and reaffirm its social commitments. Alcohol figured prominently on these occasions, enticing participants and acting as a social lubricant and removing obstacles to social discourse.

The use of alcohol in oaths reinforces the argument that alcohol had an important role in building community. Oaths could be used to repair fissures within the community. For example, a man who believed his wife to have been unfaithful might have her consume an oath drink to prove her fidelity (Bosman 1705: 149–50). Oath drinks could also actualise social ties. Bosman (ibid.) wrote:

When they take the oath-draught, 'tis usually accompanied with an imprecation, that the fetische may kill them if they do not perform the contents of their obligation. Every person entering into any obligation is obliged to drink the swearing liquor. When any nation is hired to the assistance of another, all the chief ones are obliged to drink this liquor, with an imprecation, that their fetische may punish them with death, if they do not assist them with utmost vigor and extirpate their enemy.

Basden (1966: 206) also noted that oath drinks established allegiances among Igbo warriors prior to raiding and other military expeditions. Because of its link to the spiritual world, alcohol was often central in oath drinks.

The importance of alcohol in communicating with the ancestors and in community-building ceremonies made the control of alcohol a significant factor in the distribution of power. Tribal chiefs and elders held the land and labour necessary to produce palm wine. Their power ensured that they would receive alcohol in the form of tribute from the community, as well as trade liquors from slave merchants and dealers. Alcohol was so important in defining power that warring tribes would often destroy their enemy's palm groves in their attempt to destroy the source and symbolism of the enemy leader's power (Curto 1996: 47). Ethnographies from the Gold Coast also indicate a strong link between alcohol and the Akan war gods *(abosom Brafo)*. Afua Pokuaa (the female head of a matrilineage) of Amoanman believed that Akan war gods liked the red colour of 'Buccaneer rum'. Akyeampong believes that the war gods' preference for red rums reflects the relationship between warfare, blood and alcohol. He illustrates this connection by suggesting that the rise of alcohol and blood libations along the Gold Coast correlates to the rise in warfare during the slave-raiding period (Akyeampong 1997: 28; Dumett 1974). Igbo tribal chiefs also maintained power through the control and distribution of alcohol. For example, Basden (1966: 219–22) noted that the Igbo god, Ikenga Oweawfa (meaning 'he who splits thy enemy's shield'), was evoked with alcohol libations.

The sacred nature of alcohol survived the violence of the middle passage and transferred to the slave societies of the British Caribbean. Under the harsh conditions of slavery, alcohol allowed slaves to maintain a symbolic connection to Africa and their ancestral worlds. The ritual uses of alcohol on the plantation helped define group identity which made it an important weapon in the arsenal of slave resistance.

Alcohol use was widespread in the slave societies of the British Caribbean. Rum, a by-product of the sugar industry, became a common commodity as early as the mid- seventeenth century and sugar plantations produced enormous amounts of rum during the slavery period. For example, Edward Long argued that between 1768–71 Jamaicans produced an annual average of over 3 million gallons of rum. Long (1774: 496–9 vol.1) estimated that about 530,000 gallons were consumed in Jamaica for a per capita consumption of 2.7 gallons. In Barbados in the mid eighteenth century, Richard Hall (1755: 13) estimated that the inhabitants consumed 1875 gallons of rum daily – equal to a half-pint a day for about a third of the population. The huge amount of alcohol available provided Africans transported to the British Caribbean as slaves with the opportunity to continue traditional drinking practices.

But how accessible was alcohol to slaves? As in Igbo and Akan society, alcohol was generally controlled by a small ruling class who held the means of production. Planters doled out rum to slaves as part of their weekly rations (Long 1774: 490). Slaves received portions of rum as reward for particularly difficult and unpleasant tasks. Jamaican planter Thomas Roughley (cited in Craton and Walvin 1976: 80; see also Thistlewood cited in D. Hall 1989: 43) argued that as an incentive to the principal headman to do his duty well 'a weekly allowance of a quart or two of good rum ... will be found of salutary effect'. Planters, believing in the salubrious qualities of rum, often distributed it during bad weather (Governor Parry of Barbados cited in Craton and Walvin 1976: 88; Roughly cited in Craton and Walvin 1989: 82; Thistlewood cited in D. Hall 1989: 37). In order to rid the cane fields of destructive rat populations Charles Leslie noted the practice of rewarding slaves with a bottle of rum for every fifty rats caught. Slaves could also get rum through barter or purchase at weekend markets. For example, Jamaican planter Monk Lewis (cited in Craton and Walvin 1976: 126) wrote that slaves often sold their provision of ground produce to wandering higglers or at the weekend markets at Savannah la Mar in exchange for spirits. Jamaican plantation manager Thomas Thistlewood (cited in D. Hall 1989: 18) gave rum to his female slaves in exchange for sexual

favours. Plantation owners also dispensed rum on important plantation holidays, like Christmas, or at special slave ceremonies like births, marriages, and
funerals (Thistlewood cited in D. Hall 1989: 37, 47, 185). There were also more
clandestine ways of securing alcohol. For example, in 1788, Governor Parry of
Barbados (cited in Craton and Walvin 1976: 91) claimed that slaves commonly
stole rum.

Early writers paint a complicated picture of slave drinking behaviours in the
British Caribbean. Planters often developed stereotypes concerning the character of particular African ethnic groups. For instance, Moreau de St Mery
(1797: 48–49), a French Creole planter from Martinique, wrote that slaves from
the Gold Coast were 'drunkards' while slaves from Senegal were 'very tem-
perant'. Long (1774: 374) stated a more general view of slave drinking behaviours, arguing that the slaves of Jamaica are 'void of all genius ... they have no
taste but for women; gormandizing, and drinking to excess'. Governor Parry
of Barbados (cited in Craton and Walvin 1976: 91–93) believed that many
health problems he observed among Barbadian slaves were attributable to 'the
too free use of rum'.

But where did slave drinking behaviours fit among the various social groups
in the British Caribbean? Long (1774: 29 vol. 2) believed British Caribbean
Jews were 'abstemious and it may be supposed to owe their good health and
longevity, as well as their fertility, to their very sparing use of strong liquors'.
In contrast he argued that 'The free Negroes and mulattoes are not so averse
to spirituous liquors; for both men and women are frequently intoxicated ...
and live shorter than Jews because of their intemperance' (ibid: 30). Long
(1774: 29) also observed that 'The greater mortality, observable here among
the soldiers and transient Europeans, must be ascribed to importing with them
the English custom of eating and drinking in excess, but chiefly the latter'.
Health was an important consideration for new European arrivals in the
Caribbean and Sir Henry Colt (1631: 65), writing from Barbados in the seventeenth century warned 'You are all young men, and of good desert, if you
would only but bridle ye excesse of drinkinge'. The worst reputation for excessive alcohol use in the British Caribbean went to the poorer classes of whites.
Many of these poor whites lived in the port towns, such as Port Royal, Jamaica
and Bridgetown, Barbados, which were often described as wild and unruly
frontiers characterised by gambling, brawling, and drunkenness. In the seventeenth century, South Carolina Governor Joseph West (cited in Bridenbaugh
1972: 393) condemned servants from Barbados stating 'they are so addicted to
rum, that they will do little but whilst a bottle is at their nose'.

The preoccupation of early writers with the drinking behaviours of various
social classes reveals that alcohol was an active symbol used to define group
identity. British Caribbean society recognised that the types of alcohol used,
the preparation of the drink, and the volume of consumption helped distinguish the drinker's social class. Thus, a wealthy planter drinking expensive
Madeira wine mixed with exotic spices could separate himself from the poor
white servant tilting back a cup of homemade potato wine. The African slave

too brought to the British Caribbean concepts about the socially defining uses
of alcohol based on class differences. José Curto (1996: 60) pointed out that in
the Kongo lower classes consumed millet beer while palm wine was reserved
for the ruling elite. Long (1774: 409) may have recognised this symbolic use of
alcohol in Jamaica when he wrote:

> I have often thought, that the lower order of white servants on the planta-
> tions exhibit such detestable pictures of drunkenness, that the better sort of
> Creole Blacks have either conceived a disgust at a practice that occasions
> such odious effects (drinking), or have restrained from it out of a kind of
> pride, as if they would appear superior to, and more respectable than, such
> beastly white wretches.

The link between alcohol and the ancestral world is evident in the religious
practices of British West Indian slaves. Obeah was a common form of slave spirituality in the British Caribbean that incorporated ancestor worship and a traditional system of doctoring. Joseph Williams (1932: 120) argued that the
practice of Obeah derived from Akan religious practices. However, Douglas
Chambers (1997: 88) challenged the Akan origin of Obeah claiming that the
word stems from the Igbo *dibia* meaning a doctor or diviner who had close
contact with the spirit world. In all likelihood, Obeah largely represents a
mixing of Akan and Igbo religious practices that venerated ancestors and
sought spiritual assistance in worldly endeavours. Obeah rituals relied heavily
on the sacred use of alcohol. For example, colonial whites saw Obeah as a threat
to the stability of the colonies and tried to outlaw these practices. The laws
made numerous references to the use of alcohol in Obeah, fetish oaths, and
ancestor worship. For example, in 1782, Neptune, a slave, was transported off
Jamaica 'for making use of rum, hair, chalk, stones, and other materials relative to the practice of Obeah, or witchcraft' (cited in Williams 1932: 191).
According to Bryan Edwards (1794: 111–12), colonial officials identified Obeah
practitioners by their fetishes which frequently included rum. In the context of
British Caribbean slavery, rum replaced the traditional palm wine as the vehicle
to the spiritual world. The use of rum in Obeah may reveal the strength of Igbo
and Akan spirituality and, thus, the cultural adaptability of the Akan and Igbo
to their new environment.

The sacred nature of alcohol persisted in the heavily Akan influenced
maroon societies. For example, after defeating British troops in battle during
uprising in Jamaica in 1795, the maroons 'returned to their town to recruit their
spirits by the aid of rum' (Dallas 1803: 191). Alcohol continues to be important among modern day maroon societies. For example, Diane Vernon noted
that maroon groups in Surinam use concoctions of rum, eggs, parrot feathers,
red corn, peanuts, rice, a red tuberous vegetable, and a live rooster to 'wash'
away evil spirits (Vernon 1991: 19). Kenneth Bilby (1981: 68–73) noted the
spiritual use of alcohol among the modern Windward maroons of Jamaica who
pour rum libations and make rum offerings to their ancestors. This practice is

also found in the contemporary Jamaican Convince and Kumina cults (cults combining various African religions) which offer concoctions of blood and rum to appease ancestral spirits (Simpson 1970: 171). The traditional use of alcohol at birth ceremonies continued among the slaves of the British Caribbean. Long (1774: 479) wrote that the nine-day moratorium on naming was due to the high rate of slave infant mortality which he blamed on the practice of giving rum to newborns. As late as the 1920s, Martha Beckwith (cited in Braithwaite 1971: 214) recorded a birth ceremony in Jamaica in which 'On the ninth day, a bath is prepared for the child, a little rum thrown into it'.

In 1750, Griffith Hughes of Barbados (1750: 15) argued that Barbadian slaves maintained traditional African marriage ceremonies, but does not specifically mention the use of alcohol. However, Mrs A.C. Carmichael (cited in Dirks 1987: 123) writing about slave marriages in St Vincent stated 'On occasion of a marriage, it is often necessary to build a house, and there is usually a merry-making; the master or manager deals out rum and sugar to those who have helped build it'.

Alcohol also figured prominently at slave funerals. According to Long (1774: 421–2), 'drinking, dancing, and vociferation' characterised the funerals of British Caribbean slaves. In 1688, John Taylor (cited in Burton 1997: 18), a visitor to Jamaica, recognised the important role of the ancestors and observed that after offerings, including rum, had been placed in the grave, they 'fill up the grave, and eat and drink thereon'. In 1740, Charles Leslie (1740: 307–10) noted that slaves were buried with 'a pot of soup at the head, and a bottle of rum at the feet'. In 1994, David Watters conducted archaeological excavations at the Harney slave cemetery in Montserrat. Watters and his team recovered a bottle among the grave goods that may confirm this practice (Watters 1994).

The ceremonial role of alcohol reproduces a pattern of community-building established in West Africa. Birth, marriage, funeral, and other plantation ceremonies required social organisation, the acquisition of food and drink, supportive participants, and spiritual experts. Alcohol played an important role at these occasions, not only as a link to the spiritual world, but as a social liberator encouraging the participation of the plantation's slaves and weakening any barriers to social discourse. As in Igbo and Akan society, these events helped release social tensions, reaffirm community goals, and reinforce social commitments within the slave community.

The sacred importance of alcohol, its role in shaping community bonds, and its traditional link to power in West Africa made it an important instrument of slave resistance. Also, Igbo and Akan styled oaths transferred to the British Caribbean and became common features in slave uprisings and conspiracies. For example, during the organisational stages of the heavily Akan influenced slave conspiracy in Antigua in 1736, the participants consumed oath drinks that consisted of rum, dirt from the graves of deceased slaves, and cock's blood (Gaspar 1985: 244; Craton 1982: 122). These oath drinks signified commitment and group allegiance. David Barry Gaspar (1985: 245) believed 'taking the oath with grave dirt signified that the world of the living was intertwined with that of the dead, that they were united with their ancestors, by whom they swore to be true to their solemn obligations or incur dreadful sanctions'. Although Gaspar emphasises the influence of the Akan slaves in the Antigua conspiracy and in the use of oath drinks, Igbo slaves were also clearly involved in these ceremonies (ibid: 244). During the Jamaica slave conspiracy of 1765, slaves consumed oath drinks that consisted of rum, gunpowder, grave dirt, and blood (cited in Williams 1932: 163). Even after emancipation the oath drink continued to be an important part of resistance. During the peasant uprising at Morant Bay, Jamaica, in 1865, captured police officers were forced to consume oath drinks of rum and gunpowder to show loyalty to the peasant rebels (Heuman 1994: 6). The use of alcohol in oaths may reflect a pairing of Akan and Igbo traditions and beliefs about the spiritual power of alcohol and the loyalty-building role of oaths.

This sacred and symbolic power of alcohol is also evident in the treatment of white victims in slave uprisings. For example, during Tacky's rebellion in Jamaica in 1760 the slave rebels, after killing the white servants at Ballards valley plantation, drank the blood of their victims mixed with rum (Edwards 1794: 78). Long (1774: 447) wrote that during a revolt at a plantation in St Anne's parish, Jamaica, the owner 'defended himself for some time with a broad sword, but being overpowered by numbers and disabled by wounds, he fell at length a victim to their cruelty; they cut off his head, sawed his skull asunder, and made use of it as a punch-bowl'. According to reports of the 1701 slave uprising in Antigua, slaves cut off the head of a white victim 'and washed it with rum and triumphed over it' (Craton 1982: 118).

The drinking behaviours of British Caribbean slaves reveal West African concepts of alcohol as a sacred fluid with links to the spiritual world. This is evident in the symbolic uses of alcohol at events and ceremonies marking important stages in life. This symbolic use of alcohol may indicate that Igbo and Akan ethnic groups had a significant influence on slave drinking behaviours and the substitution of rum for palm wine at ceremonies suggests the adaptability of Igbo and Akan slaves to their New World social context. The distribution of alcohol at plantation events encouraged community participation and may have weakened social barriers, including ethnic group differences. These events, coupled with Igbo and Akan styled oath drinks, reinforced shared goals and reaffirmed social commitments. The spiritual and community-building uses of alcohol, coupled with the historic link between alcohol, ruling classes, and warriorhood in Akan and Igbo societies, made alcohol a powerful fluid in slave conspiracies and revolts.

References

Akyeampong, E. (1997) *Drink, power, and culture change: A social history of alcohol in Ghana, c. 1800 to recent times.* Heinemann, Portsmouth, New Hampshire.

Arinze, F. (1970) *Sacrifice in Ibo religion.* Ibadan University Press, Nigeria.

Barbot, J. (1732) *Barbot on Guinea: The writings of Jean Barbot on West Africa 1678–1712,* two volumes, Eds. P.E.H. Hair, A. Jones and R. Law, London: published by the Hakluyt Society, 1992.

Basden, G. (1966) *Among the Ibos of Nigeria.* Frank Cass and Company Ltd, London.

Bilby, K. (1981) *The Kromanti dance of the Windward Maroons of Jamaica* Nieuwe West-Indische Gids, 55: 52–101.

Bosman, W. (1705) *A new description of the coast of Guinea, divided into the Gold, the Slave, and the Ivory Coasts.* London.

Brathwaite, E. (1971) *The development of Creole society in Jamaica, 1720–1820.* Clarendon Press, Oxford.

Bridenbaugh, C. and R. Bridenbaugh (1972) *No peace beyond the line: The English in the Caribbean 1624–1690.* Oxford University Press, Oxford.

Burton, R. D. E. (1997) *Afro-Creole: Power, opposition, and play in the Caribbean.* Cornell University Press, Ithaca.

Chambers, D. B. (1997) My own nation: Igbo exiles in the diaspora. In, D. Eltis and D. Richardson (Eds.) *Routes to Slavery: Direction, ethnicity and mortality in the transatlantic slave trade.* Frank Cass and Company, London: 72–97.

Colt, Sir H. (1631) The voyage of Sir Henry Colt. In, V.T. Harlow (Ed.) *Colonising expeditions to the West Indies and Guiana, 1623–1667.* Reproduced in 1967 by permission of the Hakluyt Society from the edition originally published by the Society in 1925, Kraus Reprint Ltd.

Craton, M. (1982) *Testing the chains: Resistance to slavery in the British West Indies.* Cornell University Press, Ithaca, New York.

Craton, M. and Walvin, J. (1976) *The British slave trade, slavery, abolition, and emancipation: A thematic documentary history.* Longman Group, London.

Curto, J. C. (1996) Alcohol and slaves: The Luso-Brazilian alcohol commerce at Mpinda, Luanda, and Benguela during the Atlantic slave trade c. 1480–1830 and its impact. Unpublished Phd. Dissertation, UCLA.

Dallas, R.C. (1803) *The history of the Maroons.* 2 vols. Reprinted 1968. Frank Cass and Company Ltd, London.

de Marees, Pieter (1602) *Description and Historical Account of the Gold Kingdom on Guinea.* Translated and edited by Albert van Dantzig and Adam Jones, 1987, Oxford University Press, London.

Dirks, R. (1987) *The black Saturnalia: Conflict and its ritual expression on British West Indian slave plantations.* University of Florida Press, Gainesville.

Dumett, R. (1974) The social impact of the European Liquor trade on the Akan of Ghana (Gold Coast and Asante), 1875–1910. *Journal of interdisciplinary history,* 5 (1): 69–101.

Edwards, B. (1794) *The history, civil and commercial, of the British colonies in the West Indies.* London.

Gaspar, D. B. (1985) *Bondsmen and rebels: A study of master-slave relations in Antigua.* Duke University Press, Durham.

Herskovits, M.J. (1937) *Life in a Haitian valley.* Alfred A. Knopf Inc., New York.

Herskovits, M.J. (1941) *The myth of the Negro past.* Harper and Brothers Publishers.

Herskovits, M.J. (1966) *The New World Negro: Selected papers in Afro-American studies.* Ed. F. S. Herskovits, Indiana University Press, Bloomington.

Herskovits, M.J. and Frances Herskovits (1947) *Trinidad village.* Alfred A. Knopf Inc.

Heuman, G.(1994) *'The Killing Time': The Morant Bay rebellion in Jamaica.* University of Tennessee, Knoxville.

Ilogu, E. (1974) *Christianity and Ibo culture.* E.J. Brill Press, Leiden.

Hall, D. (1989) *In miserable slavery: Thomas Thistlewood in Jamaica, 1750–86.* Macmillan, London.

Hall, R. (1755) A general account of the first settlement and of the trade and constitution of the island of Barbados. Unpublished manuscript transcribed and with a forward by E.M. Shilstone, Barbados 1924.

Hughes, G. (1750) The natural history of Barbados. London.

Isichei, E. (1978) *Igbo worlds: An anthology of oral histories and historical descriptions.* Institute for the study of human issues, Philadelphia.

Jones, A. (1995) West Africa in the mid-seventeenth-century: An anonymous Dutch Manuscript. Transcribed, translated, and edited by Adam Jones, African Studies Association Press.

Leslie, C. (1740) *A new history of Jamaica.* London.

Ligon, R. (1657) *A true and exact history of Barbados.* London. Reprinted 1970, Frank Cass and Company Ltd., London.

Long, E. (1774) *History of Jamaica or the general survey of the ancient and modern state of that island.* 3 vols., reprinted 1970, Frank Cass and Company Ltd., London.

McCusker, J. (1989) *Rum and the American Revolution: The rum trade and the balance of payments of the thirteen Continental colonies.* Garland Publishing Inc., New York.

Mintz, S. W. and Price, R. (1992) *The birth of African-American culture: An anthropological perspective.* Beacon Press, Boston.

Moreau de St Méry, Médéric Louis Elie (1797) *Description topographique, physique, civile, politique et historique de la partie française de l'isle Saint-Domingue.* Reprinted 1958, Société de l'histoire des colonies françaises, Paris.

Morgan, P. D. (1997) The cultural implications of the Atlantic slave trade: African regional origins, American destinations and New World developments. In, D. Eltis and D. Richardson (Eds.) *Routes to Slavery: Direction, ethnicity and mortality in the transatlantic slave trade.* Frank Cass and Company, London: 122–45.

Pan, L. (1982) Alcohol in colonial Africa. *The Finnish foundation for alcohol studies,* Helsinki, v. 22.

Parrinder, E. (1961) *West African Religion, a study of the beliefs and practices of Akan, Ewe, Yoruba, Ibo, and kindred peoples.* Epworth Press, London.

Sheridan, R. (1974) *Sugar and slavery: An economic history of the British West Indies, 1624–1775.* Caribbean University Press, Barbados.

Simpson, G. E. (1970) *Religious cults of the Caribbean: Trinidad, Jamaica, and Haiti.* University of Puerto Rico, Rio Piedra.

Vernon, D. (1991) Bakuu: Possessing spirits of witchcraft on the Tapanahony. New West Indian guide 65 (1): 1–38.

Vogt, J. (1979) *Portuguese rule on the Gold Coast 1469–1682.* University of Georgia Press, Athens, Georgia, U.S.A.

Watters, D. (1994) Mortuary patterns at the Harney site slave cemetery, Montserrat, in Caribbean perspective. *Historical archaeology,* 28 (3): 56–73.

Williams, J. J. (1932) *Voodoos and Obeas: Phases of West Indian witchcraft.* Dial Press Inc., New York.

19. DRINKING IN LA RÉUNION
BETWEEN LIVING, DYING AND FORGETTING

Annie Hubert

Introduction

This island of the Indian Ocean, with a population of 600,000, is said to be rampant with alcoholism. The local and international media point out all the terrible aspects of overdrinking, characterising a part of its population as mentally retarded because of inbreeding and alcohol. After several years of fieldwork among the Créole population of the 'Heights', this over-simple picture seems not only unfair, but also destructive, since the Réunionnais of modest origin, and mixed descent, are ready to accept this totally negative view of themselves. I will try here to trace the history of intoxicating drinks on this island, and to analyse the state of affairs today, attempting to put into perspective and context the rather polemic approach of the media and public health institutions.

It all began with drinking water. La Réunion was a desert island, known to the first Arab navigators, then to the Europeans, who used to stop there and stock up with drinking water and fresh supplies. Wild goats roamed the mountains, tropical fruit was abundant, and sea and land turtles provided excellent meat. Its first name was explicit – Eden – and indeed it must have been to the early navigators after months of seafaring. The climate was healthy and cool up in the mountains; the rivers, waterfalls and springs were numerous on the sides of the steep volcanoes rising to nearly 3,000 metres, right out of the sea.

The island was first inhabited, in the mid-seventeenth century, by six French settlers and a few Malagasy helpers, who fled a rebellion at Fort Dauphin, in the south of Madagascar. In a few years it became a royal colony, and was then called Isle Bourbon, in honour of the royal dynasty. The French India Company established warehouses and administrators: it was an ideal stopping place between France and the Far East. Eventually, came a Governor. Settlers slowly arrived from impoverished French rural areas, from the North, Normandy and Brittany, poor farmers who hoped to make a living on the fertile land. Pirates of all sorts also chose to stop there. Then slaves were imported from the east and west coasts of Africa, and from Madagascar. By the eighteenth century, the population had acquired its characteristics: black slaves, the lowest of African origin, the higher ones from Madagascar, and a very few Indians, taken as house servants and cooks, brought over from Pondicherry.

White or nearly white Créoles, the rich landowners (usually younger sons of noble families), came to make a fortune, while the poor farmers, cultivating small surfaces, were driven higher and higher up the mountain sides by the encroaching plantations. At the abolition of slavery, many southern Indians, of Tamil origin, came as plantation workers, followed by Chinese who established small shops all over the island. Today, we can add a sizeable population of French administrators, teachers and businessmen.

The various categories mix, but not much, and everyone keeps more or less to his or her colour, especially if they are white and very low on the socio-economic scale.

Plantations in a Colonial Past

The first plantations already involved a production linked with drinking: coffee. Landowners imported more and more slaves; the coffee beans were exported via the India Company. Bourbon coffee, aromatic and of excellent quality, has a good reputation. Up to this day, coffee remains an important local drink in La Réunion, and most farmers cultivate enough for their personal consumption in the small gardens surrounding their homes. The beans are dried on mats on the ground, roasted in a revolving pan over a wood fire and ground with pestle and mortar, as was done two centuries ago. However, the prosperity of coffee plantations did not last. In 1806, a terrible hurricane, frequent in these parts, destroyed the totality of the plants. It was the end of coffee production (Billiard 1990).

The next trial was with sugar cane. Cane had existed in the wild, before the island was inhabited. It was probably brought by passing Arab navigators coming from Asia; they not only left goats and chickens, they also left plants to develop for collection on a return visit.

The Malagasy, who had accompanied the first French settlers, knew the cane and how to ferment its juice to produce an intoxicating sort of wine, the *betsa-betsa*. Using the cane growing spontaneously in Bourbon, the settlers and their helpers made *fangourin,* a replica of the Malagasy fermented drink. They called it cane wine. The canes were pressed between heavy stones, the juice was collected and mixed with water, and after four or five days of fermentation, the drink was ready, described as 'a sweet and generous wine, comparable to the European wines' (Durot, undated archive doc.). Numerous settlers produced quantities of this drink and sold what they did not drink themselves. The Malagasy, again, showed them how to distill this *fangourin,* to obtain a strong alcohol, or *rake* (from the word *arak,* used in Asia).

By 1690, six settlers had built special stills and they were the principal providers of the drink on the island. The settlers also made wine, or mead, with the honey of wild bees. This was done by each household, in small quantities. Mixed with water, it was left to ferment for eight days, and would keep for several years. It is quite possible that this beverage was first made by farmers from Brittany where it was, and still is, a traditional drink. It was said that it tasted as good as the best wines of Malaga. Barrassin (1989), in his work on the daily life of the seventeenth- and eighteenth-century settlers, quotes passages from Company reports mentioning the dangerous effects of this drink on the health of the drinkers, without actually describing these terrible effects. More educated settlers and Company officials recommended fangourin rather than mead for daily consumption. Often, the best of these wines were kept for special occasions.

In 1705, a Company employee, the geographer Feuilley, sent on a mission to Bourbon, was preoccupied by the dangers of mead and recommended several times that the Company import 'healthy' alcohol from France. This is the list he required for one whole year: half a large cask of *fenouillette* (spirits distilled with fennel or aniseed, recommended to help the digestion), eight casks of plum brandy, four casks of red wine, six casks of Spanish wine. Of course, these beverages imported at great cost from the motherland were reserved for the white settlers.

Feuilley again writes 'la *raque* made in the island of Bourbon is very dangerous to the health when drunk regularly'. The six still owners made good business selling their produce. Antoine Boucher, the Company secretary in 1702, took a census of the population and he mentions that 'drunkenness is a real plague in the island'. He names forty-three heads of households as drunkards, that is more than 4 percent of the white population, plus seven freebooters based on the island, and five 'mothers of families'. Certain inhabitants, constantly drunk, were unable to work and five of them had become paralysed through drink. Absolutely no reference is made to the slaves, and they were not mentioned in the census. Anyway, for the whites, 'immorality and drunkenness were their "natural" traits'.

At the beginning of the eighteenth century, Auguste Billiard (1990), a French traveller who wrote of his travels to Bourbon for the Minister of Colonies of the time, said that numerous ships brought quantities of good cognac, to the great joy of the settlers at each arrival.

What about the slaves, then? It appears that before the cane plantations, they were rewarded from time to time with la *raque* or arak, most often given once a week, on Saturday, after work. They were said to have developed a great taste for it. In 1703, reports from the Company describe the very dangerous effect of arak on those who drank it, especially the slaves. They describe it as low-quality alcohol, but for the slaves, especially the men, arak was a reward. It was said to give them strength and it became a physical and psychological need. They asked for small coins, to buy *un petit coup de raque* (a shot of arak) from the travellers they helped disembark from the boats by carrying them on their backs. In their songs they sing of arak, and of the stinginess of their masters in giving them some. The main trading centre for arak was established at the Gol, near Saint Louis, where the remains of one of the most important sugar and rum factories can still be seen.

Sugar Cane and Rum

The success of sugar production in the French Antilles in the Caribbean encouraged planters to try the same in Bourbon, whose climate and soil are comparable. After the disaster of 1806 with the coffee plantations, landowners started to cultivate sugar cane with great success. Rum had been invented in the French Antilles by a Dominican monk, le père Labat (see Cuisines du Monde 1994). The difference from arak is that the fermented molasses are distilled, not simply the cane juice. As soon as the first sugar factories started production, they also produced rum. Admittedly, it was alcohol of a better quality than the old arak, but in La Réunion rum will always be produced industrially, and there is pratically no equivalent of the small-scale local production of the so-called *rhum agricole* common in the Caribbean.

Billiard tells us that in 1806 the population was 83,000, of which there were 6,000 whites, 60,000 slaves and some Indians. The figures mentioned for trade and produce give 100,000 piastres for rum and arak, representing about 65,000 francs of the time, which is a considerable sum of money, knowing that these drinks were not exported but all drunk on the island. Billiard goes on to say:

> The making of brandy from cane under the name of rum and arak is, as in the other colonies, very important as far as taxes are concerned, but also for public morality. The blacks consume great quantities of arak, and they need to be thus strengthened and encouraged in their work. The whites drink these also, but without the need for it. The drunkenness produced by this brandy when it is not properly made causes a sort of furor; its frequent use leads to the most coarse degeneration. It is with arak that disorder can be contrived among the slaves. One could forbid the production of such drinks, but it is a great source of revenue for the government; it is also indispensable to the needs of the blacks, for the passing sailors, as there are no other or better spirits available.

We are confronting here a problem as old as the first settlement of the island.

The Situation Today

In La Réunion today (it was given its name after the French Revolution), the population is pluri ethnic, and divided into recognisable categories: the Créoles, descendants of the old landowners, founders of plantations, representing the 'great families' – white, of course. Then the white Créoles, less distinguished, those who were pushed up the mountains into the cirques and the ravines by the encroaching plantation owners, called by Billiard almost two centuries ago *Créoles des Hauts*. Most of them were very poor farmers, uneducated, and they have remained uphill, supposedly intermarrying. Today they are called by the other Réunionnais *Petits Blancs des Hauts*, which can be best rendered by the American expression 'white trash'. They are considered as a totally alcoholic and degenerate population, mentally retarded for the most part because of inbreeding. This view, largely expressed in the local press and media, as in France, is totally wrong. Recent genetic studies have proved that there was no such inbreeding, that this population moves and goes far to marry. There is no more alcoholism than in the lowlands, as we will see, but the power of this popular cliché is such that the Créoles des Hauts have come to consider themselves as less intelligent, less capable, and less good than the other inhabitants. Then there are all the descendants of the slaves, Malagasy or African, for the most part in the lowlands or half way up the hills and in most towns, followed by the Tamil, who came as plantation workers, found in the towns and on the west coast of the island around the old sugar factories, and, finally, the Chinese, who arrived in the late nineteenth and early twentieth century.

The Clinical Outlook

Today, La Réunion produces 206,000 litres per year of pure alcohol from industrial rum and 1,223 litres from *rhums agricoles*. Of this large production, 25,500 litres of pure alcohol are drunk on the island, which represents an average of 12.5 litres of alcohol at 45° per person per year. In comparison, for metropolitan France these figures are 20 litres of alcohol at 45° per person per year.

So, apparently, people drink less in La Réunion than in France, yet they are described as a population of heavy alcoholics. Why? The reason is first of all clinical. Alcoholism in La Réunion has terrible consequences on mortality and health. It affects young people. Deaths by alcoholism of those under fifty-five represent 35 percent of the total deaths (Observatoire régional de la Santé 1990). It represents also 65 percent of the deaths of those under forty-five (for only 37 percent in France) and 13 percent of those under thirty-five (for 2 percent in France). Generally speaking, in France the number of deaths linked to alcoholism are half of those for La Réunion.

Sixty-two percent of the liquor consumed on the island corresponds to strong drinks (47 percent being industrial rum at 49°), and 22 percent to local or imported spirits (such as whisky or brandies) at over 20°. The rest are beers, of which at least two brands are produced locally. Now, these strong spirits have a greater neurological toxicity, the weaker drinks tending to be of hepatic toxicity. This alone explains why in La Réunion the mental symptoms of alcoholic psychosis are predominant and represent 53 percent of the deaths.

Among men, alcoholic psychosis and alcoholism are twice as frequent as cirrhosis. For women, the data shows a short peak of deaths linked to psychosis, followed by a trend towards cirrhosis. The risks are, therefore, different for men and women, and are linked, as we will see, to the way of drinking.

Men, more particularly rural workers, meet at the *boutique* owned by a Chinese. The smallest establishment in the cirques or ravines has this sort of general shop where groceries, kerosene, agricultural supplies and, of course, drinks (of which rum is the most important) can be found. These small shops are not only the trading structure of the rural parts of the island, they are also the main place for meeting and socialisation, actually the only space in which exchanges and communication take place. They have an important social and cultural role. Women go there to buy whatever they need for their household, they also buy rum, but never drink it publicly. The men, after work, or from the morning onwards if they are unemployed, congregate at the shop, and hang around, sitting outside or inside on old kerosene tins, wooden benches or plastic crates. They buy *un petit coup de sec* (a shot of rum), served in small glasses. Each one takes his turn in buying a round, and the rum is drunk in one gulp, thrown down the throat, and never lingers in the mouth. Thus, in less than half an hour, a man can drink what amounts to over one-tenth of a litre of pure ethylic alcohol. It is a speedy and extremely strong alcoholisation. This leads to discussions, exchanges, and sometimes ends in fights. The men then go home to eat, most of them passably drunk.

The women, in Créole society, are not supposed to drink. At least not in public, otherwise they can be taken for 'loose women'. They drink inside their homes, alone, far from the public eye. The quantities will be less.

As far as social drinking behaviour is concerned, we can note that if rum is drunk at home, it is drunk outside. In other words, if friends visit, or there is a special occasion, the guests or friends sit in front of the house, not inside, and there they are served their glass of rum or other drinks. It is never drunk inside, only the women do that, secretly. This inside-outside dichotomy is very strong in La Réunion, and is present for most important actions of daily life.

Women in the past, at least those who worked in the plantations, and all the female slaves, were given traditionally a large glass of porter before work. This very strong, malted beer was supposed to give them strength. We find here again the idea that alcohol gives strength to the individual, but if arak was given as a reward to the men, we see porter given as a tonic before work to the women. Then, from porter to rum, the step is but a small one. Today the feminine drink is Marie Brizard, an aniseed liqueur, drunk by the women for any special occasion. Men do not like it, saying it is 'too sweet!'

I have not, of course, mentioned here the city Créole élite, knowing that there is a high-class alcoholism, but no longer based on rum. Their drinking patterns, men and women, are similar to those of the inhabitants of the métropole – whisky, brandy, beer, and especially wine are socially important drinks and have higher class connotations. To sum up the 'traditional' situation: men drink in conviviality, women drink alone, the former for fun and strength, the latter to forget and calm anxiety.

What about the young? In traditional society, young people did not drink. Young boys, when considered sufficiently grown up by their fathers, would be taken to the boutique and given a drink in public, as a sort of rite of passage. Thus they became men, and could work like men. Girls did not touch alcohol.

This pattern was still true at the end of the Second World War, but things have changed. Young people today have taken to beer, wine, and foreign drinks, less strong than rum, of course, but often mixed with smoking marijuana at their parties and gatherings. The combination of both, and playing and dancing to the *maloya* style of music, issued from the African slave music, has a strong effect. Many road accidents are due to this.

From Chinese Shop to Supermarket

In the past ten years, hyper and supermarkets have sprouted around all the towns of the island. They have not yet replaced the traditional Chinese shop, which remains a social gathering place, comparable to the *bistrot* in France. However, they have made available, at very low prices, all sorts of goods, among which, of course, is rum, but also beer and wine. Pricewise, the cheapest is rum; in 1994 you could buy a litre of Charrette rum, industrially produced, for 18 francs. A bottle of whisky cost 180 francs... A new trend is appearing: a group of men, having received their pay or their unemployment allowance, will buy a crate of rum, and they will sit outside in their village or town, and get themselves thoroughly drunk. We are speaking here of the poorest and most fragile part of the population: out-of-work, no prospects, no land, no hope, no past and no future. Drink seems to be the only way to forget.

The Rhum Arrangé and Rhum Marron

In the past, the India Company watched over the production of drinks and collected taxes on it, replaced later on by the government. Such a system led, of course, to clandestine brewing and hidden stills, high in the mountains, to produce *rhum marron*. Marron is the word used for the runaway slaves (maroons) who settled in the wilds. The rhum marron was distilled from fruit produced in the mountain fields by the Créoles des Hauts: goyavas and bananas, to which some fermented maize was added, and the whole thing was distilled in small stills hidden in the high valleys. In later years, the 'moonshiners' used to burn old tyres to hide the smell of spirits. This particular rum was highly appreciated, and the older men talk of it with nostalgia, describing it as so much better than the industrial rum.

To improve on the basic rum, the Créoles have for a long time produced *rhum arrangé*. It is a flavoured rum, each household having its own recipe, improved on by each generation. Industrial rum is put into a large bottle to which are added pieces of vanilla, cloves, bitter orange, coffee beans, litchis and so on. It macerates several weeks before being drunk. It is a pleasant, sweeter drink than straight rum. Every guest is offered a glass. A very special sort of rhum arrangé mixes combawa *(Citrus histrix)* and salt with the rum. It is supposed to give appetite and strength. The Créoles des Hauts say that 'it pulls out fatigue'.

Wine

The first settlers brought vines from France, grew them, and made wine from the seventeenth century onwards, but in such small quantities that it was never commercialised and, indeed, not all farmers grew vines. This type of culture developed mainly in the Cirque of Cilaos, which became famous for its wine production. The inhabitants of that remote part of the island drank more wine than rum, and it could be bought at the Chinese shop. Today, still, I have seen in all the houses the presses and casks where the farmers continue to make it. It is a very sweet wine, more like sherry, and very strong. The French agronomists sent to the island a few years ago declared that the very ancient cépage (plant) used for it is 'toxic', and recommended new strains. Some old people have kept to their old wine, which is sold in bottles at the roadside to tourists and visitors, but the younger ones have created a cooperative, developed a real winery, and obtained an AOC. The wine produced is not exported, as there is too little of it; it is a dry white Chardonay, and has nothing in common with the old sweet intoxicating drink of their ancestors.

Rum, Alcohol and Living on the Island

Since the Company, local governments have, one way or the other, tried to curb excessive drinking on the island. Lately the government has gone through the usual authoritative and forbidding attitudes: drinking is a social scourge, it is a capital sin, usually indulged in by the lower classes. The bourgeois and powerful have the right to establish morality. Drinkers and drink-sellers are stigmatised. Alcohol is established officially as poison in a society where it is part of its roots, of its archetypes. The alcoholic is seen as vicious, sinful, bad, perturbing the social order. He is guilty of everything. This attitude has been constant for many years in La Réunion, and only recently has the outlook changed. A symposium on alcoholism was organised in 1989, and several research teams have started working on this subject, mostly, of course, in alcohology, public health and so on. Social sciences have not done much so far.

The Faces of Rum

Today, alcohol, and more particularly rum has, in the minds of the people, two faces: at the same time God and the devil, the good and the bad. It is said to eliminate fatigue, to take away the dust from the throat, to calm the nerves, to eliminate shyness, to kill worms, to be useful medicine. But everyone knows

also its power to kill. Social interaction in La Réunion, since the very beginning, the ethnic and cultural contacts, has always been linked to alcohol, this
substance being a sort of mediator of the differences, but also a creator of deep
imbalances. In fact, it is the way in which alcohol is drunk traditionally on this
island, and not just the quantities involved, which leads to public health problems.

Rum appears as a substance imposed on a colonised population by a central
power for its economic benefits. It has, from the beginning, been associated
with the lower categories of the population: slaves, plantation workers, poor
whites. It is a substance which gives courage, oblivion, heat; it is a sort of
popular panacea. The island's population, descendants of slaves, poor farmers
driven to the mountains, exploited plantation workers, have in common an
absence of deep historical past, of roots of identity, a lack of prosperity, love,
pride, or status. Rum provided the remedy to this state of mind. We are in the
presence of an alcoholisation linked to the fate of people in difficulty in a
society destined to unhappiness.

Rum has been used as a salary and a gratification, legally as fuel for the
human machine, while being taxed and submitted to regulations. It has provoked double representations: happiness and despair, misery and wealth.
Today it gives a new shine to the Réunionnais cultural identity, links the
inhabitants of this land, and expresses their faith in their short past and culture.

Having rum as a tradition does create a public health problem, not so much
by the quantities consumed, but by the way it is drunk. The observed over-
mortality touches the lowest and poorest layers of the population, and is not
so much linked to the toxicity of alcohol as to the misery, distress, and the ill-
being of those concerned.

References

Barassin, J. (1989) *La vie quotidienne des colons de l'île Bourbon à la fin du règne de Louis XIV.*
    Académie de La Réunion.
Billiard, A. (1990) Auguste Billiard, 1822. *Voyage aux Colonies Orientales.* Collection Mascarin,
    ARS Terres créoles, La Réunion.
Cuisines du Monde (1994) *Dossier spécial sur le rhum* No.16: 90.
Durot (undated Archive doc.) Journal de Voyage. *Recueil trimestriel des documents et travaux inédits
    pour servir l'histoire des Mascareignes.* Fondation Carnegie, Curepipe, Mauritius, Tome II:
    381–92.
Observatoire régional de la Santé (1990) *Document sur l'alcoolisme,* Saint Denis, La Réunion.

20. WHEN IS AN ALCOHOL-CONTAINING SUBSTANCE SOMETHING ELSE?
SOUTHEAST ASIAN DEFINITIONS

Christine S. Wilson

Introduction

The reader does not need reminding that Muslims are strictly forbidden 'strong drink' – Muhammad so decreed in several sections of the Koran. Islam was brought to mainland (and island) Southeast Asia by traders from India and ports further west in the early years of the twentieth century (Coedes 1971). Thus Terengganu, the state of West Malaysia where I first worked three decades ago, was a Muhammadan kingdom by the fourteenth century (Reid 1993). Although the adult population of this fishing village on the South China Sea may best be described as preliterate in the late 1960s, compulsory weekly 'reading' of the Koran by groups of young children tutored by older women helped them as adults to read local newspapers printed in Arabic, while it administered and taught Islamic principles required to be the knowledge of all in this Muslim state and country (Wilson 1970).

There was great concern not only not to ingest alcohol, but a fear that a person or persons from other religions might introduce containers of it into the dwelling they rented, to contaminate drinking vessels and similar household goods, making them unsafe and forbidden for future use by Islamic Malays. Since glasses and similar utensils required purchase from limited cash funds, I asked if they could be purified in some way. The answer was yes, but only by cleansing three times with mud, not easily found in a sandy seaside community, then rinsing with 'pure' water (from the brackish, not too clean wells), a reaction Mary Douglas (1966) might have added to her collection of examples of purity and danger.

These people knew about *minuman keras*, 'hard' drinks, and their inebriating potential. Yet I found they made an alcohol-containing food for celebrations accompanying the highest religious festivals of the year, a cake of glutinous (sticky) rice steamed with yeast, before being placed in folded leaves to be kept several days in a large, covered container, and subsequently consumed with relish.

Observations and Experiments

My field research in this village had been planned to examine food beliefs and food behaviours of what I naively expected to be a traditional diet predating contact with cosmopolitan Western food and diet patterns, and the resulting food and nutrient intake patterns and health of the population. The eating pattern I found consisted of two large meals taken about midday and evening, based chiefly on rice (much of it grown locally, in the state), with small amounts of fish, and an occasional 'relish' such as a spicy fish sauce, or less often a vegetable. Morning food was commonly a cake of flour or rice taken with coffee (Wilson 1970).

Other animal protein foods were taken less frequently. Meat was dear, and obtaining it required cycling or taking a bus two or more miles to a market. Though villagers kept chickens, they were valued chiefly for the eggs, which might be sold to a neighbour in need of one for an animistic propitiation, for example, or as a substitute protein source in times of fish scarcity.

As in developed as well as other developing cultures, meat of larger animals was reserved for festive occasions in the life cycle as well as religious ones. Its preparation was a community collaboration. For these occasions a variant strain of rice, notable for its glutinous texture when steamed or boiled, was tinted with turmeric (to resemble expensive saffron), to achieve the royal Southeast Asian golden colour, and served with curries of meat or chicken, according to the significance and import of the celebration.

This rice, called *pulut,* was used also to make two favoured types of cakes, *ketupat* and *tapai.* After steaming, the rice for ketupat was mixed with *santan,* coconut milk, and placed in a *palas* leaf *(Licuala* species), boiled again briefly, then fried or toasted in a wok-like *kuali* (frying pan) in its own (coconut) oil, over wood coals, achieving a nut-like flavour (Wilson 1986).

For *tapai* the rice was steamed together with one or two buttons of locally made yeast, *ragi,* before being folded into a rubber tree leaf pinned with a piece of coconut leaf rib and placed in a pot or bucket wrapped in cloths to avoid 'chilling'. They were left untouched and unopened for three days. In the usual ambient tropical heat – the village is 4° north of the Equator – fermentation occurred readily. When urged to try one, my Western palate stimulated the thought that someone had slipped a little gin into it. Other Westerners, upon tasting these cakes, have likened them to Japanese *saki,* another Asian product of fermented rice taken as wine.

Pulut-based tapai, as well as other sweetmeats made of sticky rice, were not common fare. The rice had to be bought from a shop or market away from the community. In the late 1960s it cost twice as much per quart or gallon as ordinary rice. Some villagers owned and worked rice plots in other communities reached by bus or a more affluent relative's car. Few grew this special type of rice. Thus this unusual form of the venerated staple food acquired added values from its expense, rarity and presence on occasions honouring the religion as well as the people of the town.

Sweetness too is a valued quality here, and magical characteristics are familiar concepts to these people. During one religious holiday – the end of the fasting month or the Prophet Muhammad's birthday – a neighbour, the man of the house, offering a tapai cake to me commented: 'they are a mystery; they are sweet without the addition of sugar!' This indicated to me that my village friends did not know the 'sweetness' was a result sought by other societies to make a substance the Islamic religion forbade to them. A less expensive form of tapai was made by these villagers from sliced boiled tapioca (manioc) root *(Manihot utilissima)*, mixed similarly with local yeast. This foodstuff is not considered appropriate for honorific occasions, but is sold by vendors at markets and in coffee shops for breakfast or as a snack food.

Toddy, the commonest and perhaps the earliest alcohol-containing beverage in Southeast Asia, has been made in this region from both rice and the boiled sap from the inflorescence of several species of palms, including *Cocos nucifera*, the most widespread and widely used of these nuts throughout Southeast Asia. The immature inflorescence is tied and the sap is collected from a cut end (Burkill 1996). Malaysian Malays boil the liquid to obtain brown sugar; left in the atmosphere the sap quickly ferments to wine before becoming vinegar, another locally made substance used in cooking and eating. The wine, called *tuba* in the Philippines, was termed *tuak* or *duak* as well as *tapai* by aboriginal people in East Malaysia. When distilling was brought to the region before the sixteenth century, this wine was a local source of *arak*, a brandy-like liquor (Burkill, 1966).

During my 1970 study period, a medical colleague (an expert in tropical anaemias who had found evidence of the presence of this problem in blood samples he obtained from recently postpartum women in the village during the 1968 study phase) asked me to collect samples of typical meals and their components that he would have analysed for B-complex vitamins at the University of Malaya Medical School. One of the foods for which he wished to see the nutrient composition was tapai.

Two young women, who were skilled food preparers and understood the purpose of my research, agreed to make a batch of tapai for me and the camera using glutinous rice, local yeast and most of the usual food preparation equipment. We measured the rice, they steamed it, then when it was still warm, added local yeast crushed into powder, placed a handful (measured on my gramme scale) of the mixture on a cleaned rubber tree leaf, and fastened the leaf with a coconut rib. The proportion of ingredients was one pellet of yeast per quart of sticky rice. We made a typical household's amount, three quarts of pulut and three yeast pellets. We placed the cakes in a clean plastic bucket, wrapped it round with a couple of bath towels, and pushed it out of the way in the kitchen where heat from the (gas) cooking fire would not affect it.

The three experimenters all took peeks and sniffs during the next two days to see how things were going, but we waited three days for the unveiling. The first test cakes were pronounced *sedap* (tasty), and the remainder were carefully placed in plastic sacks for transport to Kuala Lumpur. When he came to collect them, my colleague was very pleased (he liked the cakes, too), but annoyed with the young women, who had thrown the measurable amount of rice wine remaining in the bucket outdoors on the ground, because it did not taste good and would soon become *masam* or *pahit* (sour or bitter). He had been looking forward to that rice wine before dinner some night.

Because of administrative difficulties at the University of Malaya Medical School, my colleague did not give me the results of the biochemical analyses of my food samples, including the ethanol content of the 'magical' cakes, but I had that information from the (U.S.) nutrition survey made in the country a few years earlier (ICNND 1962). These researchers found it to be about three percent, not enough to cause the *pening* (reeling) 'dizziness' or intoxication *(mabok)* villagers might expect from ingesting more seriously strong beverages. Thus their innocence of the true cause of the 'sweetness' of these cakes remained when I worked there in 1984.

Conclusion

Although the Malaysian government is nonsecular (all Malays are expected to be Muslims and obey its strictures), and the police had the duty as well as the right to determine if there were containers of alcoholic substances in a household, which they were to confiscate on discovery, the chiefly Malay government officers were relatively unconcerned about their consumption of it. In 1984 the increased presence of illegal drugs, and other mind-bending ingestants, had led to extremely harsh penalties. Possession of *ganja* (hashish and similar products) was legally punishable by death.

At this time, moderate drinking among educated Malays exposed to Westerners and their ways was seldom condemned. With greater incomes from the oil profits, further study at university as well as technical colleges was encouraged by families, ensuring greater exposure to cosmopolitan ways. It is also worthwhile to recognise that toddy and rice wine contain other nutrients, both minerals and vitamins (Tee 1982).

References

Burkhill, I.H. (1966) *A Dictionary of the Economic Products of the Malay Peninsula.* Ministry of Agriculture and Cooperatives, Kuala Lumpur, Malaysia.

Coedes, G. (1968) (Translated by S.B. Brown) *The Indianized States of Southeast Asia.* University Press of Hawaii, Honolulu.

Douglas, M. (1966) *Purity and Danger: An analysis of concepts of pollution and taboo.* Routledge & Kegan Paul, London.

ICNND (1964) *Federation of Malaya. Nutrition Survey, September–October 1962.* A report by the Interdepartmental Committee of Nutrition for National Defense, U.S. Government Printing Office, Washington, D.C.

Reid, A. Ed. (1993) *Southeast Asia in the Early Modern Era. Trade, power, and belief.* Cornell University Press, Ithaca, N.Y.

Tee, E. Siong (1982) *Nutrient Composition of Malaysian foods – A preliminary table.* Division of Human Nutrition, Institute for Medical Research, Kuala Lumpur, Malaysia.

Wilson, C.S. (1970) Food Beliefs and Practices of Malay Fishermen: An ethnographic study of diet on the East Coast of Malaya. Ph.D. dissertation, University of California, Berkeley.

Wilson, C.S. (1986) Social and nutritional context of 'ethnic foods': Malay examples. In, L. Manderson (Ed.) *Shared Wealth and Symbol. Food, culture and society in Oceania and Southeast Asia.* Cambridge University Press, Cambridge.

21. EPILOGUE

Helen M. Macbeth

I have been asked to write a 'Conclusion' with an overview of the previous chapters in this volume. However, as nothing is concluded but, I argue, a beginning to a more holistic approach to the study of drinking has been made, let this just be an 'Epilogue' to a fascinating conference and a very interesting book.

This volume emerged from a very successful conference of the International Commission on the Anthropology of Food, and it is essential, but not necessarily obvious, that such an academic association should consider drink as well as food within their remit from the International Union of Anthropological and Ethnological Sciences. There is no easily definable boundary between what is *food* and what is *drink*. Clearly drink is in fluid form, but that is an insufficient classification. Presumably in recognition of the more solid contents (and one does not drink solids), it is agreed that one eats a stew. However, in English, the situation with soup is more complex: one *eats* soup off a soup plate but *drinks* soup out of a mug. According to the *Nouveau Larousse Gastronomique* (1967), the French origin of the word *soupe* referred to a piece of bread on to which the fluids from a savoury boil up were poured; this, of course, one would *eat*. Although its English (and French) successor may only occasionally contain bread, the dinner party version is still *eaten*. Yet, the late twentieth century mixture of boiling water and instant soup powder in a cup or mug must surely be *drunk*. The distinction does not seem to lie in the cooking procedure, but in the vessel in which the soup is served: one eats from a plate and drinks from a mug. Sauces, salad dressings and melted butter are also fluids which are consumed but not drunk. So, there is something in the manner of consuming a fluid that designates drinking. However consumed, liquids are biologically essential to human life and in many instances the lubricant of social communication and/or symbolically significant.

There is a further complication in defining drinking in that the term is used to refer not only to the intake of all drinks, but also more narrowly, to the intake of exclusively alcoholic drinks. Mendelsohn's (1966) *The Dictionary of Drink and Drinking* is only concerned with alcoholic beverages. It even states under the heading 'Milk and Cream': 'These words are hallowed by usage when linked to alcoholic beverages' and there follows a discussion of Bristol Milk and of sweet French liqueurs called *crèmes* (Mendelsohn 1966, p. 223). There is no mention at all about the drink that comes from cows. Similar references only to alcohols were found when words associated with other non-alcoholic drinks were checked.

A drink, then, is a word that can be interpreted in quite different ways. Furthermore, the discipline of Anthropology has very broad coverage encompassing the sciences, social and biological, in regard to humans. There are many diverging specialisms, in all of which the topic of drinking can be, but seldom has been, considered. One would, therefore, anticipate that the opportunities for anthropological discourse on drink and drinking would be highly diverse, and that is indeed the situation in this book. It is important that the value in reading these perspectives brought together in a collection of cross-disciplinary chapters is recognised, and it is beneficial that the editors have not sought to impose a veneer of unrealistic unity. Yet, as will be shown in this chapter, similar points reappear in different contexts throughout the book. In the last couple of decades the benefits of breadth as well as of specialism have been accepted as essential in the academic treatment of a topic.

The contributors to this volume are indeed specialists and the breadth is achieved in the juxtaposition of their chapters. Several authors emphasise the importance of crossing the conceptual boundaries between the social and biological sciences, and demonstrate the relevance of doing so with clear ethnographic examples. While some contributors have explained the physiological needs for fluid intake or the relevance to health of some drinks, others have sought to clarify the significance of drinking in social and symbolic structures. Yet for humans, the interaction of all these processes is inescapable.

As de Garine's eloquent Introduction to this volume explains, 'Drinking is a primary human need' and the biological functions of fluid and thirst are clearly set out by Vargas in language accessible to non-biologists. The interaction between physiology, personality and culture in these functions is emphasised and exemplified. Interest in the physiological mechanisms is pursued by Ulijaszek, who draws attention to the relevance of environmental conditions, especially those of hunter-gatherer populations at risk of heat stress. Results of quantitative studies of sweat loss among Australian hunter-gatherers are given to support his argument. The human need for potable water is also the theme for the next and very different chapter concerning populations in the Southern Pacific area, for Pollock is a social anthropologist, who points out that there is a serious gap in anthropological literature in regard to non-alcoholic drinks. She is concerned with the accessibility to thirst quenching beverages, since on many Pacific islands, especially the atolls, potable fluids are a scarce resource whether from rainfall or from coconuts. Demographic increases impose more stress on supplies, and the social controls, contexts and options, Pollock argues, require a great deal more study. Her chapter provides some initial information and analysis.

It is indeed unusual for anthropological interest in drinking to focus on non-alcoholic beverages, but this volume includes several chapters that discuss the topic, for example the next three very different chapters are concerned with milk. The first of these by Little et al. is centred upon the importance among the Turkana and other pastoralists from East Africa of milk not only as a dietary staple but also as preferred within their culture. Little et al. are interested in the consequences for the human biology of these populations, not just in their contemporary anthropometry and energy, but also in their evolutionary adaptation. Den Hartog then considers changes in milk consumption and attitudes to that consumption in a west European context, specifically in the changes in Dutch government policies from the 1937 'Milk-in-School' programme to later worries about fat intake and cardiovascular risk. The very recent interest in the benefits of lactic acid bacteria is again bringing modifications to attitude to these liquid milk products. The chapter highlights the power of the food and drink industry and the nutrition and health sectors of government in influencing individual choice and so consumption. The third chapter about milk is by Macbeth, who discusses its traditional and contemporary high consumption in the Pyrenees, which contrasts with Anglo-American ideas of southern Europe and the concept of a 'Mediterranean Diet'. Again the analysis of research data is provided and cultural changes over time are suggested.

Both soft and alcoholic drinks are discussed in the next two chapters. The primarily ethnographic chapter by Igor de Garine concerns the Masa and Muzey of northern Cameroon. 'Water, blood, milk, traditional non-alcoholic drinks, home-made sorghum and millet beers, home-made spirits ... and manufactured drinks' are discussed, allowing comparison of the two communities with regard to culture and welfare condition. Ibrahim follows this with a chapter focused on the traditional drinking rules, rituals and habits of the Maasai of northern Tanzania. Much of this chapter too is concerned with milk in this cattle pastoralist society, but the remainder concerns the rituals in which alcoholic drinks play a significant role. Points about such African beliefs are reflected again in later chapters.

From Spain, it is not surprising to find that the emphasis is on wine, and in the next four chapters Spanish authors contribute very different perspectives. Troncoso et al. embellish the welcome news that first reached the health conscious in 1993 that the moderate consumption of red wine reduces some cardiovascular risks. Gonzalez Turmo, on the other hand, writes an elegant overview of the 'individual and social fact' of drinking wine with special reference to Andalucia. Her fascinating chapter covers many angles about drinking and about wine and fortified wine, including gender differences. The topic of gender differences is central to the chapter by Cantarero Abad, who provides both quantitative and qualitative data on sex differences in drinking in Aragon. Once again the reader is provided with information on both alcoholic and non-alcoholic drinks and the socially constructed values attached to them. In different societies the time and places for meeting for drinks differ, but spreading throughout Spain is the Andalucian custom of snacks (*tapas*) with drinks in bars and taverns. Millan writes about the custom of tapas referring both to the foods and to the wines, but he draws it all together in relation to an expression of identity in Spain.

On leaving Spain, the following chapters provide ethnographic examples that are widely dispersed in geographic terms but again contain comments that echo earlier points made in different contexts. Avila Palafox considers the Mexican *cantinas* and their patrons. He considers explanations for heavy drinking of alcoholic drinks in Mexico. As in Mexico, the centrality of drinking in Georgian society is emphasised by Chatwin, who shows that social cohesion is achieved through drinking, feasting and hospitality. Eric Garine finds the Duupa of northern Cameroon an 'interesting example of a small-scale agricultural society that is "driven by drink"'. Again the centrality of drinking alcohol is shown in this society. A more salutary perspective on drinking beer in an African context, this time among the Abagusii of western Kenya, is provided by Subbo. Problems are outlined and some suggestions for improvement made. The African context of drinking alcohol is again an important feature in the next chapter by Smith on the historical ethnographic approach to Caribbean slave life. The linkage between the secular and the sacred worlds achieved through alcohol in traditional African life was mentioned above by Ibrahim and is claimed by Smith to be found in the slave societies of the Caribbean. Smith argues that this had profound cultural and political effects on Caribbean history.

After a general introduction to the populations of La Réunion in the Indian Ocean and an overview and history of alcohol drinking there, Hubert shows how rum drinking has come to provide a cultural identity on the island. Once again points made in earlier chapters by Millan and by Avila are echoed here. However, among the poorest in Réunion society, this is strongly linked to misery, distress, ill-health and earlier mortality. This epilogue started with a discussion of the unclear boundaries between what is 'food' and what is 'drink'. So, it is fascinating that much of the last chapter by Wilson describes the consumption of alcohol in festive foods, which is deemed quite acceptable in the Muslim west Malaysian society described, despite the Muslim prohibition of other alcohols in liquid form.

Those who are not so familiar with the need in the human sciences to be holistic, and to do this to cross traditional disciplinary boundaries, may look for greater linearity in the progression of chapters in a book. To do so may ignore the value of collecting together in one book chapters which at first glance seem so disparate. At the end of this book one realises not only how much one has learned about the topic, but also how many links do exist between comments within the chapters. In many cases the contributors themselves will have been unaware of the links until they too become readers of the whole book. Yet, similar points are made arising from quite different settings and there is even some repetition of sources referred to. Only by specialists of different disciplines and different nations meeting together in cross-disciplinary conferences, such as the one from which this volume arises, and through the juxtaposition of their different perspectives in a book, can the processes for a truly holistic approach be started. It is hoped that this book and this epilogue are but a beginning.

The editors should be thanked for their early perception of the opportunities and needs for cross-disciplinary discussion of the topic of drinking.

References

Mendelsohn, O.A. (1966) *The Dictionary of Drink and Drinking*, Macmillan, Melbourne.
Montagné, P. (1967) Nouveau Larousse Gastronomique, Librairie Larousse, Paris, p. 978.

INDEX